This is the first comprehensive overview of the Native people
of Puget Sound, who speak a Coast Salishan language
called Lushootseed. They originally lived in communal
cedar plank houses clustered along rivers and bays. Their
complex, continually evolving religious attitudes and rituals were woven into daily life, the cycle of seasons, and long-
term activities. Depsite changes brought on by modern influences and Christianity, traditional beliefs still infuse
Lushootseed life.

Drawing on established written sources and his own two
decades of fieldwork, Miller depicts the Lushootseed people
in an innovative way, building his cultural representation
around the grand ritual known as the Shamanic Odyssey.
In this ritual cooperating shamans journeyed together to
the land of the dead to recover some kind of vitality stolen
from the living. Miller sees the Shamanic Odyssey as a
central lens on Lushootseed culture, epitomizing and vali-
dating in a public setting many of its important concerns
and themes. In particular, the rite brought together a
number of distinct aspects or "vehicles" of culture, including the cosmos, canoe, house, body, and the network of social relations radiating across the Lushootseed waterscape.

Jay Miller is the former associate director of the D'Arcy
McNickle Center for the History of the American Indian
and the author of Tsimshian Culture: A Light through
the Ages (Nebraska 1997).

University of Nebraska Press
Lincoln NE 68588-0484
nebraskapress.unl.edu

LUSHOOTSEED CULTURE

AND THE SHAMANIC ODYSSEY

An Anchored Radiance

JAY MILLER

UNIVERSITY OF NEBRASKA PRESS   *Lincoln and London*

Library of Congress Cataloging-in-Publication Data
Miller, Jay, 1947–
Lushootseed culture and the Shamanic odyssey:
an anchored radiance / Jay Miller.   p.   cm.
Includes bibliographical references and index.
ISBN 0-8032-3200-4 (cloth : alk. paper)
1. Puget Sound Salish Indians—Rites and ceremonies.
2. Puget Sound Salish Indians—Religion.
3. Puget Sound Salish philosophy.
4. Shamanism—Washington (State)—Puget Sound.   I. Title.
E99.S21M53   1999   299'.789—dc21   98-38249 CIP

To Lushootseed

whose embodiment is

Vi taqʷsəblu Hilbert

and

whose motto is

"Write all you want

because

you can never learn

culture

from a book."

CONTENTS

ILLUSTRATIONS

ACKNOWLEDGMENTS

Once again, it is a pleasure to thank Vi and Don Hilbert for all their help and encouragement, along with their family of Lois, Ron, Jay, Bedelia, Jill, John, and all the grandchildren. Within the larger Lushootseed family, thanks go to Peggy Dunn, Andie Palmer, Alf Shepard, Robbie Rudine, Janet Yoder, Pam Cahn (*wiw'su*), Crisca Bierwert, Carolyn Marr, Brad Burns, Carolyn Michael, Barbara Iliff, Dean Reiman, and many more.

Among other degreed members, appreciation goes to Drs. Thom Hess, Pam Amoss, Dale Kinkade, William Seaburg, Laurel Sercombe, Dawn (*ɬup*) Bates, Robin Wright, Bill Holm, Greg Watson, Laura Dassow, Bob Walls, Astrida Blukis Onat, Ann Bates, Carol Eastman, Fr. Patrick Touhy, Viola Garfield, and Erna Gunther.

Among the native community, many elders have been most helpful. While they cannot all be named, or wish to be, I must single out the late Isadore Tom, Ed Davis, Lawrence Webster, Martin Sampson, Susie Sampson Peter, Morris Dan, Theresa Willup, Helen Ross, Lottie Sam, Walter Sam, and Dewey Mitchell. Younger members include Lona Wilbur, Dobie Tom, and the families of Andy Fernando and Jack Fiander. Of note, three mother-son teams have been involved in the final production of this information.

To these and all others interested in their traditions, I lift both my hands in thanks and praise.

ORTHOGRAPHY AND PRONUNCIATION

The Lushootseed words in this book are approximations of correct forms cited in two dictionaries (Hess 1976; Bates, Hess, and Hilbert 1994), a collection of texts (Bierwert 1996), and the volumes of Lushootseed Press (1995a-c).

The ə represents schwa (ə), a vague vowel.

The ɬ is pronounced around the tip of the tongue set against the back of the upper front teeth.

The ʷ is said with rounded lips.

The x is formed in the very back of the throat.

The ' marks glottalization, a consonant produced with the glottis (voice box) closed to create a forceful puff of air.

Lushootseed Culture
and the
Shamanic Odyssey

INTRODUCTION

Resilience, especially through healing ritual, is the focus of this study addressing the "missing middle" of my prior book (Miller 1988) assembling all accounts of the shamanic odyssey among the Lushootseed Coast Salish of Puget Sound and comparing these with shamanism, rituals, and beliefs throughout Native North America. Entirely missing, however, was any discussion of the place of this rite within its own context of Lushootseed culture. Considering that the last full-form journey to the land of the dead was held in the winter of 1900, I might be excused from such an ethnographic lapse; but living among Lushootseed people, I am all too aware that although this ceremonial has gone, Lushootseeds continue to suffer from soul loss, to consult shamans, priests, and ministers, and to need the solace of healing rituals to return errant spiritual features of their individual existences.

What seems an apparent loss or lapse, therefore, on closer examination is actually continuity in substitute forms, both traditional and Christian. Identifying a rite as "traditional," a term in academic disfavor, recognizes Lushootseed use of this word to mean "anything that supports the continuity of the community," expressed equally by current shamanism and by Pentecostalism and the regional Indian Shaker Church founded in 1882 near Olympia.

Throughout composition, my working title was "Saleehalee/Soulside" to emphasize the fundamental spiritual aspects of this universe, confirmed even in the historical record, albeit written by outsiders. The compound word *səlihali* is composed of *həli* 'be alive, living' with the noun-forming *s*-prefix to make 'soul, life, spirit,' compounded with *-ali*, "place where something is kept, place where something is typically located" (Bates, Hess, and Hilbert 1994, 28). Indeed, Lushootseed culture is permeated by just this sense of place, of localization—of buoyant anchoring, represented by the security of a house and the stability of a canoe, both made from trees, the very rooted-ness of which epitomizes this profound spatial sense. Once harvested, more-over, such local bounty radiated outward as planks and tools to enhance the security and prestige of person, kin, community, and region.

Overall, Lushootseed organizes cultural information as reflexes of this equation of cosmos, canoe, house, and body, a universal theme that is herein given a Lushootseed phrasing. In the rainy Northwest, such cultural elabo-ration on the theme of more expansive "coverings" makes particularly good sense. Indeed, within the greater Northwest Coast culture area, Lushoot-seed data can be clarified and expanded by comparison with adjacent tradi-tions, particularly other Coast Salishans.

As Sergei Kan (1989, 54) has already made clear for the Tlingit at the northernmost Northwest Coast, a noble upper class provided an ideal that was characterized as dry, hard, and heavy, to which Lushootseeds added the quality of warmth, represented by valuable blankets woven from the wool of mountain goats and a special breed of wooly dogs (cf. Bierwert 1996, 103). Today, initiates (called "babies") of the winter smokehouse religion continue to wear hoods made of such twisted wool strands.

When I moved to Seattle in 1973, I had finished a dissertation on the Keresan Pueblos of New Mexico, had begun research with the Oklahoma Delawares, and was planning to follow up undergraduate contacts with the Tsimshian of British Columbia. I was well aware that my new home was Salish territory, but I had no special desire for local fieldwork, except to make sure that my teaching included reliable information on nearby natives.

My lack of enthusiasm changed drastically when I met Skagit elder taqʷsəblu (Vi Anderson Hilbert), who was then teaching the local language, literature, and culture of Lushootseeds, usually known then as Puget Salish. With a momentum all her own that has catapulted herself (and those around her) into international prominence and led to her being named a U.S. Na-tional Heritage Fellow, I was soon swept along into Lushootseed research. As her car driver, sounding board, and advisor, I was allowed to enter winter ceremonials in local longhouses, known from their open fires as smoke-houses, and to observe shamanic cures, first salmon ceremonies, and rituals to mark namings, marriages, and deaths. With her, I attended events from the Fraser River of British Columbia to Washington reservations at Lummi, Swinomish, Upper Skagit, Tulalip, and Puyallup, meeting and learning from many of her aged relatives.

Many ethnographic details included here are the products of these expe-riences. In some cases, to assure my own continuing good relations with these elders, teachers, and adepts, I have remained vague about attributions. Throughout, I have preferred to use my own sources first, before turning to the published citations used herein. Firmly embedded in Lushootseed and other native traditions is the principle that any expert deliberately hold back a critical bit of information to assure a long life to its keeper. No published study, even a second one, can therefore make any claims to being definitive or exhaustive.

By the 1980s, I was sufficiently known among Lushootseed communities that I helped with a 1981–82 petition for Duwamish tribal recognition, still pending, and was expert witness in a 1983 federal trial for Suquamish, Port Gamble Klallam, and Muckleshoot fishing rights. As such I was able to review relevant publications and tribal records, including an initially frustrating quest for the notes of Hermann Haeberlin, the first academic to work in the region.[1] By making contact with Warren Snyder in Sacramento, I was able to repatriate his unpublished ethnographic notes to the Suquamish Tribal Archives. At both Suquamish and Muckleshoot, Vi went with me as translator and advisor. She and Lawrence ("Web") Webster, Suquamish chairman and grandson of chief Jacob Wahalchu, became good friends until Web's death in 1991. An account of Jacob's own questings and spiritual life concludes this chapter to inform everything succeeding.

While at Port Gamble, I heard about the last family of Chimakums who lived there. Looking for more materials, I was grateful when Dale Kinkade of the University of British Columbia showed me his microfilm copies of John P. Harrington's notes, which also included materials from Chehalis. Later I typed the more than four hundred pages of 1927 Chehalis ethnography by Thelma Adamson into computer files and edited a condensed version, which is the source for Chehalis references used here.

In 1984, Vi Hilbert, in response to continuing neglect of her traditions and her own growing impatience with scholars (styled "academic barnacles"), incorporated Lushootseed Research as a native-owned not-for-profit corporation. As an indication of her larger impact, these documents were filed by a Yakama lawyer who had been her student. In preparation for this new executive position, Vi cleaned out the separate room in her house that had been her hairdressing salon and turned it into the "brain room," installing computers in place of hair dryers.

While Vi had long been working closely with Thom Hess, the linguist who taught her to be literate in her native language, she soon embarked on her own publication efforts. In 1985, after self-producing two volumes of Lushootseed Literature, she published with University of Washington Press

Vi taqʷsəblu Hilbert,
Lushootseed elder,
Washington State Living
Treasure, and National
Heritage Fellow, wearing
a cedarbark dress made
by Alice Williams under
a wool blanket by Crisca
Bierwert. (Courtesy of
Lushootseed Research)

a volume called *Haboo: Native American Stories from Puget Sound*. I undertook the labor of transferring computer files into a format usable for camera-
ready copy to print the book.[2]

The great concentration and academic discipline needed for this effort
conflicted with the interpersonal priorities so important in a native context,
putting strain on relations between Vi and myself that were resolved at the
final push toward publication. In brief, acts she regarded as kindnesses—
offering food, drinks, and conversation—I regarded as irritating interrup-
tions. Shortly after, I took a fellowship and then a job in Chicago, taking
along two manuscripts related to Washington State Salishans of evergreen
coast and sagebrush interior (Miller 1988, 1990).

During 1985, I presented two preliminary papers based on comparative
Salishan data that have since developed into the consideration of decedence

kinship terms (at the end of the Body chapter) and these two volumes on the odyssey. As a result of my research to testify in the fishing rights trials, Vi and I met a remarkable Snoqualmi elder named Ed Davis, a fluent speaker who, as a child, had helped with the preparations for the midwinter soul recovery ceremonies at Lake Sammamish.[3] Recording his unique perspective on what was then known in the literature as the "spirit canoe" rite (more properly shamanic odyssey), I was drawn to assemble all versions, general and specific, available in print or manuscript. To complement these hundred pages of description, I added another hundred of comparisons dealing with its three major themes of death, power, and cooperating shamans. Missing from the middle, however, as indicated, was any attempt to situate the ritual within cultural traditions of Lushootseed tribes.

My commitment to Salish research extended in 1988 to acting as organizer of the Twenty-third International Conference on Salish and Neighboring Languages at the University of Oregon, no small feat to accomplish from Chicago. This forum for yearly sustained discussion of Salish language and culture is among the best in the academic world.

My involvement with Interior Salishan is more complicated. In 1977, I went to the Colville Reservation near Grand Coulee Dam to do an ethnographic survey of the lands to be flooded by heightening Chief Joseph Dam. In part, I was interested in a chance to compare Coast and Interior Salishan traditions. As an unexpected dividend of that research, I met Charles Quintasket, a superbly articulate elder. By another set of coincidences, I acquired the miscellaneous pages of an autobiography written by his half sister Christine Quintasket, whose pen name became the title of my 1990 editing of *Mourning Dove*.

Using the occasion of the 1992 Columbian Quincentennial to popularize native issues, I reconsidered Salish materials for overview chapters on Native American kinship systems, including three pages on Skagits of 1492, and on native astronomy, with two pages on Quinault (Miller 1992a–d).

Since returning to Seattle, committed to writing up twenty years of diverse fieldnotes, I have again been drawn into Vi's orbit, taking time to review, edit, and correct a series of volumes based on tapes made in the 1950s by her best–informed relatives. Published by a group of her students and friends as Lushootseed Press (1995a–c, 1996), with improved computer equipment (CARTAH 1997a–f) and her own funds, this series presents a uniquely native perspective on local culture and history by distinguished elders such as Susie Sampson Peter, a Skagit who was Vi's aunt; Ruth Shelton, a Sehome Klallam married at Tulalip; and Isadore Tom, a Lummi and Skagit native doctor. Brief excepts from my study of Lushootseed culture have appeared in these books to provide background, but the sustained treatment occurs only in the present work.

Every writer is advised to have someone in mind when composing. In the case of this volume, that person, Vi Hilbert—Lushootseed elder extraordinary—was also my reader, as indicated by a few footnotes expressing our most divergent opinions. Throughout, Vi upholds the highest ideals of her traditions, which are not always borne out in everyday practicalities and conflicting intentions. Nevertheless, it is just those ideals that are all too often slighted and maligned by scholars who lack sustained contact with these traditions and with the people for whom they are all consuming and all important. Though uncomfortable at the time, it is nevertheless heartening to hear other Lushootseeds criticize Vi for "bothering with white people" and "making money" off her publications. Routinely, these same charges are also made against other academics, who, like Vi, have lost money but strengthened their personal convictions.

Throughout the impending discussion, a reader would do well to have an image of constant rain and a steady drip in the background, ever present during my writing of it. On average, the Puget basin receives over three feet of rain and over a foot of snow each year. During Seattle winters, steady precipitation can continue for almost a month without a break. The rest of the year, rainfall is never far away, and in good Native American fashion, Lushootseeds delighted in this characteristic of their environment by thoroughly elaborating its reflexes in all-pervasive symbolism based on the concept of the slope-roofed house.

Each chapter begins with a brief historical sketch to bring past into present before concentrating on traditional concerns of the early 1800s, when the culture was more consistently integrated among its members and environments, before both suffered from the consequences of Euro-American destruction.

Throughout, attention is paid to the importance of grounding within a locale to benefit wider relations among the freeborn social class, particularly the regional elite. Specialized and expert knowledge was a privilege confined to families belonging to the upper social class, believed to have been long resident along the same river drainage. Overall integration was the responsibility of leaders holding names famous throughout a region because of their frequent appearances in houses and canoes, as dramatically emphasized during the shamanic odyssey. Until 1900, inside a plank-style house, such a vehicle was depicted by painted cedar planks, carved effigies of Little Earth

spirits, and a marked perimeter. Shamans, once dressed in cedarbark clothing, more recently wore purchased work clothes.

All told, therefore, the crucial frames in this culture, as a system, were the
coverings of body, house, canoe, and cosmos, each with a central blazing
nexus of heart, hearth, or sun. Breaches, intrusions, or invasions (by elements like rain, wind, and cold or by hostile beings) of the integument
of these coverings induced sickness (dis-ease) of the body, soul, spirit, or
community.

Thus, ultimately, the curing of a patient, the bailing out of a canoe, and
the cleaning of the house became a renewal of the world.[4]

The closest prior approach to that herein was by Anne Galin (1983), who
analyzed Lushootseed culture in terms of a triple series of configurations she
characterized as encompassed, transitional, and extended. Encompassed had
a central point and surrounding periphery; transitional had two distinct
parts separated by a boundary; and extended stretched in time and/or space.
These three cognitive systems pervaded all of Lushootseed language and culture, with strong imaging, respectively, as house, beach, or river. Among
rituals, she viewed the vision quest as encompassed, winter dance as transitional, and potlatch as extended.

Better knowledge of the culture, however, casts doubt on her analysis
since the house is believed to be the more pervasive image, located and inhabited by all life forms, particularly immortals dwelling under beaches, sea,
and rivers, as the mythology makes abundantly clear. Moreover, her three
culture-specific configurations seem to owe more to pan-human matrix relationships based on marking as exclusive, inclusive, or inclosive (Miller
1979a). Her theory, thereby, appears too powerful for her data, missing
much of the Lushootseed cultural (emic) perspective.

Similarly, when various authors have called attention to Lushootseed ritu-
als, they were never the same ones. In an introduction to her own culture,
Vi Hilbert (1980b) briefly considered the Longhouse (Winter Dance), First
Salmon, Naming, Power Boards, and Bone Game (Slahal).

While Galin emphasizes a lapsed past, Hilbert concentrates on the present
day, when initiation into a winter dance smokehouse allows family spirit
helpers to be inherited. The First Salmon has been reintroduced in the aftermath of the long battle in federal courts to receive recognition of that treaty
right. Namings continue, particularly in elite families protective of their hereditary claims to these valuable possessions. Similarly, shamans with proper
family rights continue to use carved and painted power objects for the benefit of the greater native community. The bone game is most often regarded

as a secular gambling diversion, yet native peoples view the two teams as testing the relative strengths of their own spirit helpers (Hilbert 1976), thus revealing the all-pervasive religious inspiration that tinges the most mundane of native activities.

Many conversations with Vi have clarified her reluctance to use the term "potlatch" for what she views as simply "an invitational," strongly reacting to her perception that many academics and others delight in negatively comparing Salish traditions with those to the Canadian and Alaskan north with their more explicit traditions of masking, drama, and display. Instead of recognizing the finer distinctions motivating the languages and cultures along the entire North Pacific Coast, outsiders have tended to stereotype in favor of northern matrilineal clans, formline heraldic art, and trans-Pacific trade.

The Lushootseed potlatch was more subtle, requiring greater cultural understandings by all of those involved, as their art was more diffuse and unrevealing. Suggestion was much more significant than explication.[5] In the past, as now, Lushootseeds held these invitationals less frequently, with fewer gifts than became common elsewhere after the fur trade introduced an expanded inventory of goods.

Nevertheless, neither Hilbert nor Galin broached the topic of the shamanic odyssey. Since abbreviated, individualized recovery rites are still held, belief in the power of immortals is as strong as or stronger than ever before.

A recent exchange of articles (Tollefson 1987, 1989, 1996; B. Miller and Boxberger 1994; Boxberger and Miller 1997) debating the degree of political development among aboriginal Lushootseed was flawed by misconceptions that wrongly emphasize Eurocentric stereotypes about personal individuality instead of situating a family within their anchoring landscape, that overly democratized a strong elite, and that were woefully irreligious (Miller 1997).

A lingering sense of dissatisfaction with my prior book led me to the current effort, seeking to explain not the role of the ritual in explicating the culture, nor the reasons for its passing, but rather how the vitality of Lushootseed culture has coped with the very real and continuing concern with spiritual loss or damage so aptly treated by these former intertribal odysseys. While this ritual has lapsed, its reason has not.

Knowing this, living in close proximity with the culture, and assessing present conditions, it soon became apparent to me that native-inspired Shakers and Christian Pentecostals now have the public, intertribal duties once filled by cooperating shamans. Shamanic careers continue to run in recognized families, but the more primal pattern of intershaman "jealousy" still holds forth, so that only those who are closely related by marriage or birth now work together.

My aim is a portrayal of this dynamic vitality of Lushootseed language, culture, and traditions, using the demise and replacement of the shamanic odyssey as a case example. Lushootseed souls and spiritual qualities still become endangered. How they have in past and present coped with these concerns is the thrust of my study.

To amplify sometimes sparse Lushootseed data, comparisons are drawn to Salishan, North Pacific, and more distant cultures. Several of these nations and tribes have provided native terms for themselves that are not as yet widely known, such as Nuxalk for Bella Coola. While respecting their right of self-designation, I sometimes use adjective forms of Kwakiutlan instead of the preferred Kwakwaka'wakw, and of Nootkan instead of Westcoasters or Nuu-chah-nulth for the sake of clarity.

USAGES

Close attention to the ways in which Lushootseeds talk about their own traditions has forced me to depart from some earlier technical usages. For example, prior anthropologists have distinguished spirits and their powers as being lay or shamanic. While such a contrast was and is correctly drawn, natives themselves continue to talk about spirits ("just plain like," "ordinary") that help them do their duty at a specialized career or about doctoring spirits who enable "real Indian doctors" to perform cures.[6] To be recognizable, therefore, these immortals are here called *career* or *curing* spirits.

While the freeborn members of society, apart from slaves, have been distinguished as lower or upper class, the latter including almost everyone, careful attention must be drawn to the holders of renowned names, who constituted a nobility at the core of elite families. These noble families passed on the most famous names of all. In addition, members of this elite possess sacred words that I call "enchantments" instead of magic formulae or ritual words because, although magic has the technical meaning of being compulsive, such usage is demeaning to this native system of "mind control."[7] More generally, members of the upper class possess what has been called "advice" (Suttles 1987), too weak a translation for this native "knowing, wisdom, teachings, knowledge, traditions, and depth of understanding" about the perceived spiritual and social workings of the world.

Among Lushootseeds, these words are much closer to the meaning of the native terms, which include *xʷdikʷ*, *xʷdigʷid*, *gʷədzada*, and *'ugʷusaɬ*, the last specifically meaning 'teachings' (cf. Hess 1976, 681). People who consistently transmitted and practiced these teachings became appropriate members of the upper class. People who did not were either low class or slaves.

These teachings included the full range of the traditional heritage and family treasures, including stories, dances, songs, and artistic expressions, all linked to a stock of immortal names requiring the expression of great "respect" through proper etiquette, elite protocols, moralistic narratives, and information about the effective (spiritually sanctioned) use of prime resource areas.

Further, calling any and all winter settlements "villages" hides the complex pattern of interranked communities along a waterway and region, communities ranging spatially from towns as regional centers through villages and hamlets to temporary seasonal camps and resorts used every year over centuries. Towns were administrative and religious nodes in the settlements along a waterway, often with huge longhouses to accommodate large ingathering crowds. Towns had the ability to receive a large influx of visitors, sometimes everyone living along a drainage, when hosting public events. A town was thus characterized by such maximum intake of visitors over space and time.

Because the immortals (misknown as supernaturals) play a central role in these cultures, their own identities as "shape shifting persons" will be indicated by the use of capital letters for the names of spirits that were progenitors of various species. Thus, Wolf, Duck, Salmon, and Basket Ogress refer to spirit beings before the capsizing instant at the World Change, when things became much as they are now. Afterward, wolf, duck, and salmon became species distinct from their undifferentiated counterparts of the Epic Age.

Benefiting from research in other areas of Native North America and from insights gained in the developing field of religious studies, it is clear that these spiritual beings are best understood as other-than-human persons who were immortal, as is so well phrased in A. Irving Hallowell's analysis of the cosmology of the Ojibwa of the Great Lakes.

In his most explicit statement about the Ojibwa category of person, both human and other-than-human, Hallowell (1992, 64–66) noted that each of these beings had an enduring vital part (a spirit or soul) and an outward form (appearance) with attributes of intelligence, will, and speech, enabling all of them to communicate. Each form was merely typical (rather than absolute) since any person could metamorphose between coverings. For example, the "person" of each biological species was its "owner" (or boss), possessing speech and transformative abilities that were lacking among the ordinary mortal members. Similarly, transpersonal perceptions varied according to species, although each had parallel traditions as to what constituted a proper home, customs, and foods.

While Lushootseed people, of course, adhered to their own version of this belief, its comparability with all Native America should not be overlooked.

Although precautions of fasting, praying, and purifying were necessary to make contact with these immortals, the reason has nothing to do with a separate supernatural realm but rather with proof of probity by humans seeking contact with these beings. So that my text can avoid misreference to any such supernatural, these persons are alternatively called beings, spirits, and immortals.

JACOB'S QUESTS

The most intimate view of these beings—bonding person, place, and power(s)—was provided by a Suquamish chief whose own longevity at the time probably contributed to his willingness to divulge, under a cloak of denial, his own youthful encounters to Edward Curtis (1913, 97–100), a controversial source because his commercial interests in photography outweighed any commitment to ethnography.[8]

Jacob Wahalchu (1799–1911) signed the 1855 Point Elliott Treaty. Though he carefully denied that most of these powers were successively acquired by him, some of this rhetoric was pro forma protection of his partnerships, obviously proven by his own long life.

Jacob did not begin questing until he was a young adult because he dreaded the ordeal, despite great social pressures to do so. Finally, after a long night of hunting deer by torchlight, he found his mother opening a pit oven filled with fish and clams. Hungry, he grabbed a steaming rock cod, which his mother slapped from his hands, scolding him that children should not take the best food until the elders had eaten. She called him worthless and insensitive. Hurt, angry, and ashamed, he began to cry as he ran into the woods. That night he decided to undertake a quest and went to the cemetery at Eagle Harbor, where he climbed into a burial canoe. Nothing happened, so the next morning, he removed the bones and tried to use the canoe to go across the inlet; but this craft was so useless that he put it back.

Instead, he walked until he was across from Oleman (Oldman) House. Remembering a lake in the woods where others had quested, he made a log raft, crossed the channel, and found a marsh where the lake had been. Such wetlands were the preserve of Little Earths, the dwarf immortals who own the earth and give shamans the ability to travel safely to the land of the dead.

Determined to succeed, he spent four days fasting nearby, tying himself upright to a fir tree each night so that he would not sleep. The fourth night, a human voice called to him to look north, where he saw a light that directed him thither.

The next morning he went north to Point No Point and then to the beach below Foulweather Bluff, where he saw a huge oncoming wave hurling logs before it. Turning to run, he was transfixed by the sound of howling wolves. Realizing spirits were near, he stood to receive them. Two ducks, one white and one black, approached him on the water. Unimpressed by what he took to be minor powers, he backed away, knowing that turning his back would expose himself to their wrath. The ducks submerged, but the howling continued, gradually changing into the words of a song that said he had made a mistake in refusing this power. Jacob knew the tune to be that of an important wealth spirit. Depressed, he tried for another five days to have the power return but gave up, too starved to continue. Just south, he met people camping, who gave him food and shelter. When he regained his strength, he borrowed a canoe and went home.

After a time, he decided to quest again, going to Fletcher Bay and walking along the beach. Nothing happened until a log drifted in, struck the point, and fire flashed toward him. Immediately, the gravel turned to quicksand and his feet sank. Three more flashes came toward him, but he dodged them, watching smoke rise from the spots were they struck behind him. A woman's voice called out in woe that they had missed him and failed. From the tune, Jacob knew that this was a curing power, but since his parents had advised him against this profession, knowing full well the life-threatening dangers to himself and his family from rival doctors, he backed away.

A year or two later, Jacob went to Alki Point after fasting, ostensibly to hunt ducks. He paddled out to pick up his spent arrows and, while leaning over the side, saw a large house on the bottom of the sound with many salmon resting on its roof. Herds of elk stood around the outside. Excited, Jacob went home to get help, but his father, the proper aide, was away. His mother, grasping the situation, sent him back alone; but by then the house was gone. A faint refrain told him that this was the greatest wealth power, a requirement for a successful, generous leader.

The next time, Jacob fasted at Deception Pass for eight days before he dreamed he was in the middle of a canoe between an old couple. The man looked back and the woman forward. The old man told Jacob that he would live to be very old, like them, and that no one could harm him because these elders could see in all directions. In this way, Jacob got long life power, confirmed by his own longevity.

Again, Jacob quested by swimming from Whidbey Island to a small island at the north end of Deception Pass. Exhausted, he crawled onto the beach and, recalling that Cowlitz dug into the ground with their hands to make contact with "the other side," he did the same.[9] All night he moved sand, praying for clams, mussels, elk, fish, and plenty. The next day, he walked the beach to stay awake. He dug all the second night until, just before dawn, a voice called out and he looked up to see a standing war spear begin to dance. Then it changed into a stone war club, which also danced and sang that it was hot tempered and ate men quickly. This was a warrior power.

Jacob soon became prosperous and influential. Then he married and his questing came to an end because marital relations were incompatible with spiritual purity.

LANGUAGE

Lushootseed, used in the singular, refers to the language spoken by the various tribes of Puget Sound belonging to the Salishan language family, aboriginally spread from the Pacific shore into western Montana, with twenty-three interlinked languages of Coast (sixteen members) and Interior (seven members) divisions separated by the Cascade Mountains. Coast Salishan branches, from the north, are Nuxalk (Bella Coola), Central, Tsamosan, and Tillamook. Central Coast Salishan includes Comox, Sechelt, Pentlatch (extinct), Squamish, Nooksak, Halkomelem (including Chilliwack, Musqueam, Cowichan), Straits (including intergrading Sooke, Saanich, Songhees, Lummi, Samish, Semiahmoo, and, more apart, Klallam), Twana, and Lushootseed. Tsamosan, once called Olympic, includes Cowlitz, Upper (including Satsop) and Lower Chehalis, and Quinault.

Interior Salishan comprises dialect chains, from the north, of St'at'imcets (Lillooet), of Nlakapamuxcin (Thompson), and of Sexwepemxcin (Shuswap); and of Mid-Columbia dialect chains with "upriver" Methow-Okanogan-Nespelem-Sanpoil-Colvile-Lakes and "downriver" Chelan-Entiat-Wenatchi-Columbian; of Kalispel-Spokan-Selish (Flathead) and of Coeur d'Alene.

Lushootseed has northern and southern dialect chains. Those of the north were Skagit (including the Sauk-Suiattle), Swinomish, and the Snohomish (including the Skykomish); while south of Whidbey Island were Snoqualmi, Duwamish (including Muckleshoot), Puyallup, Nisqually, and Sahewamish, together with Suquamish on the west side (Suttles and Lane 1990).

Important distinctions are separate names for salmon species, respective accents on the first or second vowel of the basic root of a word, and the use of 4 as the pattern number in the north and of 5 in the south, presumably a borrowing from the Columbia River Chinooks and upriver Plateau tribes.

Within Salishan, Lushootseed is characterized by an ancient reworking of the two sets of transitive person markers, regularization of the suffix system, and an elaboration of prefixes. Over a century ago, Lushootseed and others shifted away from nasals so that M > B and former N > D. Thus, any snowcapped mountain is now called *taqʷoba*, which is the source for what the settlers heard as *takoma* (Tacoma) for Mount Rainier and a nearby city. Since Lummi and Klallam, nasal-using Straits Salishans, were expanding their territories around 1800, the shift from nasals by Lushootseed, Twana, Chimakum, and southern Nootkans (Makah and Ditidat, called Nitinat in English) may have been a counterresponse to Straits depredations. For example, the name of a famous warlord killed in battle, a man from the Bow Hill area near Samish River, has been transmitted to two of his descendants in Lushootseed and Straits forms. Thus, Ron Hilbert's real name is Chadəsqidab in Lushootseed, while Kenny Cooper at Lummi is known as Chanəsqinam. Such an oral/nasal distinction would have provided a ready means of distinguishing friend from foe.

1 PANORAMA

SENSE OF PLACE

The basin around Puget Sound, with Seattle at its center, was and is the home of the Lushootseed Coast Salish.[1] The rivers cascading from its rim of mountain ranges were dotted with winter towns, villages, hamlets, and seasonal camps (resorts) of a distinct tribal community, which fully interacted with all the others near and far to give order and meaning to Lushootseed culture.[2]

The sound, 40 miles wide, 170 miles long, and encompassing 1,000 miles of shoreline, includes such ecologically diverse habitats as islands, deltas, tide flats, marshes, estuaries, shallow bays, and beaches. Away from the shore, terrain is hilly, interspersed with lakes, and dense with undergrowth beneath a mixed forest of Douglas fir, red alder, grand fir, bigleaf maple, and cottonwood. Scattered parklands, kept grassy by annual burnings set by natives, included oak and Douglas fir. Edible plants ranged from a host of berries to clover, cow parsnip, fern, *wapato* (wild potato), and camas. Plentiful game, living in diverse microenvironments, comprised shellfish, ocean fish, porpoise, seal, sea lion, waterfowl, deer, elk, bear, otter, raccoon, beaver, mountain goat, and the seasonal runs of salmon, smelt, and herring (Nelson 1990, 481).

Salishans of the coast emphasized class, while those of the inland, upriver, and southern sound held Plateau ideals of a kin-based society. "Southern Puget Sound culture emphasized spirit quests and had a lesser emphasis on inherited privileges than the Northerners" (Roberts 1975, 32, 35, 77). Each "tribe" occupied an overall river drainage, the flow of which provided cohesion and identity to an otherwise diverse collection of communities and camps, except on the east and west sides of Puget Sound.

The drainage of the Duwamish had a complex outlet with an H trellis pattern, fostering an important population concentration on the interconnecting Black River, since obliterated to build downtown Renton.

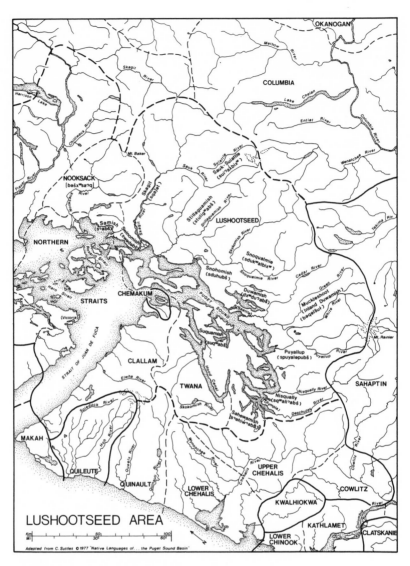

LUSHOOTSEED AREA

Adapted from C. Suttles © 1977 "Native Languages of... the Puget Sound Basin"

Lushootseed area map, properly oriented according to waterways.
(Courtesy of Lushootseed Research)

The Sahewamish, now based at Squaxon Island, derived their name for
the portage (*ʔəhiwʔ*) between the southern sound and Hood Canal. After
epidemics devastated their community, particularly when they were confined to the island during the 1855 Treaty War, the toe of the canal was re-
settled by Skokomish Twana (discussed later).

The Suquamish ancestral territory was the Kitsap Peninsula between the sound and upper Hood Canal. Their homeland, significantly, lacked any major rivers, so their subsistence adaptation required extensive travel to collect resources needed for winter, in addition to the harvesting of local foods from sheltered bays, creeks, and streams.[3]

For Lushootseed peoples, closely related yet linguistically distinct Coast Salishan neighbors were, to the north, the Nooksak; to the west, the Twana (particularly the five interrelated Skokomish towns at the elbow of Hood Canal); to the south, the Chehalis; and to the northwest, the Straits (of Juan de Fuca) Salishans of Samish, Lummi, Songhees, Saanich, Sooke, and Klallam.

Although this has seldom been reported, all traditional territories were carefully tended by their occupants.[4] As eminent ecological historian Richard White noted (1980, 20), "The Salish used fire not only to maintain their nettle grounds, but also as an instrument for shaping the ecology." While among Chehalis, Harrington (1942, reel 017, frame 0024) was told by a local minister that tribes in Puget Sound trimmed the lower branches off trees to make some of the forest beautiful, shaded, and parklike.

After epidemics spread by diseased Europeans devastated native populations, survivors scattered to safe locations as insulated upland or island communities expanded into depopulated areas.

STOCKADERS

Throughout Native America, land usage was a sacred trust, derived from ongoing relations with resident immortals, as is well illustrated by the movement of Lummi to their present location a few centuries ago (Curtis 1913, 26–30).

Living on Orcas Island, Lummis had routinely taken clams and elk from the mainland, where the aboriginal residents on Bellingham and Lummi bays, probable Nooksak speakers (Amoss 1978, 4), were known as Stockaders, benefiting from huge salmon runs through the delta of the Nooksak River. With other Straits speakers, Lummi ancestors had coveted this abundance but specialized in the use of reef nets suspended from canoes at fixed locations (Stewart 1977, 93–94).[5] Therefore, they did not know how to build river weirs, knowledge that more properly involved prayers and rituals than mere technology.

Their eventual claim is expressed in a story about a Lummi husband who insulted his Stockader wife (noting her fat legs from eating steelhead) and was beheaded by her brothers. Later his own brother quested for great power and received a club that killed whole villages.

After such depopulation from raids (and more devastating epidemics), Lummi colonists hired Stockader survivors to continue to build weirs. At the end of each season, Lummi pulled up the frameworks and hid the pieces on the north end of Lummi Island, but, knowing this location, Stockaders retrieved the posts to resell them to the Lummi every spring. Eventually, a few Lummi married, adopted, or befriended Stockaders to learn for themselves how to make weirs. Subsequently, this knowledge was passed down through families with Lummi descendants (Riley 1955).[6]

What accounts failed to grasp, however, was that while Lummis could easily build such a fence trap, they believed it would be ineffective because they lacked necessary enchantments for success with local Stockader immortals.

Duhlelap

As these Straits speakers settled at river mouths on the decimated mainland, so some Twana moved to the tip of Hood Canal, using a famous portage along a trail from Gorst on Sinclair Inlet to Belfair. Elmendorf (1960, 271) was told that a Twana looking for a lost canoe between 1800 and 1810 "discovered" this good village site, rich in waterfowl, so he led a colony from the Skokomish to settle the village of Duhlelap on Big Mission Creek, where, in respect, these Twana retained its Lushootseed name.[7] Suquamish maintained links with this area by using Mission Lake and nearby mountains for vision quests. As recently as the early 1900s, Suquamish were camping and fishing at the mouth of the Tahuya River, southwest of Belfair.

Other trails between the sound and canal crossed the Kitsap Peninsula from Dye Inlet, from the villages at Chico-Erland Point to Seabeck, from Poulsbo (called Mapleville in Lushootseed), from the village at Suquamish to Port Gamble, and from Silverdale, a route so useful that it has been paved as the Anderson Hill Road.

Because water travel predominated, portages were crucial throughout the area, highlighted by the self-designation of the Sahewamish. The Skagits had extensive contacts with their neighbors because those upriver had to portage over to the lower Samish or Stillaguamish rivers to reach salt water (Collins 1974, 39), bypassing a logjam two miles long, that blocked the river above Mount Vernon until it was dynamited away in 1878.

Across the Cascades were the Interior Salishans and Sahaptians of the Plateau culture area. Though such mountain walls have often been regarded as a barrier, sloping river valleys and upland trails enabled selective exchanges. In ancient times, moreover, this range seems to have been a common territory where a resident population remained intermediate between coastal and inland traditions. Certainly, the historic closeness of the Skagit and Chelan suggest a long period of such interactions.

Indeed, given a large prehistoric population and seasonal mobility, including summer sojourns in the peaks, the Cascades may have been a distinct subcultural region. Both Onat (1990, 12) and Bruseth (1950, 13) suggest that there was a dense, ancient, and permanent occupation of native peoples along some peaks, but little research has been devoted to its range and extent. Farther south, the California Sierras did indeed form such a separate and distinct province.

In terms of the overall Puget Basin, Marian Smith, relying on her fieldwork with the Puyallup and Nisqually, devised a spatial model, based on increasing levels of integration, for describing how native peoples related to their watersheds.[8] She explicitly recognized that the greatest allegiance and loyalty coincided with the entire drainage system.

Within each watershed, group affiliations became more expansive in terms of (a) hearthmates eating together, (b) households of all residents, (c) birthright locals—those born there in contrast to in-laws, visitors, and foreigners, (d) settlements and resorts, (e) community networks, (f) tributary drainages, and (g) the entire drainage.

Culturally, these units, increasing in size, included notions of person (combining body, mind, and soul with spirit allies); of house (including hearthers, locals, and distant kin); of canoe (transport across time and space, distinguished as forest, prairie, river, or sea); and of world (the drainage linked both to resident immortals and to more remote peoples and places through marriage, ritual, and trade). Membership within each unit derived from the subtle, discerning, and valued appreciation of customs such that insiders, in contrast to outsiders, understood the complexities of "the feud, the snub, the verbal innuendo" and accordingly "were appropriate guests for a ceremonial feast" (Roberts 1975, 79).

Major nodes in this overall system were cedar plank houses located along the shore near spots rich in local resources, such as a salmon stream, berry patch, and hunting territory. Even spirit beings lived in such houses, though this has rarely been reported (see "Jacob's Quests" in introduction) with the detail characteristic of the more northern Tsimshian, Haida, and Tlingit. Beyond this house node were at least three concentric rings occupied by allies, by competitors for regional status, and by strangers (Roberts 1975, 82).

The mountains were thickly coated with evergreen trees, including the western red cedar, the straight grain of which made it ideal for woodworking. Native technology relied on this tree, which provided planks for houses, tools for tasks, boxes for cooking and storing, and canoes—the primary transport around impenetrable undergrowth.

Lushootseed natives had an extremely complicated social life, comparable to the complex towns of farmers elsewhere, yet they largely lived by harvesting what nature provided. Bounty was enhanced as people unobtrusively left seeds and roots in well-watered locales. After traders from the Hudson's Bay Company introduced natives to potatoes, these prior talents at tending wild foods allowed them to adopt readily such tubers as a cash crop (Suttles 1987, 137–51). Traditionally, people moved with the seasons to camps near available natural foods. The climate being mild, due to the offshore Japanese and California currents, and extremely wet, the region abounded with plants and animals.

Chief among these foods were five species of salmon which (more properly, who) spawned and died in the rivers each year, although in some years the runs were more abundant than in others.[9] By working hard for a few weeks, a household could catch and dry enough fish to last the winter. Yet people did not live by fish alone. After the summer fish runs, families went into the uplands to collect dozens of kinds of berries, which were also stored for winter use. Men hunted a variety of mammals, on both sea and land, during the fall and winter. In the spring, fresh greens and early fish runs enriched the diet.

Because the dense vegetation and the rugged terrain left few level spaces where people could live, each house in every town had about fifty occupants, with placement in the house reflecting rank in local and regional society. Thus, the owner of the house and his family had the best spot in a front corner, away from the drafts at the doorway, and constituted a nobility, providing the varied leaders for community tasks. These adepts were previously known as task leaders, but this overly economic terminology is here replaced by "sigers," derived from sig (special interest group) and the -er suffix (Miller 1997).

Along the sides and back were common folks, who contributed food and upkeep to the household in return for the prestige of living with wealthy relatives. The least desirable and most exposed places in the house were available to slaves, who owed their lot to capture in raids, purchase, or birth from tainted parents. Each family had its own hearth fire along a side of the house, since eating together as a commensal unit was what defined close relations.[10] Nobles usually had more than one wife, but each seems to have had a separate fireplace to feed her children.

On important occasions, particularly during winter, the head of the house hosted public events on behalf of all the residents. Accordingly, most families moved out to other accommodations, either nearby homes or tents, to make room for guests, and two or three large fires were lit along the middle axis of the house. Huge amounts of food, gathered by slaves and housemates to be prepared by women under the direction of the senior wife of the host, were served throughout the festivities. Changes in status—such as naming, puberty, marriage, or death—provided the occasions for inviting in guests. The more prominent a family, the more people would be invited from farther away. Important families had far-flung networks of friends and kin, forged by marriage, adoption, trade, and social obligations. By prudently using resources locally "anchored," a household could add to their regional "radiance."

The crux of the entire system and the basic reason for gathering people together was the display of bonds with particular immortal powers. No one could be successful without such help. For centuries, leading families had bonded with the most powerful spirits in their locales. Lesser family members, some commoners, and even a few slaves could also have spirit partners, but these were less powerful than those of the leaders.

SPIRIT BONDS

Among Salish as well as other native cultures, the hallmark of life was the existence of immortals, intermeshed within a web (rather than a hierarchical chain of being), their positions depending on differential access to a diffuse concept of vitality, which, while deriving from a unitary source in the high god, can variously be called force, energy, potency, and power. Members of the elite, especially shamans, understood it best.[11]

Furthermore, in Lushootseed, the word for land also means nature, world, and the whole globe of earth, so "to learn from the land" was to learn from the earth and generalized nature, above all via its spiritual aspects. Even things like rocks and tools, considered inanimate by most Americans, were recognized as having spirits and the potentiality for self-motivation.

A basic premise of this cosmos, therefore, was and is that everything was alive, had access to power, and was within the sphere of responsibility of a local spirit. At crux, the basis of power in this universe derived from an ultimate entity, being, or creator, known in Lushootseed as *xa'xa*, more commonly now as *shaq si'ab* (Above Chief, Above Lord), equated with the Christian God and intermeshed with individual spirits, collectively called *sqəlalitut*, each associated with an allocation of power derived from the font of memory possessed by the Creator (Miller 1980).

In derivation, this word for spirit(s) comes from the *s-* nominalizer applied to the word meaning 'dream,' which breaks down into *qəl* 'stop,' -*al-* 'during,' *-'itut* 'sleep' (Bates, Hess, and Hilbert 1994, 18, 174) and means "an interlude during sleep." The *s-* indicates that this is "someone/something that comes during a dreamlike state," referring both to all immortals in general and to those conferring careers in particular. The other subset of such powers, much the stronger, are those for curing possessed by specialists called shamans or Indian doctors. Both the powers and these practitioners are called by the same name.[12]

According to Lushootseed mythology, all of these immortals were and are "persons" who shared qualities that made them akin to humans. All of them were specifically said to have human or humanoid characteristics, disguised when outside their abodes by the covering of their species or natural form. Sometimes, it was said that their form was not strictly human, only that they shared characteristics of gender, intelligence, and sensitivity with humanity.

The most important attitude toward all beings and life in general, therefore, was respect, in full awareness that any life form was capable of both good and harm (Hilbert 1985; Collins 1952b). By showing such respect a human indicated self-worth, sometimes tinged with fear of unexpected consequences. Of all, the most serious of the crimes against nature was waste because this showed disrespect both for a specific spirit and for all life.

All success involved a spirit and human bond, dramatically expressed in song and dance. Through it, a human could fulfill any task, career, or undertaking to benefit the human and spiritual community.

Thus, all of life was involved in constant negotiations within a cosmos of flux and flow. Indeed, movement was a characteristic of all life, either obviously as with animals, subtly as with plants, or unobtrusively as with thoughts. In addition, cross-generational bonds set up channels along recurrent, if not closed, circuitry.

For instance, while immortals were always in some contact with their human partners, they themselves traveled in such a way that they were farthest away from Lushootseed communities in the summer and closest to them in the winter, expressing a fundamental duality. Summer was devoted to economic activities, collecting food for storage and winter use, moving all over a territory among set resorts. In the winter, humans stayed in or close to their towns as immortals drew near to signal the start of the winter season, devoted to the communal rituals of their ancestral religion.

Prominent families indicated their profitable bonds by sponsoring such religious events as initiations and displays for the singing of power songs, and by providing shelter and food for visitors at these gatherings, spreading their elite reputation for sharing far and wide. Sometimes, such families went deliberately outside their home territory to gather or purchase delicacies from other areas, fostering intertribal networks based on visiting, trading, and ritual, which often led to intermarriage, adoption, and even closer cooperation.

The differential strengths and advantages a family derived from various partnerships elaborated into a triple system with two freeborn social classes (upper and lower) and an underclass of slaves. These classes were recognized by all North Pacific tribes. Wealthy families, with strong, ancient bonds, composed the nobility, known as *si'ab*, meaning an "endowment with family—with knowledgeable and resourceful relatives, rather than with wealth alone" (in Bierwert 1996, 103). Ordinary people, without a venerable pedigree or specialty career, made up the commoners, mostly honest yet volatile and lackluster.

Nobles had to be active and constantly diligent, every moment of their time used efficiently and wisely. By contrast, commoners worked intermittently, laboriously during fish runs and leisurely between them. Nobles were the managers of resources and community, constantly alert to needs and abuses that impacted on the well-being of all life. Their primary means for relaxing seems to have been the traveling that took them into other regions.

These freeborn classes were distinct from slaves, acquired as a birthright, purchase, or capture. Occasional reports indicate that even slaves sometimes entered into a partnership with an immortal, but elders were quick to stress that these were the least powerful sources of power. In his fieldnotes, Hermann Haeberlin (1917, notebook 39, 33) recorded the interesting fact that war captives taken into slavery went to the afterworld of their original tribe after death, but those born into slavery went to the afterworld of their masters, where they remained slaves forever.

This fate suggests the strength of the bond between a human and that person's community and locale among the Salish. Clearly, the strongest bond was that created by birth at a specific place, the abode of a particular immortal. Freeborn people had full access to whatever a place could bestow, while most slaves could only benefit via their masters. This contrast suggests that the modern distinction between culture and survival (discussed later) may somehow relate to an ancient one between master and slave, with obvious overtones about Euro-American oppressors. More than an invidious comparison between their past freedom and present role as "wage slaves," this astute observation expresses a native sense that the ultimate benefits from their fishing, logging, and carving belong to people other than themselves.

Traditionally, all classes seem to have been further modified by terrain and location along the drainage. While everyone living along the same river shared a common identity, those who lived downriver were distinguished from those who lived inland. Generally, downriver communities, especially those at river mouths, were more populous, diversified, and prosperous than upriver ones, particularly those in the mountains, whose more arduous life, however, gave them a certain prestige derived from admiration of their forbearing diligence.

In Lushootseed languages, the greater cohesion of the downriver towns was indicated by the -*bsh* ending, while the looser organization of the upriver communities was reflected in the -*bixᵂ* ending to imply a "bunch" (Hess 1976, 38.3), as indicated by one name for the little wild evergreen blackberry. Hence, nobles were more numerous and visible downriver.[13]

Moreover, each drainage constituted a "tribal" community in the sense that its inhabitants frequently and easily interacted with one another. Their relations involved economic, social, kinship, political, and, above all, religious considerations. Rather than constituting a tribe in the usual lingual-sociopolitical sense, the people living along a drainage represented a congregation with the same localized spirits but reflecting differences between downriver and upriver communities in that fierce ("black paint") warrior partnerships were uniquely saltwater, while gentle ("red paint") power relations were symbolically associated with the mountains and deep lakes.

As an important aspect of drainage solidarity, foodstuffs moved up and down the drainage to even out local specialties and periodic abundances. Thus, shells and marine foods went upriver as meat, hides, berries, and roots came down. Generally, these exchanges took place in a ritual or kinship context that set them apart from ordinary trading instances, which were regarded as overtly commercial and therefore somewhat crass. Thus, for the duration of a marriage, in-laws exchanged gifts with each other in a constant series to indicate ongoing kindness and goodwill. On a wider scale, members of a congregation always shared what they had, only trading or selling their resources to those characterized as outsiders and foreigners. The implication, therefore, was that everything "born" (indigenous) along a drainage was shared willingly and generously among all members, whether human, biotic, or immortal.

In part, this may reflect a belief that the drainage itself (more correctly, herself) was alive, demanding respect from all residents. Over the years, my persistent questioning of valued Lushootseed elders has confirmed that they regard rivers as associated with women, without elaborating further. Once, after severe flooding by the Skagit River, an elder specifically said it had acted like an angry woman.

Further amplification of such a statement is provided by other peoples of the Northwest who more explicitly equate rivers and women. In a Fraser River epic (see "Khaals," ch. 3), a sister was placed at the head of this river and her brother at its mouth. Farther north, on Haida Gwaii (Queen Charlotte Islands) natives believe that a Creek Woman lives at the head of every stream, with her head at its source and her feet at its outlet.

Today, Lushootseed and other elders still insist that the entire earth was and is alive; sometimes they have equated its vegetation to hair and its stones to bones. Moreover, throughout the landscape particular places were special to specific immortals. One shaman noted that local immortals and places gave each distinct language as a gift. While often overlooked, such a linkage was not unique to Salishans. In the biblical Old Testament, a parallel equation was made with Hebrew, Jews, God, and the Holy Land. For traditional Lushootseeds, Puget Sound and its environs were every bit as much of a holy land, most properly addressed in their own dialects.

For this reason, each winter community included certain individuals with a special ability (conferred by a spirit partner) to project thoughts at a distance and to sense the presence of strangers in their territory. Often, they watched the area around a camp or community, paying attention to the movement of every creature so as to forecast future conditions or dangers. In particular, all communal activity sites, particularly those associated with fishing—such as weirs, traps, and platforms—were closely watched, not to keep out intruders but to be aware of whether respect was or was not being shown to nature and its bounty, especially the salmon, who demanded the constant expression of respect if they were to return and stay year after year.

As with any endeavor, success was the outcome of a partnership between immortal and human. Among the events that could damage or cut this tie was the refusal of any human to share his or her bounty with other people, particularly the needy. Selfishness violated this pact because it stopped the circulation of goods, actions, and power in the world—representing a kind of waste due to the neglect or abuse of a resource.

During periods when salmon runs peaked, messengers were sent out from drainages to invite in distant kin and neighbors, both to prevent waste of salmon and to encourage visiting, hospitality, sharing, and local pride. Today such invitations continue, now issued over the phone to tribal fisheries managers who then broadcast them. Such mesh of new technology with old values has long been characteristic of Lushootseeds.

A central tenet of all Native American cultures was the need to share with others, to give to both the needy and the great. What moved up as homage came down as hospitality and generosity. It was perfectly in keeping with this ethic, therefore, that the predominant institution of Northwest societies was the potlatch or give-away feast, drawing together diverse members of a community (cf. Elmendorf 1971, 360, 363).

Social position and prestige derived not from membership within a local community but from links—forged by visiting, visibility, hospitality, and generosity—among a network of such communities. People who did not share were low class, and perhaps only marginally human. Generosity had the effect of creating in the social fabric a knot that contributed to increasing attention and regard over time.

Sharing was all pervasive, both in and out of the community. Warren Snyder (Indian Claims Commission 1952, 157) noted, "for the most part there was an ideal of individual ownership, but this has to be qualified by the fact that there was a great deal of sharing, and it was sharing which was forced upon a person in order for him to remain a member in good standing in the community. It was absolutely necessary that he share with other people, say, in the village, what he had."

While all normal social relations were based on sharing, the greatest benefits came to an individual who shared with others who were both far away and unrelated.[14] Such a host was considered "real high class, a real person."

It was therefore not in the best interests of a village or its leaders to exclude anyone. The dictionaries of Salishan languages assembled by Gibbs (1877), Snyder (1968), and particularly those of Hess (1976), of Bates, Hess, and Hilbert (1994), and of Thompson and Poggi (ms.) do not contain any words meaning "to exclude, exclusive, or exclusion." Nor have I found any native speakers who can supply such terms. The nearest equivalents were constructions based on a term meaning "to hide," with a semantic range that included being alone and selfish, both undesirable qualities for Lushootseeds. During hard times, sharing became especially important, and anything, however meager, was shared by everyone—with one exception.

Although food, artifacts, and hospitality were shared with all, knowledge was private property that was passed down only through family lines. The contrast was between survival, to which everyone was entitled, and culture, which was the privilege of the better families. Thus, while these tribes lacked terms for exclusion or territoriality, they did express the need to "seclude" valuable information, particularly details of epics, legends, rituals, and songs needed to maintain rapport with powerful immortals. Yet some of this knowledge also had a darker side, called victimizing magic by Elmendorf (1970, 152), and it too was private and secret.

Whereas the importance of seclusion as a Lushootseed cultural characteristic has not been generally acknowledged, federal court cases involving fishing rights have relied on notions of approval—expressed through invitation, permission, or kinship—to forge a coherent system of native rights and privileges within the confines of American law. These variables, however, have not been carefully treated.

Among Lushootseeds, the word usually given for potlatch literally means inviting (*sgʷigʷi*). But this does not mean that everyone attending had or needed a personal invitation. Rather, high class people invited only specific other high class people to events they were hosting, so as to be sure of their attendance. These invitees could then tell kin, retainers, and others the date of the event, expecting them to attend if they were able. Given the sharing ethic, a guest who arrived with a large retinue was particularly welcome. In other words, special invitations were a mark of elevated social status, given to others of a host's status or higher, who then confirmed his or her judgment by arriving with an entourage.

In lieu of an invitation, permission worked in much the same way but depended much more on place than on time. People unsure of the appropriateness of fishing or conducting any other activity asked permission of a resident noble, elder, or shaman who could be expected to know in what way the rules relating to reverence for the earth and its bounty applied to such a special request.

In Salish, asking to use resources might involve an inquiry such as "Do you think it is a good idea for me to take x resource in order to stay alive?" Clearly, when phrased this way, it was impossible for an elder to say no without very good reasons, such as stated taboos, offense to an immortal, or damage to continuing bounty. As elder Morris Dan expressed it, resources were available to anyone who needed them; the only consideration was that you "didn't run somebody else short."

Since the 1978 federal court (Boldt) decision on treaty fishing rights, kinship has been treated as the key that unlocked other resource areas for use. Usually, this was a marriage bond, which naturally led to a descent line with membership and "ownership" in both places. Actually, Lushootseeds more accurately regard kinship and marriage as the simplest expression of a complex system of regional intertribal bonds based on the recognition of identifiable persons, known and valued by a community.

Visitors were always welcome, but their arrival was never without dangers. Most came to visit, but a few came to scout out the community for a later raid to take booty and slaves. Use of resources, therefore, involved complex and subtle evaluation of guests as they arrived and while they were visiting. Access to resources was based primarily on proper attitudes, such as showing respect for people, resources, and spirits. The number of guests was also a consideration since a large group could quickly overwhelm the hosts, sell them off as slaves, and misuse the territory.

Feast, Flee, Fight, or Fidget

In all, my conclusion based on many discussions with local elders is that any such encounter could have four outcomes: the hosts could feast, flee, fight, or fidget. The first was preferred, while the second occurred when the visiting group was large and hostile. The third required people among the hosts with "mean" spirit partners conferring the toughness of warriors. The fourth was a temporary pose to prolong the waiting until something happened to decide among the other options.

Treating kinship as the sole criterion of access thereby oversimplified the system by allowing only the option of feasting. As kin, these visitors arrived as known quantities, already part of the ongoing system, though under suspicion if numerous, heavily armed, or surly.

Generally, community response was triggered by the manner of approach. As long as visitors approached in full view, they were welcomed politely before the hosts learned, in due time, their reasons for travel. Proper visitors came by canoe or walked along a recognized trail through tribal territory. Mrs. Paul Petit at Chehalis told John P. Harrington (1942, reel 018, frame 819), "My grandmother told me that in the old times if we saw a sole canoe coming, it would be a messenger and all awaited news."

A host's obligations included feeding the visitor(s), with subsequent meals escalating into feasting. During peak salmon runs, many visitors were invited to share the bounty of an area and feasting became quite lavish during lulls in their labor.

Occasions when people would flee, fight, or fidget depended upon the size of the group of visitors and the degree of uncertainty about their intention or reputation. In general, the closer a large force was to a village, the more likely the inhabitants were to flee or fight. As Mary Carolyn Howard noted in her testimony (Indian Claims Commission 1952, 15), "[People] might come in as a friend but they were always on the look out for trouble and so when any large party of people would come, they would very definitely investigate them."

Saltwater villages were the only communities to include members with warrior powers and to receive frequent unknown visitors. A few men from these downriver areas might marry into upriver settlements, but they were seldom called upon as defenders.

Fidgeting as a response occurred most often in areas along borders or away from habitations, where behavior was less governed by the conventions of social life. As Harrington (1942, reel 018, frame 661) remarked for the region, if not for all of North America, "Joint food-gathering grounds often separate American Indian linguistic divisions. Yet there were also intimate ties between a region and a tribe, based on the sharing of traditions in which primordial bonds are formed between ancestors and immortals before being perpetuated into the present."

Support for this highly diversified system of sharing—conferring status, position, and prestige across towns—spans more than the past century (cf. Elmendorf 1960, 268), beginning with the statement of George Gibbs (1877, 186–87), pioneer in Salish studies:

> The tribes are, however, somewhat tenacious of territorial right, and well understand their respective limits; but this seems to be merely as regards their title, and they never, it is believed, exclude from them other friendly tribes. It would appear also that these lands are considered to survive to the last remnant of a tribe, after its existence as such has in fact ceased. . . . As regards the fisheries, they are held in common, and no tribe pretends to claim from another, or from individuals, seigniorage [revenue] for the right of taking. In fact, such a claim would be inconvenient to all parties, as the Indians move about, on the Sound particularly, from one to another locality, according to the season. Nor do they have disputes as to their hunting grounds. Land and sea appear to be open to all with whom they are not at war.

Arthur Ballard, who learned to speak Lushootseed from his Muckleshoot nanny and devoted much time to research, also held that "non-village areas were open to all who cared to use them. This was a cultural characteristic of the Indians of the Sound area that they would share the area as being common territory" (in Horr 1974, 116–17).

While the Northwest Coast has been characterized as a potlatch society, given to elaborate generosity, the importance given to sharing resources over its wide area was not unique. For Plateau tribes along the Columbia River, sharing (sometimes called cross-utilization) was the rule for game, fish, roots, berries, furs, skins, stone, and "other materials not distributed evenly throughout the area" (Walker 1967, 8).

To the south, Arnold Pilling (1950) extends its range to the Monterey coast of California: "The Yokuts trips to the Monterey coast [for mussels and abalones] as here described are noticeably historic, being made by a mounted, armed group. However, similar long distance travel for Yokuts described by Latta, who tells how the Northern Hill Yokuts travelled over 75 miles by balsa to Buena Vista Lake annually, is strictly in the aboriginal pattern."

Interestingly, while the Yokuts sometimes fought with the local Costanoans (later known as Mission Indians), their caches of stone mortars and pestles at the coast, hundreds of miles from home, remained undisturbed until white settlement.

CULTURE AND SURVIVAL

When trying to explain their present condition to outsiders, contemporary Lushootseed elders often distinguish between culture and survival to express the recent changes that have greatly impacted their lives and communities.

At base, survival is what people have to do to keep themselves and their families in food, clothing, and other necessities, such as cars, boats, gas, and utilities. Since the 1850s, it has involved work for wages from lumbering, commercial fishing, carpentry, canoe ferrying, or unskilled labor. To do this, people moved out of their native community and so lost full participation in family life and public events, except for sending back money and goods.

Survival means that children are not encouraged to use native languages and traditions in the (not entirely mistaken) belief that this will interfere with their education in American schools. Today, well-meaning elders hope that if they suppress native fluency, their children will profit from the perceived advantages of white Americans. Usually, this does not happen unless elders also provide a strong sense of direction and self-confidence for finding a way through the social and emotional strains of an alien, dehumanizing modern world.

In consequence, elders have had to point out that culture, the quality of a lifeway based in the land, is not the same as survival, earning a living by exploiting that same terrain. Sometimes, the two were and are incompatible, as when a new initiate into the winter dance has to quit his or her job before having the time and energy to learn this aspect of culture. Over long winter months, elders made speeches intended to instill values, attitudes, customs, and practices that were once commonplace. While in seclusion, the initiate had to rely on family, friends, and trainers for food, money, and other necessities.

When the late Martin Sampson (Bierwert 1993), a Swinomish leader, was asked by Vi Hilbert, a Skagit relative, to define native culture, he said that it was "learning from the land."

Insightfully, Sampson captured the essential difference between culture and survival. Culture involved keen attention, receptivity, and reciprocity within the resident community of sentient, sensitive, and sensory life. Survival merely consisted of a disinterested utilization of some obvious, but less important, features of this unity. Culture was a dynamic, interactive, and receptive process of insightful learning, while survival was drudgery, mechanical and uninformative. The one recognized the primacy of the spirit and spiritual; the other ignored them for mundane reasons of practicality until things become so wrong as to require a ritual to restore proper conditions.

SHAMANS

In addition to career powers, ranging from woodworking and canoe making to berry picking and midwifery, curing powers assured the well-being of the whole community because they were constantly available.

Leaders had spirits, themselves leaders, that empowered them to give wise counsel and to acquire wealth as well as to hunt the most dangerous of animals. Most chiefs had inherited power from Thunder and passed it along to their heirs for generations, giving each a booming voice and eye-catching flair. Leaders also needed wealth or property-attracting power to enable them to be generous.

Most spirits, however, only visited their human partner in the winter months. During these long *rainy* winters, people gathered to welcome back their spirits by singing and dancing a mime of how they had first met in some remote spot on the land or in the sea. The rest of the year, the spirits lived in villages of their own "on the other side" of the human dimension, before spiraling all winter through the Salish country from the east to the north, west, and south. Towns knew their location along the route from centuries of such visits and began to prepare to host their own power displays once they had been invited to the celebrations of the towns that always preceded them on the circuit.

For most people in most places, these public displays set the seasonal pattern for trafficking with powers. In every community, however, there were and are specialists who maintained personal and permanent relations with another kind of spirit power. The Lushootseed generic word for spirits referred either to career or to curing powers, with this latter named subset constituting the doctors of the universe.

Though these were usually known as shamans, this term for both spirits and their human allies derived from Lushootseed for "name" or "call" because in the native system of medicine, to designate correctly (to "name") the cause of an illness was to diagnose the cure. Shamans and curing spirits were always at the ready, unlike career powers, whose closeness varied with the seasons.

To be effective, the head of a household and the leader of a town, who was also the head of the most distinguished house, either had to acquire such a doctoring spirit or had to have a trusted associate who was a shaman. Just as European noble families sent various sons into the church, into business, banking, or the military to widen the family power base, so too did Lushootseed nobles try to have members in all positions of authority, since leadership was multiplex, depending on the task. Leadership relied on specialization, so each activity had its own "siger" to take charge, but only for the duration of that activity.

Moreover, modern Salish families extend this strategy to include many contemporary options, particularly religious ones, believing ecumenically that the more religions you have, the better for you. Thus, while families continue to attend winter ceremonials to welcome the return of spirit partners, on Sunday they devotedly attend Protestant, Catholic, Bahai, or other services.

SHAKERS

In addition, for the past century, natives of Puget Sound and beyond have belonged to a religion uniquely their own and legally incorporated in Washington State in 1910. Known as the Indian Shaker Church, it was founded by a local man, John Slocum, and his wife Mary (Amoss 1981, 1982; Ruby and Brown 1996). In October of 1882, John died and went to heaven, but God, the Christian God, sent him back to preach a new religion, founded when his wife began to shake over his body just before he revived.[15] While many of the overt actions are like details of Catholic worship—such as altars, albs, candles, and making the Sign of the Cross by placing fingers to forehead, shoulders, and chest—the use of hand bells to accompany hymns during circular processions was a creative innovation.

When natives join the Shaker Church, furthermore, their spirit powers convert with them, thus continuing the ancestral religious tradition.[16] The primary role of Shakers in the modern native community is curing, especially of addictions, but unlike the ancient shamanic tradition that also

Indian Shakers, including four women in white garments, gathered around an altar with bells and candle atypically set up outside. (Courtesy of Lushootseed Research)

continues, Shaker curing is much more democratic in the sense that it is performed by all believers and is free of charge.

Today, shamanism continues to be the career of aloof individuals who mostly work alone. Traditionally, shamans were feared for this mood, often described as mean and selfish, but they were nevertheless respected for the good that they did or could do. Whenever a shaman enters a room or a native gathering, quiet quickly falls over the people. Since powerful spirits travel with him or her and cannot be seen, everyone has to be especially careful not to give offense of any kind.

Among the Salish, sexual equality was and remains well developed. With proper supernatural sanction, any man or woman could perform any task. Gender roles, therefore, existed only in the statistical sense that men tended to do some things and women to do others. Since the immortal spirits also had gender, a woman performing usually male roles was presumed to have a male spirit. Anyone undertaking a quest could expect to receive a spirit of either gender since there was no obligation for male spirits to appear only to men or for female immortals to gift only women. Dr. Bill, a famous Snoqualmi shaman at Tolt (now Carnation, Washington), went to the land of the dead with the aid of a female Little Earth (Miller 1988, 18).

When someone fell ill, the character and duration of the disease determined which curer would be called to provide treatment. If it was a European-derived case of measles or a problem that required surgery, then a university-trained physician was consulted or the patient went to a hospital. But natives were and are subject to many more diseases than modern allopathic medicine can treat. Bad relations ("breaches") with the cosmos, the community, the family, and the self were manifest in particular diseases. Though psychologically derived (according to Western categories), these problems were nonetheless painfully real and could be fatal.

To improve community sentiment and general well-being, Shakers are now generally called in because they cure communally and never accept money for their treatments, although they are given donations to pay for gas and lodging. For present-day instances of cosmic disharmony and spiritual disaffection, a shaman is called, loudly and repeatedly so that his or her spirits will also know that they are needed. Such a shaman is expensive, although fees are returned to the family if the cure proves unsuccessful or the patient dies.

Shamans who lost too many cases, however, were killed by their own relatives because of a belief that their powers had turned malevolent and would henceforth only kill and not cure, beginning with the youngest, closest, most vulnerable members of that family. Such a shaman became a liability to the community, but the execution had to be performed by a family member so as to prevent a blood feud. A bereaved family that did not wait for justice but instead killed the shaman themselves precipitated hostilities until they gave goods to settle up with the shaman's kin.

ATTACKS

Illnesses cured by shamans could have either external or internal causes. Sometimes, another shaman became jealous or envious of someone or was hired by an enemy to make that someone sick. Often, the onset of this illness was caused by magically "shooting" a sharp object or barbed probe into the patient's body.

A victim could be attacked at three junctures: mind, spirit, or breath. A shaman relied on his spirit helpers to indicate what was wrong with a patient and how to cure it. Lushootseed shamans had a characteristic gesture, placing the upper face near the crook of an arm, for making such a diagnosis. By placing the back of the wrist against the forehead, normal sight was blocked to gain access to a curing spirit with X-ray sight that was believed to live in the lower arm. Also, entering into a trance was helped by the rhythmic pulses of the veins at the forehead and wrist.

For the Salish, as for other Native Americans, the mind was located in the heart at the center of the body.[17] The brain stored memories, thoughts, and emotions. Therefore, sorcery applied to the heart would confuse and weaken a person, leaving him or her susceptible to worse illness. The shaman had to suck out whatever probing object had been magically shot into the body, often by using slack fists stacked atop each other to form a sucking tube. Modesty required that a shaman avoid touching the patient's body as much as possible. Once the problem was gathered inside the fists, it was either sent away, if not too dangerous, or, on rare occasions, it was drowned in a basket filled with water.[18]

The second instance, spirit illness, was a common phenomenon of winter. Spirit powers were acquired in youth, before puberty in the old days and by initiation today, but they did not begin visiting their human partners annually until middle age, when a successful career and healthy family were taken as proof of a spirit ally.

Every winter, when the spirit returned to its human, that mortal became ill ("sick to sing"). The first time this happened, a special shaman was called to "draw out" the song that had lodged in the throat of that man or woman. The shaman then sang the song of the initiate so that everyone in the house could hear and remember it, because thereafter, whenever that human became ill, people had to gather with drums to sing while the invalid danced to become attuned to and strengthened by his or her bond.

Today, at large weekend gatherings all winter long, everyone sings and dances an evocation of their (or an ancestor's) first encounter with a spirit. Type of song and gestures help to suggest the general category of that spirit, but exact details are guarded.

Sometimes, in this second kind of illness, a shaman found one of these spirit allies attractive and stole it from its human, who then became gravely ill. If a more powerful shaman could not retrieve the spirit, then the human partner died, unless he or she could quickly acquire another strong power, which was virtually impossible.

In the third illness, a spirit, shaman, or deceased loved one might steal someone's breath. Since the very word for life derived from the word for breath, such a theft led to death, either quickly, if that was what the perpetrator wanted, or after prolonged lingering with great suffering for maximum revenge. Breath was linked with the soul, so the delay in death was a consequence of the time allowed for the soul to wander to the land of the dead, where it became a ghost.

When someone died, everything that person owned was given away because any memento might make a relative fixate on the deceased and thus become a prime candidate for being lured away by a forlorn ancestor. Natives say the dead cannot help killing their descendants because they were and are believed to be lonely and to have little else to do.

Indeed, the dead remain more significant in the lives of Lushootseed people than anything else except the spirits. For people living in close and caring communities, the bonds of the flesh, like those of the spirit, continued far beyond the grave. In the same way that only specialists like shamans and "mediums" could remain in contact with their powers, so too could they make contact with the dead. To do so, they engaged in one of the most impressive and meaningful ceremonies of Native North America and the world. Though mistitled the Spirit Canoe Ceremony, its correct intent was the recovery of stolen vitality, in various intensities as mind, soul, or spirit.

Last held in the winter of 1900, the shamanic odyssey is only vaguely known to present Lushootseed elders. Yet, at various times over the past century, missionaries, scholars, and visitors have provided glimpses of the rite, assembled and analyzed for comparison with beliefs and practices throughout Native North America (Miller 1988).

In this companion volume, however, the rite is viewed within the context of its own Lushootseed culture and the regional network reflecting the equation of cosmos, canoe, house, and body.

In human societies without a tradition of scientific inquiry, the cosmos was an organic whole in which the shape of the house mirrored that of the universe, as did the body, both of biological species with essentially human underforms and of canoes as an animated means of facilitating transport and interconnections. The house frame was imagined to be a body on its hands and knees, with the face at the front. Therefore, the outer skin, canoe shell, house walls, and rim of the world were equated, as were the inner heart, hearth, and helios. In regions with gabled roofs, moreover, the ridge pole was equated with a spine, river, and the Milky Way, as were the four support posts with human limbs and sky pillars. The bow of a canoe was a head, as paddles were arms. In consequence, curing, bailing, and cleaning were all reflexes of a renewal of the world.

WEDGING RELIGION

The Northwest is a region where the all-pervasive religious inspiration of native peoples resonates throughout the historic literature, even though it has been written by and for outsiders. Similarly, again and again, natives took talents and tools learned from Europeans but then gave them native religious applications. They earned wages to host family and community rituals. In the most dramatic instance of all, John Slocum and Mary Thompson Slocum adapted the Christian God to the Indian Shaker Church (Ruby and Brown 1996), founded with John's first death on 20 October 1882 and incorporated in 1910.

With the precision so characteristic of Native American languages, Susie Sampson Peter (Lushootseed Press 1995a, 60, line 335) explained her view of how Americans, locally called Bostons, came to dominate native lands.[1] After mentioning a Kikialus settlement near Utsaladdy on Camano Island, she added that "Bostons squeezed themselves into the very middle of the clearing where natives had their homes." The morpheme she used for squeezed is *ch'ədkʷ*, "penetrate, break through the surface" (Bates, Hess, and Hilbert 1994, 70). A better translation would be "wedged," with the sense of gaining a toehold and then forcefully expanding to occupy all the surrounding space. In other words, in the native view as confirmed by the language, whites took over the Northwest by acting as expanding wedges set in the most desirable areas, generally those long occupied and developed by resident native communities. As a descriptive image, it is both vivid and telling, especially when compared with academic history.

BRIDGING SPACE, FAITH, AND TIME

In lieu of detailing that amply documented history, its cumulative assessment by Alexandra Harmon (1995) provides a useful overview to make the point about the paramountcy of religion for natives.[2]

Snoqualmi Tribal Council, federally recognized in 1997, meeting 22 February 1948 to pursue land claims. Jerry Kanim, standing in the center, publicized the Shamanic Odyssey around Puget Sound to raise funds during the 1930s and 1940s. Others in this photo include a Shaker bishop and a man who appeared in the famous set of 1920 pictures portraying aspects of a shamanic odyssey led by Kanim (Miller 1988). (Courtesy *Seattle Post-Intelligencer* Collection, Museum of History and Industry, no. 23888)

Characterizing the ever-contested "middle ground" between natives and settlers as a partial bridge with unsure footings (Harmon 1995, 253), she regarded its status as a compromise solution. "In a haphazard and sometimes acrimonious process, Indians and non-Indians mixed such elements as kinship, lineage, property law, social relations, and residence to build a rambling structure that offered some people welcome shelter, trapped others against their will, and kept out still others who wanted in" (Harmon 1995, 421). Indeed, to find common ground natives often had "to present their complex web of social relations in simplified form" (1995, 421), and leave their ongoing traditional beliefs entirely out of the discussion.

Considering aspects of this negotiation in various time frames, she began with the fur trade, before moving on to Euro-American homesteading, treaties, reservations, federal policy, and legal cases culminating in the 1978 Boldt decision guaranteeing to Washington natives half of the annual harvestable salmon. "Distinctive conditions arising from population distribution, economic activities, political institutions, or national policy therefore frame . . . each successive political and economic context, [when] the historical protagonists have pondered anew, debated, and revised the indicators and the implications of Indian identity in the Puget Sound region" (Harmon 1995, 12). By limiting herself to economic phases, however, she slighted significant historical complexities involved with native cultures interacting with varieties of Christianity.

Natives joined the labor force to acquire money and trade goods to benefit their own family prestige, not to become "white." Yet from Eurocentric sources, we learn more about native roles in the money economy than how and when they applied this new wealth to traditional activities. Indeed, too close an identification with American interests, as among the Klallam at the Port Gamble mill, led to their designation as "Little Bostons." Earlier, the 1833 founding of Fort Nisqually provided revenue to those living along the beach at Sequalitchew Creek.

Lahalet, a leader of that village, came to wider prominence, which he confirmed by marriage to women from at least five other tribes. Waskalatchy, a Snohomish leader, became known as "the Frenchman" because he adopted a métis style of dress, grew a beard, and frequented the fort. From Whidbey Island's Penn Cove came Tsalalakum and Sneatlum, both of whom later became influential Catholics.

From 1818 to 1846, the Northwest was a joint use area for British and Americans, who also played out their differences in religious terms. While natives used religion as a fundamental means of ecological regulation for the entire universe, Europeans used it as a means to a political end.

The Hudson's Bay Company (HBC), through its string of trading posts like Fort Nisqually, discouraged native hostilities in the interests of a far-flung fur trade. Overall, HBC rule was indirect, relying on native trading leaders, the native wives of employees, and, at Fort Nisqually, native judges from Yelm noted for their arbitration skills (Sicade 1940, 492).[3] Unable to make economic headway against this monopoly, Americans established Protestant missions to "serve" the native population, foster migrants from the states, and spread American presence, which eventually overwhelmed the region.

Some fur traders instructed native people in aspects of Christianity, with the higher officials being Anglican while French Canadian and métis voyagers were Catholic. About 1830, Spokan Garry, who had been sent as a boy for schooling among retired HBC personnel at Red River (later Winnipeg), returned to preach a nativized Protestantism among his neighbors in the Plateau country.

Responding to Iroquois voyagers in the western fur trade who had been baptized in eastern Canada, Flathead and Numipu (Nez Perce) men set out for St. Louis four times after 1830 to ask for "blackrobes with the Great Prayer," specifically meaning Jesuits with the Catholic mass, but such priests did not come until Pierre de Smet organized the interior missions in 1842.

Protestants responded more quickly, beginning with 1836 Congregationalist missions among Nez Perce by Henry and Eliza Spaulding and among Cayuse by Marcus and Narcissa Whitman, who were massacred in 1847.[4] In 1837, a Spokan mission was founded at Tshimakain jointly by Elkanah and Mary Walker and by Cushing and Myra Eells, whose sons spent their careers in Puget Sound.

Brief coastal Protestant missions began with Reverend Herbert Beaver, an Anglican at Fort Vancouver from 16 September 1836 to November 1838, when the Catholic mission began. From the spring of 1839 to the fall of 1842, a futile Methodist mission was located at Fort Nisqually, under the care of Reverend David Leslie and Brother William Holden Willson. In 1876, after moving as Catholics to Lummi resulted in their dispossession by settlers, Nooksaks became Methodists (Amoss 1978, 22), setting themselves apart from most neighboring tribes just as their aboriginal language had done.[5]

Periodically, novel situations led to distinctly religious responses by and for natives. The most incongruous involved a visit to Fort Nisqually on Wednesday, 21 January 1835, by a Suquamish young man who was "rising up a new religion" after a "vision of celestial beings" who gave him a written paper and eighteen invisible blankets. On 10 February, this Suquamish "juggler . . . is again doing wonders about his tribe—it is said he has a coat covered with dollars and is making presents to the natives by giving them Blankets of Cloth. . . . This is to be a yearly custom with him therefore they (his friends) will be well off." But this generosity led to his undoing for, on 19 February, Chief Tsalalakum, a Suquamish living on Whidbey Island, reported that the young juggler had been exposed for robbing grave offerings to provide wondrous goods to his followers. After much deliberation, in lieu of execution, a council of chiefs banished this "rascal" from Puget Sound (Bagley 1916, 157, 159, 160).

Presumably, this Suquamish prophet used his travels to take goods left on graves, mostly manufactured items, to entice followers, relying on the sameness of imported goods to conceal their source. As his movement spread, however, some item must have been identified as a grave offering to result in his accusation and banishment.

What is fascinating, moreover, is that Tsalalakum was soon to distinguish himself as a leading Catholic convert, adding to his fame in the fur trade, much like his colleague Sneatlum (Harmon 1995, 120). In sum, religious motivation is clear for both failed prophet and successful convert, and, indeed, the charge of one against the other contributed to the eventual success of Catholicism and other forms of Christianity.[6]

Catholic secular clergy, Fathers Francis Norbert Blanchet and Modeste Demers, arrived at Fort Vancouver on 24 November 1838 and soon established headquarters at Cowlitz Farms, "regularizing" métis marriages, instructing native visitors, and undertaking periodic tours along the coast. Surprised to learn of his fellow missionaries on the coast, De Smet reported that Blanchet had devised the Catholic ladder in 1839 (cf. White and St. Laurent 1996) as a mnemonic to instruct twelve Lushootseed visitors, led by Tsalalakum, whose success in using it was confirmed the next year when a visiting priest was greeted by a wooden cross and Latin hymns on Whidbey Island. Tsalalakum later served as guide, companion, and advisor to Father Demers during visits among the tribes of Puget Sound (Sullivan 1932, 36).

Reverend John B. Z. Bolduc (1941, 81), who joined the Catholic mission in 1842, also visited Whidbey, where Sneatlam, chief of the Skagits, had a house (28 by 25 feet) built for him in two days during late March (Harmon 1995, 123).[7] Notably, the two hundred workmen were directed by four skilled carpenters, presumably with ancient woodworking power. While the priest had his own explanation for this effort, Sneatlam was following family tradition, much as his own father had assembled workers to build a famous potlatch house (see "Owners" in ch. 4). A new religion obviously needed a new public building, and the glory went more to Sneatlam than to the church.

Missionary success eventually resulted in Francis Norbert Blanchet becoming Bishop of Oregon City; his brother Augustine, Bishop of Walla Walla; and Modeste Demers, Bishop of Vancouver Island.[8] Responding to a plea from Augustine, the Oblates sent five recruits to the Plateau, including Charles Pandosy and Eugene Casimir Chirouse, who were ordained inside Fort Walla Walla at the 1848 New Year. Father Chirouse had a long career at Tulalip, where he learned Snohomish and worked closely with the Skagit Prophet (Captain Campbell, discussed in ch. 4 under "Specializations"). After the other five Oblates were reassigned to Canada, Chirouse was assisted at Tulalip by Father Paul Durieu, who later became Bishop of British Columbia and encouraged model native governments based on Catholic tenets.[9]

From the start, native leaders befriended Europeans through their own well-developed sense of humane outreach, serving as guides, interpreters, couriers, laborers, and mobilizers. During all these historical and ethnic interactions, leaders played diversified roles enhancing their special effectiveness at these cultural boundaries. In addition to new prestige, novel goods, and increased name recognition, friendship with Europeans also included unforeseen advantages, such as inoculations.[10]

While the Hudson's Bay Company was long the dominant force throughout the region, American homesteaders moved north from California and Oregon after the 1849 gold rush, bringing along prejudicial terms such as "rancheree" to refer to native homesteads. With the 1846 compromise border, American numbers swelled, although the flood came after the Civil War and the completion of the transcontinental railroad in 1869.

During the winter of 1855, natives began to be excluded from much of their homelands when Isaac Stevens forced the series of treaties "legally" ceding land from Idaho to the Pacific. Done in a hurry, councils were held in January, at the time of the year natives devoted to their religious ceremonials, adding greater import to the treaty process. Yet the lands reserved by natives for their own use as reservations and fisheries did not become their refuges until decades later.

Racism was rampant, including a legal ban on mixed marriages from 1855 to 1866 (Harmon 1995, 372). Of course, native women and European men continued to marry and have families, but they did so without the comfort of law. When métis children tried to sue for their inheritance from a white father, this law was used against them.

Through the late 1800s, half of all Puget Sound natives lived off reservations, at their own separate homesteads and camps. Each worker and family decided how and where to live based on a variety of options, such as "the amount and quality of reservation land, the availability of government services, the proximity of towns and wage work opportunities, the activities of nearby non-Indians, and the religious affiliation of white overseers" (Harmon 1995, 314).

As elsewhere, European traders, missionaries, and government officials came with their own prejudices about what constituted acceptable behavior. In particular, natives were criticized for "polygamous marriage, . . . aboriginal healing rituals, potlatches, gambling, and liquor consumption" as disruptive of nuclear family harmony and productivity (Harmon 1995, 307). Larger issues of worldview and cultural diversity were ignored, misunderstood, disparaged, or condemned.

Yet when public events needed a regional flavor, tabooed and other native customs were favored. In 1895, the forty-first wedding anniversary celebration for David and Rebecca Denny included sixteen youngsters dressed as Indians, forming a circle, singing, and beating time against "tahmanawas boards" (Denny 1909, 260). When Teddy Roosevelt visited in 1902, native boys were paid to race canoes, while a 1903 labor carnival at the University of Washington included a working village staffed by Port Madison Suquamish. In 1911, Seattle celebrated its own founding with a Golden Potlatch. Moreover, when teacher and agent Edwin Chalcraft imposed his authority at Chehalis, he sometimes hosted a feast, "calling it a 'potlatch' to signify good will" and lessen resentment against him (Harmon 1995, 312).

Native adzed-plank houses, bastions of communal life, were early targets of American authority. In 1871, Reverend Myron Eells, missionary and agent at Skokomish, had Klallam houses on the Port Townsend beach burned in a vain attempt to force a move to his reservation. About 1874, men desiring lands already improved burned down the plank homes at Minter Creek on the Key Peninsula, and built their own cabins. Hostilities were averted because these landgrabbers deliberately kept away from the aboriginal Glen Cove fishery where this community rebuilt (Harmon 1995, 286).

Increasing native dependence on Euro-American goods and materials, albeit for their own purposes, also dampened hostilities. Log cabins and clapboard housing depended on sawmills, the lumber from which supplied California wharfs, ships, and houses. In addition, native workers helped to export shellfish and, later, canned salmon. From earliest contact, native men functioned as guides, translators, and couriers. Indeed, carrying any piece of paper was a guarantee of safe conduct throughout the Northwest, as Paul Kane (1925, 171) observed for a Nisqually who canoed to Fort Victoria in search of his enslaved wife.

At Fort Nisqually, native women worked as domestics—cooking, washing clothes, tending children, and keeping house for fur company families.[11] Routinely, men worked to pack cargo to and from the fort, cut wood, construct buildings, "shear sheep, round up cattle, build fences, plant and harvest peas and potatoes, and spread manure" (Harmon 1995, 88–89). Such labor intensified in 1841 when Fort Nisqually became the major outpost of the Puget Sound Agricultural Company and "4,500 sheep and 1,000 cattle grazed where there had been eleven head of cattle and four oxen only four years earlier" (1995, 88). Initially, foremen were Kanakas (Hawaiians) or métis Canadians, but, over time, several of these key positions were held by Lushootseed men.

Many native families also had their own gardens and fields, getting seeds and plant starts from the fort. Settler livestock was often a problem since unattended cows and pigs destroyed both indigenous and farmed foods. When cattle at Ebey's Landing destroyed Klallam potato fields, their protests in 1853 led to their receiving three hundred dollars in compensation, even though this land had been usurped from Whidbey Island Skagits.

Furthermore, Whidbey provided a microcosm of the recent economic history of the sound, beginning with logging by settlers to clear the land. They took the more familiar oaks first, then the best Douglas fir with bull teams; in the twentieth century they returned for "cedar, the remaining fir, and even hemlock, and then . . . second growth, which smaller operations harvested as mining poles, railway ties, and cordwood." Use of the open land shifted from potatoes and vegetables, made unprofitable by cheap shipments from California, to sheep raising, back to grain and potatoes, and then to "intensive farming by Chinese tenants" (White 1980, 62, 95).

Most natives remained involved with their local environment, using their well-honed talents involving the land, forest, and sea. They traded meat and fish with settlers, along with baskets, canoes, firewood, and labor. In his 1880 census of Klallam living off reservation, Eells (1884) listed incomes as "34 sawmill workers, 22 farmers, 80 fishers, 23 general laborers, 40 mat and basket makers, 17 sealers, 3 police, 15 medicine men and women, 1 carpenter, 2 wood choppers, and 1 blacksmith. Among 242 Twana were 42 farmers, 4 carpenters, 2 blacksmiths, 4 laborers, 7 hunters, 20 fishers, 21 lumbermen and loggers, 1 interpreter, 1 policeman, 6 medicine men, 7 washerwomen, 6 mat and basket makers, and 1 assistant matron" (Harmon 1995, 524).

By 1917, natives earned wages as loggers, stevedores, sawyers, farmers, fishers, clam diggers, general laborers, cooks, farm labor contractors, tailors, blacksmiths, a bridge builder, and a steamboat fireman" (Harmon 1995, 474). Note that while shamans continued to practice, they are not listed. Natives hid cherished beliefs behind conversion until negotiated compromises advanced the concern with fishing as the persistent, permissible stereotype of native identity and income. Other Americans could easily grasp such emphasis on food, family, and livelihood, hiding its religious basis.

During the 1920s, Puget Sound natives began to use federal and state courts "to begin constructing a common identity based on a common history. In public forums many individuals from diverse communities had the opportunity to describe for each other who they had been and who they had become during eighty years of interaction with Americans. As Harriet Shelton Dover said, the Indians lost that round, but at least there were a lot of meetings bringing people together. Organizing and prosecuting a case in the Claims Court meant putting people who asserted an Indian identity on display and allowing them to articulate, especially in terms of their history, what made them Indians" (Harmon 1995, 508).

While Dr. Charles Buchanan, long physician and agent at Tulalip, "believed that the indices of [native] membership were descent from Indians represented at the treaty, residence in the reservation community, and continuing association with Indians of that community" (Harmon 1995, 384), natives themselves relied more on extralegal criteria, such as shared kinship, ideology, and, above all, links with a particular plot of land, however tenuous.

Native sense of place was and is constantly confirmed throughout all records. Traditionally, each community insisted on its ownership of local territory and resources but shared them willingly. Settlers who acknowledged aboriginal claims were welcome to build and improve local lands in the native hope that they would learn to be better humans. Indeed, as recalled by Emily Denny (1909, 114–15) more than fifty years later, natives claimed kinship with all children born on their lands, saying "You were born in our 'illahee' and are our 'tillicum.' You eat the same food, will grow up here and belong to us." [12]

It was land that provided the abodes of spirits, the placement of resources, and the domain of human communities. In outline, each shamanic odyssey duplicated the route used by the souls of a particular place to their own eternal locale in the afterworld. Native religion, therefore, was mostly about place, position in this world and in the afterworld, as the anchorage from which to radiate.

In all, therefore, in trying to bridge the worlds of Europeans and those of natives on the sound, the endspan of the outsiders was founded on economic considerations of workplace, while that of natives was based in spiritual considerations of ancestral place. That these bridges ever met (to any extent) is due to the material aspects confirming belief—as a powerful spirit provided wealth in tangibles—overlapping to a small degree with aspects of Euro-American economy. As prosperity was an outward manifestation of inward grace for some Christians, so confirmed native access to spiritual powers provided for human needs, wants, and wishes. Goods were an outpouring of the good and godly, which for Europeans relates to the individual but for natives relates to family, community, and society.

The European attack on native religion was doubly insidious, trying to make people embrace a self-image motivated by financial (not spiritual) considerations, under the auspices of a white, male, all-powerful God (rather than apportioned, coordinating powers) while also tearing at the organic religious foundations that morally and socially inspired the natives' own traditional image as integral within a greater universe.

By contrast, an element of appeal in Pentecostalism for gender-equal Salishans was the prominence of women in its history. Inspired by teachers at Bethel Bible College in Topeka, Kansas, Agnes Ozman received Spirit Baptism on 1 January 1901, beginning modern expressions that blossomed during the 1906 Azuza Street (Los Angeles) Revival and Aimee Semple Mcpherson's 1921 founding of the Foursquare Gospel Church and the Angelus Temple in the same city. Before 1920, Sarah Ober actively worked to recruit Washington Shakers into the Pentecostal fold but to no avail, even among those already using the Bible. Today, members of both faiths remain friendly, recognizing that both place great emphasis on possession by "spirit" as evidence of a direct link with God, exuberantly expressed while healing the sick and afflicted (Amoss 1978, 81; Ruby and Brown 1996, 154).[13]

By historical happenstance, probably because George Gibbs (1877; cf. Beckham 1969), sometime treaty secretary, saw destitute California natives during the Gold Rush and Governor Isaac Stevens wanted natives to feed themselves with free salmon, a clause was inserted into most 1855 treaties to assure natives a legal right to take fish in common with settlers at their usual and accustomed (UnA) grounds and stations.

Isaac Stevens—simultaneously Washington territorial governor, superintendent of regional Indian affairs, and director of the survey of a northern railroad route through the United States—forcefully concluded a series of treaties: Medicine Creek in December, 1854; Point Elliott, Point No Point, and Neah Bay, all in January, 1855; Yakama, Walla Walla, and Nez Perce within three days in June; Quinault and Hell Gate in July; and Judith River in October. Congress, suspicious of Stevens's debacle at Grey's Harbor in March of 1855 and the immediate outbreak of the Treaty War, did not ratify many of these treaties until 1859.

A century later, a federal court made fishing rights the common span bridging natives and other Americans in the Northwest. For natives it confirmed their sense of place through assured natural bounty, while for federal agents it provided people with the means to feed a family and supply other necessities, regardless of its ancient and continuing cultural import. Yet natives celebrated their victory not only by buying fishing boats but also by reviving the First Salmon ceremony, acknowledging the religious basis of and for their economic success (Amoss 1987).

The multiple inabilities of local settlers to grasp or understand Lushootseed culture is sadly illustrated by an 1874 trial. On 14 December 1873, as his wife Susie lay dying, Harry Fisk shot Dr. Jackson, a Squaxin shaman, once in the head with a rifle and then twice in the body with a pistol. That Jackson did not die immediately after the first shot must have been taken as an indication of his considerable powers.

Fisk, whose father was white and mother native, worked as a translator for the local superintendent of Indian affairs, using this authority to serve as an intercultural go-between around Olympia, so his relations with other Lushootseeds were sometimes strained by his employer's demands. During a potlatch in Seattle a week before, one of Fisk's enemies hired Dr. Jackson with nine blankets to project an evil power (*masatchie tamanawas* in Chinook jargon) into Susie, presumably because Harry had his own strong allies to protect himself. Certainly, the speed with which Susie became mortally ill was another indication of the intensities of power involved.

When other remedies, such as other shamans or medicines, proved of no avail, Fisk went to Olympia, found Jackson, handcuffed him under the pretense of making an arrest, and took him to Mud Bay, an off-reservation native community five miles away, where Susie languished in the home of Indian Sandy. Confronted with his victim, Jackson was unmoved. In desperation, Susie demanded that Harry kill him to save her. Fisk fired both a rifle and a revolver at point-blank range, but the shaman resisted, then took a while to die, pleading to men standing nearby for weapons to defend himself. Lewis, who was about to chop wood, refused his ax. Half a day later, as Susie died, she gloated in the voice of Dr. Jackson claiming fatal responsibility. As a result, native witnesses concluded that Fisk had taken the right course at the wrong time, waiting a week too long to save his wife.

During white preparation for the trial, however, the judge and opposing lawyers developed legal strategies for this first case involving a native murdering another native. Their positions are instructive, if wrongheaded. Previously, such crimes had been left entirely to native justice, because as the judge explained to the jury, "An Indian is a man if he kills a white man, but loses his identity if he kills an Indian" (Asher 1995, 19). Not until 1885 was such federal jurisdiction imposed on reservations by the Major Crimes Act.

In this era of President Ulysses S. Grant's peace policy to put Christian reformers in charge of corruptly administered reservations, the prosecutor sought to use this trial to force natives into the American mold, while the defender argued that believing in witchcraft was an insane delusion justifying self-defense without criminal intent.

In twenty-two pages of instruction, the judge insisted that law was an objective search for truth, rejecting any plea of insanity, yet suggesting, taking into account the defendant's "level of civilization," the legal doctrine of mistake, an eminently reasonable and justifiable action based on misunderstood facts, according to the law "which covers the soil on which he did what he has done" (Asher 1995, 19). After a trial that allowed several native witnesses, an all-white, all-male jury, after deliberating for eight minutes, tendered a verdict of acquittal on 31 March 1874.

From a Lushootseed perspective, Dr. Jackson's guilt was obvious from his heartless disregard of prostrate Susie, his own prolonged death indicative of great personal powers, and his boastful self-confession from the grave through the dying woman's lips. Thus, Fisk was entirely justified in his actions, though they came too late to reverse his wife's condition. That he was tried and freed by Americans, however, gave some of Jackson's relatives a counterclaim of revenge that was never fulfilled. Rather, another possible outcome, suggested by present Jackson family claims to descent from an aunt of John Slocum, may have led to the founding of the Indian Shaker Church at Mud Bay, site of this murder, about a decade later.

Overall, therefore, while Lushootseed people, like their kin everywhere, have adopted the goods, clothes, boats, and housing of mainstream society, their most creative response to Euro-American society has been in terms of religion, epitomized by the Indian Shaker Church (Tollefson 1989). Most recently, among Pentecostals and Charismatic Catholics, healing and sustaining aspects of traditional beliefs have been updated by natives in ways that are more acceptable to many Americans.

3 COSMOS

THE WORLD

Literature dealing with Lushootseeds is largely silent on the form and substance of their aboriginal world, apart from the sense, common throughout the Americas, of a domed sky rising up at the horizon. While the three layers of sky, earth, and underworld were widely reported, only June Collins (1974, 209) provided a general description of the earth as a huge round island floating in a vast sea surrounded by a wall.[1] In darkness beyond lived immortals, salmon (each species in its own town), and other beings, such as a woman who cast diseases over the wall to slaughter large numbers of humans.

Old Jules told Hermann Haeberlin (1917, notebook 9, 7a–9) that people knew that the world was round because a spirit called *shobadad* (*cumanan* in his spelling) lives in a house on the edge of the world, leaving his home and "servants" during the winter to walk counterclockwise around the rim. Viewing the earth disk as a clock face, his house is at twelve, and his journey goes backward through the numbers until he reaches his farthest limit at two. All winter he walks and sings a special song. When spring comes, he changes his song and goes back home, where he stays all summer. His power is the ability to know every kind of illness, along with when and where it will strike. Human young men who encounter him receive the ability to predict the onset of illness throughout the world, but not to cure it, because he is a seer, not a shaman's spirit.

At Swinomish, Joyce Wike (1941, 70–74) was given a map of the trails to the land of the dead followed by a shaman intent on a cure. While the route of life was supposed to be generally straight, the way used by ghosts was tortuous, with bends and switchbacks, along with rough terrain filled with rivers, a lake, and slopes.

In all such instances, the prior existence of the world was taken for granted by the Lushootseed peoples. While elaborate tales do set precedents for various modern phenomena, epics treat only re-creations after a great flood rather than creation from a void. That there was such a tradition, privileged among the elite, is hinted at by John Fornsby, a famous Skagit shaman, in his rambling biography (Collins 1949, 296), where he mentions that God devoted considerable thought to how the first people were going to make a living. He created fish and animals for them and taught them how to make a variety of traps. He decreed that Europeans would have tame animals to feed them but that natives would rely on wild creatures, who required prayers and rituals before allowing themselves to be killed. In consequence, return (first) foods rituals were instituted, along with prayers and taboos appropriate for hunting, fishing, and berrying. In that one short paragraph, Fornsby suggests that shamans and other religious leaders did indeed maintain the cosmology and cosmogony of their culture via rituals.[2]

The likelihood, therefore, is that Lushootseeds, like many other peoples of the Americas, believed that the world was thought into being by a deity, who then populated it with various life forms. For Lushootseeds, the last of these forms to appear was human beings, whose way was prepared by changers (transformers) who set the precedents still followed in the modern world. Most people knew of the actions of these changers and tricksters, but only members of elite families—whose members practiced specializations that ranged from crafts and leadership to shamanism—knew the epic of creation.

EPIC AGE

Featuring "Animal People," beings from the dawn of the world "when animals were people," a variety of epics describe the onset and continuity of Lushootseed traditions.

Neither fully animal nor human or spirit, not fixed in time or space, these Animal People were protean, with many simultaneous attributes that only got sorted out when the world changed or "capsized" in preparation for the arrival of modern humans. As the "epic age" closed, each being assumed a final form and became associated with a particular location. Many transformed into particular landmarks where they still exist as aspects of geography, unusual acoustics, or appearance. In this manner, mythic people became mountains, echos and surf reverberated, and birds became colorful. Others became species of plants or animals occupying particular ecological niches. For most elders of today, the epic age is believed to have continued for countless eons until a sudden flurry of activity prepared for the change, set off by rumors that human people were "coming soon." Sometimes, the agent for these events was a being called Changer, who turned Animal

People into species, rocks, river rapids, and many other things. For example, he would encounter Deer, who was sharpening stakes to kill the Changer before he could transform the world. Changer would ask to examine these slats and suddenly poke them into Deer's head, creating antlers and forever making this animal timid and a prey of hunters.

During this transitional period between what was before and what is today, everything was in flux. Somehow, each known narrative picked up the story in the midst of things. There was, for Lushootseeds, no point of beginning (except perhaps in esoteric shamanism). Instead, all narrative was and is continuous and proceeds in terms of connections. Things were already in existence, but they led separate lives until a link was made and other events followed in due course. Various genesis stories around Puget Sound serve to account for the many different village, ethnic, and tribal differences. All versions underscore, from a native perspective, the great language diversity in the area. Some storytellers attributed these linguistic differences to Thrush, while others gave it an explanation more like that of the Tower of Babel.

As historic conditions changed in the region, so did the versions of the epics. Among the most remarkable was that about the heroic figure known as Dəwi who saved most of the Animal People from a flood. Since Lushootseed has regularly shifted the sound of *n* toward that of *d*, it seems likely that Dəwi began as a Salishan version of the Noah story before going off on its own course. But that was their only point of similarity. At base, this story was about competence.

Dəwi

During a time of drought Dəwi asked both River Bullhead and Beaver to bring rain. Either one of these "persons" was capable of doing that, so asking both of them together was sure to bring trouble. Indeed, Beaver warned Dəwi to be prepared with a large canoe. Dəwi was explicitly punished because he doubted the ability of both of them. Thus, it not only rained—it poured, and the earth flooded. Dəwi got males and females of all the Animal people into the canoe.

In the version told by Susie Sampson Peter, there was a hilarious moment when Lizard and Snake slithered into the canoe and hid in its cracks, sure to float to safety in a wreck. They had no confidence in Dəwi and were sure he would capsize them before the flood was over. As an added precaution, the canoe was tied to the top of the only exposed mountain.[3] Six other tribes also survived by tying their canoes to that same peak. After the water crested, one of the seven canoes drifted away from the mountain and eventually landed across the ocean to begin the Chinese population. Passengers of the other six canoes settled along the shores of western Washington State. In the aftermath of the flood, Thrush gave all of these peoples different languages, including the various animals, who were changed permanently into modern species. Thrush kept for herself the song to make berries ripen and still continues to use it.[4]

Robe Boy (txʷuyalitsa)

After the flood, according to another account, a boy was abandoned by his family because he refused to fast and quest for spiritual help. Starving, he was forced to purify and, thereby, made contact with God, who instructed the boy to make a special blanket from the skins of many small animals (Sampson 1938, 14–16, Matson 1968, 29–38). Then he gathered up all the refuse from the flood and waved the blanket over it, creating an abundance of food. People too were revived, but they had no sense, so the boy made brains for them from the very soil of that place, according to Andrew Span Joe (Snyder ms., tale 68).[5] When he waved his blanket over them, these people revived but spoke many languages and so scattered all over the earth.

Grizzly Wife

While some Animal People were changed on a case by case basis, as when Mrs. Grouse left eggs all over the Northwest so that everyone would have grouse to hunt, some transformations were wholesale. In one of the most terrifying of all Skagit stories, Grizzly Bear woman so terrorized her household that many of its members decided to transform permanently into modern species.

According to the Skagit version, two sisters, a Grizzly and a Black Bear, were married to Eagle, and each wife had a son and a daughter. Black Bear was an ideal wife, but Grizzly was deranged. When Black Bear offered berries to the family for dessert, Grizzly, in a matter-of-fact way, offered her own feces as though they were berries. Fearing the worst, Eagle kept Grizzly's teeth and claws hidden away.

Coyote was Eagle's father and he grew intolerant of Grizzly, so he arranged for some worms to chew through the log that she used as the seat of her latrine. In consequence, when she sat to use it, the log broke and she fell into a deep pit filled with her own offal. Furious, Grizzly announced from afar that she had begun menstruating and took to her secluded hut, where she cleaned up. She sent her daughter to retrieve her teeth and claws from Eagle, who reluctantly returned them. Shortly afterward she came roaring out of the hut, sending everyone into panic.

Black Bear and her children hid in a tiny hole in a rock, holding a supply of red paint and oil. The other housemates met quickly and decided that a strong man was needed to guard the door. Raven, ever the braggart, volunteered, but he turned coward at the first sight of Grizzly. Everyone in the house instantly changed into modern species in their haste to escape her vengeance. Coyote, the instigator of the attack, changed himself into maggots living under a stone mortar used to grind up dried meat. Grizzly considered chewing up the maggots, but then thought better of it. Thus, Coyote too escaped.

Grizzly then located her sister in the rock and jabbed a spear into the hole. Black Bear smeared it with oily red paint that looked like blood, and thereby fooled Grizzly, who went away.

Grizzly's two children fled during the attack. Later, they found themselves all alone and decided to marry. The brother-husband took up hunting. During one outing, he met Grizzly and she realized who he was. She talked sweetly to him and showed him the breast where he had suckled. Enticed, he laid his head in her lap, went to sleep, and was killed.

Then Grizzly went looking for her daughter, who had a son (plus nephew) of her own by this time. Knowing the worst, the daughter used a spell to make Grizzly very thirsty.[6] When she arrived, Grizzly again spoke soothingly and showed her breasts, but she kept being distracted by her thirst. Finally, she asked for a drink and the daughter showed her a spring. When Grizzly bent over to drink, the daughter shoved her in and Grizzly drowned.

The woman and her baby left their home, wailing for their murdered brother, husband, and father. Coyote was also looking for the girl, wanting to marry her, even though she was his own granddaughter. When they met, the woman was aware of his plan but pretended to be taken in by a stranger. Just before bed, however, the woman grabbed her baby and jumped into the fire, where they were consumed. This woman (or her spirit) now exists as a specter of death who visits certain families just before a member dies.

In such a manner, therefore, the transformations of the epic age continue to be relevant in the present, after the influences of Catholic and other missionaries have become grafted onto native traditions. Changes in history become changes in narrative, but the native voice remains strong.

For the whole region, however, the most significant narrative for explaining the world is that of Star Child, the son of a sky father and an earth mother who began the connection that led to the present form of the world; Star Child's descendants are said to be the chiefly families.

According to Susie Sampson Peter's oldest son, Martin Sampson (1972, 51–55), Star Child and Diaper Boy detail the origin of the Nookachamish (now pronounced Dukʷachabsh), a major division of the Upper Skagits who lived around Clear Lake, where two noble sisters wished to marry Stars and where a hill with banded rock is called *yədwastə* (heart) because it marks the place where their escape rope from the sky fell to earth and coiled up.[7]

Among the Snoqualmi, a small hill near Mount Si also marks the place where their own rope ladder fell down. In this version, the rope hung in the air for some time and the Animal People used it as a swing until Rat, angered that he did not get enough turns, chewed through the rope and it fell to earth. Rat, of course, was thereafter condemned to repeat his act forever. Thus we have the same epic in neighboring tribes, each grounding it in their own lands.

In Star Child, also known as Star Husband, action focuses on neither sky nor earth but rather on the link between them created when a pair of sisters married distant Stars, forging the world of the Lushootseed peoples and still defining all important aspects of their life and belief.[8]

Two sisters of high rank were camping on a prairie, digging fern roots. The world was new and there were few males so, one night, each fantasized marrying a white or a red star. The next morning they awoke in the sky next to their husbands. The older sister was married to an old man with white matter in his eyes; the younger sister was married to a handsome man. They continued to dig fern roots in their new home, but their husbands warned them not to dig any root that went straight down.

The older sister was soon pregnant by her wiser, older, kinder husband but, dejected, she wanted to escape. Digging deeply, she broke through the sky and looked at her home below. She convinced her sister to dig twice as many roots so that she could make a cedar bough rope to lower herself down. Her sister stayed in the sky when she escaped.

On earth, she was advised by a voice to change a log into an old woman to babysit her newborn boy, Star Child, and to build a house and a fish weir to support them.[9] Easily confused, the grandmother sang lullabies appropriate for a boy instead of a girl, as the mother had demanded.

Meanwhile near the Chehalis River, a lone changer made a weir and a canoe, but he could not be at both places at once, so he left his anus (or feces) at the trap.[10] As dumb as the log grandmother, the anus confused the situation until a salmon was finally caught and eaten by the changer. Denied any food, the anus puckered up.

The salmon's milt (or eggs) was saved, warmed, prayed over, and, days later, it became two girls. Though the changer began by calling them his daughters, while canoeing he called them his wives several times. Alarmed, these girls fled until they came to the grandmother swinging Star Child and stole him upriver to the east. Eventually, both married him, one sister producing all the trees and shrubs and the other all the fishes.

Rushing home, the mother kicked the grandmother back into a log.[11] Devastated, she took a soiled diaper left behind and washed it in the river. Blinded by tears, she was startled to hear a baby cry and discovered Diaper Boy in her hands, cross-eyed, bald, and twisted from her agonized efforts.

Raven took the defenseless mother and babe to be his slaves, treating them badly. This enslavement was punishment for abandoning her husband in the sky. Diaper Boy was warned never to go east, as Star Child's wives warned him never to go west. Thus the brothers eventually met, the younger was healed, and they planned revenge on Raven. Star Child came to the town with an elk in his canoe; the girl who lifted it out would become his wife. Dainty Green Frog won and everyone feasted. Raven gorged on elk-fat-rich feces and transformed into the bird of today.

At the wedding, the brothers decided to finish the modern world. They threw everything that they could find—tools, clothes, baskets, bowls, and house planks—into a huge fire that burned for many days. Later the cooled ashes were placed in a pouch and scattered over the earth so that humans would ever after be able to find most of what they needed wherever they settled. Thus, the brothers made the world ready for humans, towns, and tribes. Trees and stones were now available at most locations to allow humans to make a variety of necessary tools, clothes, buildings, and traps.

In addition, during this scattering, the brothers confirmed the sacred qualities of the world and acknowledged the supreme importance of immortal beings for achieving success. As they re-created the world, the brothers named all of its aspects with special words (instituting the "enchantments"), which were only learned in the most important chiefly families.

These words controlled the world because they linked together minds by the sheer force of disciplined will power to accomplish a variety of personal ends.[12] Animals were summoned and killed, people's moods shifted, and catastrophes were averted with this power. Sometimes, by its harmful application, people were made to do things against their will.

When the brothers finished, an old woman asked about light and they decided that the earth needed a soul, so they prepared to create sun and moon. Star Child attempted to be the sun, but as he rose into the sky, the earth became very hot and people jumped into the water to cool off. When he returned, Star Child was told that he would not do. Instead, Diaper Boy became the sun and Star Child became the moon, going into the sky with his wife, who became the Frog on the back of the moon. She was somehow involved in every woman's monthly discharge of blood and also kept track of the months until a baby was born.

Things continued for some time until Mink claimed to be a son of Moon and went along through the sky. Moon took along a cane to vault over the river in the sky, which was the Milky Way. A few days later, Mink decided to go alone as the Moon, but he forgot the cane. When he came to the river, he tried to jump but missed, fell into the Milky Way, and drowned, causing the first eclipse.

The brothers met and decided that they needed to move away from the earth so that they would have no more unwelcome visits from people like Mink. Besides, the world was now ready for humans. They gave names to every bay, nook, cranny, bend, confluence, and prominence. They named every lake, hill, mountain, and spring, allowing some duplicates. They named the tribes who would live in each place, taking the name from the characteristics and spirit of that location.

Humans arrived and occupied the land. They grew and prospered. They filled the region and learned from ancient traditions, while adding some of their own.

Thus it continued for many years until people living along the coast saw a strange floating island with a few tall trees and billowing white clouds. Hairy beings like bears ran along the vines that hung from the trees and along the surface of the island. A smaller, spiderlike island launched from the big one and had many legs that pushed against the water like paddles.[13]

The bears came ashore, looking like hairy humans. They offered food like what ghosts would eat, such as maggots, rotten flesh, and strange water. To avoid offense, these foods were fed to a slave, who liked their taste. The water, however, made the slave die for a time. Reviving, he claimed to have visited the spirits. Years later, natives learned that the maggots were rice, the flesh was biscuits, and the water was alcoholic liquor. By then, reservations had become refuges from diseases and dislocations, though salmon continued to decline. Giving up plank houses and seasonal camps for frame houses and jobs, natives earned money to buy food and clothes. Today, engulfed by uncaring strangers, people find that their culture helps in their struggle to survive.

The original inhabitants of the Lushootseed world became the present immortals who "own" the land and steward all of its resources, occupying appropriate plank homes at various locations. As "persons," they also travel widely and visit; humans might encounter them anywhere. While fasting and praying on vision quests, human children sought them out in hopes of visiting the immortals' homes, where the youngsters received a full dose of power allowing success.

Because many of these spirits had been people transformed in anticipation of human arrival, they have many characteristics desired by natives. Like humans, spirits observe a basic dichotomy in their talents between careers and curings. In other words, spirits were divided into those with career powers—those who enhanced mundane abilities—and those involved with curing, who intervened in social affairs either to heal disease or to snuff out life.

In present conversation the animal metaphors of bird, dog, and snake are regularly used to refer to these immortals. Spirits are frequently compared to birds because they hover and fly in the air. Each new initiate in the winter dances has a nest for his or her own spirit to rest in when it is near the human partner. After the death of the human partner, the spirit is often compared to a lost dog seeking to attach itself to another close member of the family. And whenever the subject of religion and spirits is broached, elders say that these can never be fully understood because every time you try to come close to them, they wiggle away from your mind like a snake.

Authors of prior academic treatments of Salishans (Haeberlin and Gunther 1930; Smith 1940; Collins 1974) endeavored to list all spirits and powers they could learn about, but this was both ethnocentric and inappropriate. In the native view, spirits exist in infinite variety—no list can ever be definitive. Powers belong to certain family lines—mixing all of them together is not culturally appropriate. Moreover, native peoples rightly object to revealing unnecessarily such significant details of their religion, having already suffered attacks, abuse, and criticism of their own beliefs from intolerant Americans.

For all Salishans, what defined the overall categories of spirits was not the plethora of individual "persons of power" arrayed in many species but rather the type of song being conferred (Suttles 1951, 357).[14] Because someone gifted with a power could not display it alone, others had to drum and sing while the spirit possessed that visionary (making him or her "sick to sing" and dance). Since the song activated the bond, its rhythms had to be generally known. Thus, the dozen or so musical styles were common knowledge, so that whenever someone was overcome with their power, most people could help that person express it in song and dance.

The earliest and most detailed Lushootseed listing for the subset of career spirits was provided to Hermann Haeberlin, with some later revision by Erna Gunther (Haeberlin and Gunther 1930, 69–75). Members are divided on the basis of functional types to distinguish the enhancement of (a) hunting and fishing, which included Badger, Pheasant, Clam, Duck, and various anthropomorphs; (b) industrial activities, benefiting from a manlike being who appeared to women from the east or to men from the west to give tokens to excel in the making of baskets or weapons, and various man or woman spirits who sanctioned crafts and gambling or kept diseases from spreading; (c) warfare—monsters, Loon, a man covered in red paint, and a birdman who gifted fierce men and strong women; warriors also cured their own wounds with the aid of Raccoon, Grizzly, Black Bear, Cougar, and Wild Cat; (d) wealth and property—manlike beings who lived in large houses filled with riches and slaves at inaccessible locations; and (e) ritual prominence—Wolf for undertakers, Little Earths to go to the land of the dead, Disease prevention but not cure, Happiness expressed in song (acquired even by slaves), Thunder for a booming voice and command, and various sacred artifacts that were animated by song.

Curing spirits came to humans who then became shamans (or doctors) after they had acquired several of these powers, often four, in addition to career spirits. For shaman powers, Haeberlin and Gunther (1930, 76) specifically list Otter, Beaver, Mountain Lion, Hawk, Eagle, Shark, Whale, Salmon, Trout, Dog, Snake, Lizard, Owl, Cougar, Bear, Redheaded Woodpecker, and Kingfisher. In addition, there were several powerful humanoid beings who gave power.

For the Snohomish, the foremost of these lived in a house surrounded by a fence to keep out other shamanic spirits.[15] A shaman with this power could stand at the opposite end of a human house from a patient, stretch out his hands, motion to grasp the disease, and thus remove it. He did not have to touch or even be near the patient.

Other great powers looked like giant snakes with retracting antlers or like giant lizards ("alligators") who lived on mountains. These were fearsome, remote, hostile beings who only gifted a human who suffered great hardships and deprivations. The longer one quested and the farther one went away from civilization, the more powerful was the spirit acquired. Most spirits were apathetic to the human condition, so their powers were neutral. Only human emotions and intent directed them to some special purpose, which might be either helpful or harmful.

June Collins (1974, 146) provided a list from the Upper Skagit, which included almost all animal species, trees, natural elements, lakes, strangely shaped rocks in the Skagit River, and Mount Baker. The curing spirits included those named by Haeberlin and Gunther, in addition to Minnows and Skunk.

Marian Smith (1940, 68), though advanced among early anthropologists in properly beginning her study of the Puyallup and Nisqually with a first chapter on religion, nevertheless listed their powers (separated into birds, animals, trees, and unusual features) in alphabetical order according to English name, an entirely inappropriate procedure.[16]

In his insightful study of the Twana, William Elmendorf (1960, 489) divided career spirits into those for wealth, war, soul recovery, messengering, gambling, land mammal hunting, sea mammal hunting, and ceremonial (which gave abilities to levitate the body or to animate artifacts). The powers that aided soul recovery included Blowfly, Graveyard Post, and Little Earths. All other authors explicitly include Odyssey power among the curing spirits, so Elmendorf's own placement of it seems incorrect. For Twana (Elmendorf 1960, 499), curing spirits were distinguished on the basis of their intensity and function, with the greatest of all identified as a huge antlered snake and reptiles who live on the sides of high mountains, sliding down talus slopes. Along with shamanic abilities, some of these powers (Sea Lion, Cougar, Squirrel, Grouse) also gave magical weapons to cause illness or to slay a victim by sorcery.

The complexities involved in trying to understand these various spirit powers can be illustrated by three examples, one a famous wealth and property spirit, the second a being whom John Fornsby called "guarding power," although more usually known as "power boards" or by its native name of *sgʷədilich*, and the third the earthlings or Little Earths who own the land.

Among the tribes who lived near the river mouths on the salt water, chiefs were expected to have a wealth power called *tiyuɬəbaxad*, who lived in a huge cedar plank house deep under the water. Those brave enough to quest for him had to dive from a raft hugging a heavy stone. Once a quester was taken into the house and instructed in how to use this power, he became very wealthy because this spirit caused neighboring tribes to provide the man with gifts and wives, and made game drop dead at the door outside the man's house, particularly when he was hosting a winter dance. Usually, the power was inherited from father to son.

According to Little Sam, a famous Snohomish shaman, the first man to get this power, back nine generations, was his own grandfather, who fasted for forty days, dove into the salt water holding a rock, and landed on the roof of the spirit's house. Welcoming him inside, the spirit gave him everything in the house and sent him away. When he rose to the surface, the tide covered Skagit Head and so he floated to Mukilteo, where he slept on the beach for five days. Then he went home. His mother gave him soup, but he could only hold it down on the fifth try. When he was better, he made a suspended air net and called his relatives to watch. After he swung a stick carved with an elk hoof on the end, elk herds appeared and ran into the net, as people rushed to hamstring them. He was also successful with whale, seal, sturgeon, and salmon. When the Swinomish, Skykomish, Skagit, and Snoqualmi came to visit him, he fed them lavishly and gave them food to take away. In return, they gave him shell money and hides, making him wealthy. Every tribe gave him two wives until he had married twenty women.

Little Sam's account holds only for the Snohomish, not for other tribes in the region, for whom this spirit has its own local residence. For example, the Upper Skagit know that this wealth spirit resides in a deep pool in their river near the Dalles at Concrete. The Allen brothers told Elmendorf (1993, 167) that it lived underwater in a big house under the bluff near Aberdeen, Washington. When a Skokomish boy got this power, it "telephoned to Port Townsend, to Dosewallips, everywhere, to give this young fellow sea animals whenever he wants them" (Elmendorf 1993, 177). According to a Lushootseed dictionary (Hess 1976, 505.1), this is the spirit of abundance, found at great depth for tribes along Puget Sound but high in the mountains for inland communities. Bierwert (1996, 196) added that this wealth power (*tiyuɬəbaxad*, considered greater than *dxʷhi'idə*), "was known to every tribe along the shores of Puget Sound. (In fact, various forms of his name seem to be known in an area extending from Musqueam in British Columbia to Kalapuya in Oregon.)" Thus, within a larger context for the intertribal importance of this spirit, beliefs about him remained strictly local, as was characteristic of all powers in the region.

More fascinating but also more problematic—at least for scholars—was the being known as *sgʷədilich*.[17] During the epic age, he came through the Skagit Valley with three brothers to place men and women in various locations to create coming generations. His brothers were Knife, Fire, and Baby, each of whom gave special powers to people according to their names

(Snyder ms., tale 73, Collins 1974, 158–59). Knife taught the proper way to butcher and prepare game, while Fire taught how to cook it. Baby showed how to fix various family talents and abilities on children. When the others went away, *sgʷədilich* became a rock in the river, where he can be heard singing at about 3:00 A.M. Those who have fasted and purified can receive power from him to hunt and fish successfully (Amoss 1978, 66–70).

According to the Snoqualmi and Snohomish, however, this power always remains underwater in a river or Puget Sound. He never travels. He confers on both men and women the ability to catch fish, especially salmon in large quantities. The first person said to have received it was Johnny Wheeler's great grandmother, a Snohomish. She was fishing with a net attached to a pole from a canoe and suddenly saw many fish. Then she fainted. When she came to, she found a painted board floating on the water and took it home. After this, fish became plentiful in the river where she lived. Later, this woman gave the spirit to her daughter, who passed it to Johnny Fornsby's mother. When she died, Johnny went out and slept on her grave, fasting for four days to inherit the spirit.

The board that represents this power is a flat piece of cedar, a foot and a half long, painted black and red. Before it is used at a dance, it is warmed at the fire and "fed" dry salmon fat thrown into the coals. In addition to helping ensure bountiful game and serving in public displays, the boards were used to locate lost or stolen goods and to find the bodies of those who drowned or disappeared.

The Snoqualmi used only a single board, regarded as male, while John Fornsby added that it was all head. Snohomish and Skagit used two boards, called elder and younger brothers or number one and number two. When these double boards were "run," two men held each one through holes in the sides of the planks. The elder one led the way around the house, moving counterclockwise. If they danced clockwise, their owner died. While the four men worked the two boards, the owner sang, standing or sitting on the sideline. The boards moved through the house looking for lurking spirits, bad feelings, or potential dangers, and removed these difficulties. Afterward, each holder was paid a blanket and gifts. In the past, when the *sgʷədilich* were run, people sang and danced for four days and nights. The songs were sung four times in fast tempo, then four times slowly. In November, at the end of the potlatch season, as an act of generosity, the owner's family spread out lots of property along the shore and invited people to take away whatever they wanted.

Other powers related to this one were the power poles or *tustəd*, which never left the house where they lived, and a ducklike wooden effigy that got fish, ducks, seal, and sturgeon for its human partner. These other spirits were regarded as siblings or close kin (cousins) to the guarding power.

In addition to the board shields, *sgʷədilич* is also represented by twisted vine maple, cloth, cedarbark, cedar withes, and special rocks. Among northern Lushootseeds these objects were paired and "run" at the same time to cleanse and purify a building, person, or event (Amoss 1978, 66). These sacred artifacts become, at least for a time, the "home" of that power during the public ritual, and some aspect of them remains resident there even when the objects are in storage.

When I asked elders what other spirits had houses like these, the reply was unanimous that all powers had their own homes, appropriate to their characteristics, whether or not humans realized what these were. Variously, the body of an animal of its species, a hollow in a tree, or a rock in the river might constitute such a home. Each spirit had an abode (a "holy home") where it could host visitors and instruct questers in the use of its talent and abilities. Indeed, for Lushootseeds, as for all native peoples, it was impossible to imagine a being without a home, a creature without a dwelling. While there were a few communities in the epic age where people did not have homes, a changer saw to it that they were assigned a residence before humans arrived. For example, among Katzie, Khaals sent one homeless group to stay under a lake (fuller discussion of Katzie tradition follows). In fact and image, therefore, the house was a basic expression of this culture, or any other.

The minimal requirements of culture seem to be clothing and fire, since at least two groups of "wild" people were mentioned in accounts which are taken to be historic. Often called "stick Indians," these beings were described as giants without houses (using only flimsy arbors), who played tricks on people and stole food, mostly fish from caches.[18]

The Little Earths were another order of beings who "owned" the land and deplored any waste of resources. According to Smith (1940, 130–32), they lived in overgrown marshes, gullies, and creeks, where an encounter with them led to insanity if proper precautions were not taken. Their voices were heard as the sound of gurgling water. When someone was away from home and drank from a spring or creek, he or she uttered a low guttural sound to warn off the Little Earths who were assumed to be coming close.

Among the Twana, Doctor Monkey, an Odyssey shaman, was empowered by a Little Earth who walked along the tops of trees and never traveled on the ground (Elmendorf 1993, 89, 227). A shaman befriended by a Little Earth had the ability to go to the land of the dead and return because the dwarf was so closely tied to the land that he or she also held the shaman tightly to the everyday world.

COAST SALISHAN COMPARISONS

To compensate for detail lacking in the available documentation of Lushootseed cosmology, we are fortunate to have two comprehensive accounts from other Coast Salishans in Canada, the Katzie Halkomelem just to the north and the Nuxalk on the midcoast.

Fraser River Halkomelem

The most fully articulated Salishan genesis came from a Katzie shaman named Old Pierre (1860s–1946) to Diamond Jenness of the National Museum of Canada in 1936. A few significant details were provided in 1952 by Simon Pierre (a son born in the 1880s) to Wayne Suttles, who wisely deduced that while local villages had far-ranging social ties through marriage and kinship, along with wider ceremonial relationships encompassing the entire region, the basic economic and spiritual bonds with a home territory were conversely both extremely narrow and intense (Suttles 1955, 14), enabling an anchoring for radiance.

His shaman mother sent Pierre out questing from the age of three and paid three of their oldest and best-informed relatives to teach him these sacred epic traditions from the age of eight. As a result, among his powerful helpers was the father of all trees, the only arboreal being who could grant power. Once, he tripped over a rock that turned out to be the pillow of the leader of the earth, gaining power in his hands and wrists to draw out sickness, power in his mouth to swallow it, and "power to see all over the world and to recover minds that had strayed from their bodily homes" (Suttles 1955, 67); note the explicit regarding of a body as a home.[19]

Pierre learned to diagnose sickness depending on its causes: lost vitality or mind; impurity or offense to a spirit or ghost; or a probe shot into a victim by a hostile shaman.

All Katzie were instructed to pray to deities in sequence, beginning with the Lord Above, then moving to the Sun, Khaals (addressed more fully later in this chapter), Moon, and personal spirit powers. Humans owed their existence to the Lord Above, who created each of them with a soul, vitality-thought, a certain talent-power, and a shadow-reflection. At death, the breath and special talent perished with the body, the soul returned to the

Lord Above, and the vitality and shadow merged to produce the shade or ghost that roamed as a barely visible form in the neighborhood of its old home, feared by the surviving relatives.

Though this is debated by academics, Salish belief in a supreme deity, this Lord (Chief) Above, was probably ancient, although subsequently influenced by beliefs about the Christian God (Miller 1980). Earlier, this deity was closely associated with the sun, although frequently overcast skies kept him distinct from the solar orb itself. He was considered to be good but was not concerned with ethics, except that He took back the souls of those who did wrong.

For Katzie, of all the beings that have existed, only humans and sockeye salmon still have their own souls since all others were sent back above by Khaals, although he allowed these other animals, plants, and beings to retain their vitality-thought, talents, and shadows. Humans receive their souls from above as soon as they cry out after emerging from the womb.

Vitality, which was inseparable from thought, pervaded the entire body. Any loss of the body was accompanied by a proportional loss of vitality. The loss of a limb or the cutting of the hair, therefore, decreased its manifestation as warmth, closely linked with the sun. While vitality was diffused throughout the body, it was especially concentrated at the heart, the center of thought and emotions for native peoples (Miller 1981) and the locus of shamanic power. Though this is unstated, it seems likely that Salishans believed that the heart contained a fire (fed by food) that heated the body, just as a hearth (fed by wood) warmed the house.[20] Gifts of blankets and food, therefore, were intended to "warm the heart" in the fullest possible sense.

The Lord Above created evergreen trees at the beginning of the world so that humans would have a strong source of vitality, manifested by the constant green of such foliage. Khaals created the deciduous trees with lesser vitality, which, during winter, retreats into the roots of these trees to await spring strengthening from the rays of the sun. Humans gain their warmth from the sun and from fire, storing it during daylight and using it up during the night. As an aid to memory, the vitality would visit a place or person to help its possessor recall an incident or name. Sometimes the vitality wandered away from the body, whereupon the person fainted or went into trance. If it stayed away for too long, the person sickened. During the winter, when the world was cold, ceremonials were held because they also provided warmth.

Sometimes, a human was reincarnated, particularly when the Lord Above pitied those who mourned so unceasingly that He revived that body or gave the same soul to a newborn. In the case of a reborn shadow, however, that person had only the appearance of the deceased.

Because they were transformed from the first people, the original members of the various species were sacred and able to share their talent-power with particular humans. The more remote the home of the being, the more powerful it was. Humans needed these powers to cope with the unseen hazards and dangers that filled every life.

A human without power was like a cork floating helplessly in the water, subject to all kinds of pulls, crosswinds, and undercurrents. Humans could also inherit power from their ancestors, but then they only received an "echo" of the talent. To get power in full strength, people made themselves ritually pure so that they could actually enter the home of the spirit and receive instruction there at first hand.

People undertaking quests had the potential of receiving any and all spirits. As proof of this, a man at Abbotsford received power from a train locomotive. When people scoffed at this new power, he decreed that the valley would become cold for two months, and it did. Thereafter people believed him.

The integrity and flexibility of these beliefs was explained in the sacred traditions, which Pierre shared with Jenness. Indeed, the manner in which the Fraser River valley became like a huge dish filled with food was the work of the Lord Above, who decided to send specific groups of people under a named leader to particular locales along the river. Instead of one pair like Adam and Eve, there were many couples, each entrusted to form a set community: at Musqueam (north of the river mouth), Point Roberts (south of the mouth), and upriver at Port Hammond, Sheridan Hill, and Pitt River.[21]

ANCESTORS. Initially, the Katzie world was grim and silent, with only invertebrates such as shellfish to feed these first people. There were no birds, animals, or winds. The Lord Above made the sun to give warmth, which the people needed and craved; the moon to measure time; and the rainbow to indicate that the next day would be nice and sunny.

People built their houses and towns to settle in their locales. The leader at Point Roberts married and had a son, who was very powerful. Every day, the wife went out to dig roots for their meals, but then for several days she returned emptyhanded. Curious, her son followed and found her with a young man. Devastated, he took to his bed and cried all night. The next morning he got up and went outside. He decided to make a sling. Testing it out, he flung four white rocks, three of which landed near Victoria, Sechelt, and Semiahmoo; the fourth went out of sight.

Now he was ready. The son took his mother's lover and flung him to the east, beyond the mountains (as Eastwind?). He catapulted his mother to become the Southwind, where her tears are now expressed as raindrops. Summoning his father, the leader at Point Roberts, he sent the man's vitality into the deep water off the peninsula so that it could always help his people, then flung the father's body to become Northwind. The son himself became Westwind.

At Musqueam, people lived well on clams, mussels, flounders, and other seafoods. The only gift they gave to humans was the Sxwayxwey mask, along with its special costume and rattle. The powers for these masks came from Thunder, Raven, Two-headed Snake, and Sawbill Duck.[22] The song used for the masks floated down from Above.

Those at Port Hammond supposedly contributed little to the world because they were considered foolish by others.

At Pitt Lake, the leader and his wife had two children, a son and a daughter, who always stayed around the water and did not eat. Finally, deciding that she should do some good, the father changed the girl into the first sturgeon. Ever since, sturgeon with the best flavor have been found at Pitt Lake. Mourning his sister, the son changed into a bird that appears when sturgeon run. His followers were supposedly stupid and so were changed into servants for the good families.

SWANASET. At Sheridan Hill lived the greatest leader of all. He was Swanaset and he made the sloughs on Pitt Meadow so that it would drain, allowing resources to thrive along the banks. He did this by drawing the lines of the sloughs on his own face with red ocher. Then he prayed to the Lord Above and raised his right hand, and instantly the sloughs formed in accord with the diagram on his face. He gave each of them a name. Many berries and roots grew up, and people gathered to harvest the bounty, including two sisters who were Sandhill Cranes. Swanaset convinced them that he was not a relative—because he could perform many miracles that they could not do—and then married them. Every day, while gathering wild potatoes from the mud, they rudely flung ooze behind them. When Swanaset saw this filthiness, he became ashamed and decided to leave them.

He called everyone to Sheridan Hill to shoot arrows at a hole (smokehole?) in the sky. After an arrow stuck, others were shot to form a chain. Swanaset climbed up into the sky, met two old blind women eating onions, and restored their sight. In gratitude they warned him of coming dangers and covered him with stone armor. After thwarting various traps and tricks, he married the two daughters of the sky leader. In time, he left his elder wife to take care of her own parents and took the younger one, Spider, back to earth. Her father gave her as a dowry a partitioned box, one half holding seagulls and the other with candlefish (eulachon, hooligans).

On his return, Swanaset shattered Sheridan Hill so that no one could climb to the sky again. His wife founded a village where the Pitt River met the Fraser and released the seagulls one day and the eulachon the next. She caught these fish with a net made of fine webbing, which humans were never able to reproduce.

Eventually, Swanaset left his wife to help the people and went on. He led a canoe full of men to the south, where he gambled at several villages, winning many goods. The man who later became Mink won a diving contest by breathing at a knothole in Swanaset's canoe until long after all the other men had surfaced. They visited Dog Salmon, people whose houses were painted with red stripes and whose clothes also had red or black bands. Humpbacked Salmon explained that they traveled every second day, which meant they spawned in alternate years. Finally, the canoe got to the town of Sockeye Salmon, who lived along a beautiful coast and spent their time playing games. There Swanaset married the daughter of the chief, gifting him with all of his gambling winnings in return for the bride.

Swanaset took his new wife home. Thus sockeye came to Pitt Lake. Spider had a son, who passed on her lessons to his children. Sockeye also had a son, whose birth was the occasion for the first swarming of sockeye in the Fraser River. The Sockeye wife taught people to observe the first sockeye rite, using the stalks of consumption plants because that was what the Sockeyes used to fuel their fires.[23] She instructed the women to make a dip net of nettles. Lastly, she taught one man in each tribe the enchantments, rituals, and taboos demanded by Salmon. Each of these men became the native priest of his community, passing on the wisdom only to his own son or selling a few details to worthy nobles.

Thus the world began with people sent down from Above who settled in communities made distinctive and livable because of divine gifts and extraordinary deeds. Yet, even so, people did not observe all that was required of them and some became so foolish that the Lord Above took action against them. He prepared the way for humans by sending Khaals to set things right again.

KHAALS. From the west, Khaals came with two younger brothers and twelve servants. Through the power of his thought, he could transport them anywhere and change anything. At Boundary Bay, he met a couple and transformed each of them into a boulder after raising his right hand to send their souls back to the Lord Above. These stone people would give humans fair weather if they were greeted with fair words.[24]

At Tsawwassen, he changed a greedy woman into a carved stone image, which still bears her name. Khaals fought with and killed a giant octopus, cut it up, and threw the pieces to places along the coast where large octopi are now found. Then he joined Tsawwassen to the mainland. At New Westminster, he petrified a man called "killer," turned a solitary hunter and his family into the first wolves, and made the first ravens from a family of scavengers.

He petrified a deaf warrior at Coquitlam and changed a foolish man on the Coquitlam River into mink. Then he made other species such as kingfisher, black bear, raccoon, and crane. He sent a baby into a deep pool of water so that it could grant power to future seers. When the Coquitlam leader boasted of his exalted station, a rude breach of etiquette, Khaals changed him into the master of the Fraser River, placing him at its mouth. He placed the man's sister at the headwaters but allowed them to visit back and forth through time.

At Pitt River, he changed a warrior to stone and put a one-legged fisherman in charge of the fish runs along the Fraser, turning him into a rock at Davis Pool.

At Alouette River, Khaals created suckers out of the remnants of Swanaset's people, who had foolishly stayed behind when he moved to the river town of the Katzie. Siblings who spent all their time grabbing feathers out of each other's headbands were transformed, after feathers were repositioned as tails, into beaver and muskrat.

At Sheridan Hill, Khaals met the Sandhill Crane wives of Swanaset still digging potatoes and changed them into these shore birds. He transformed other people into geese. At the base of Sheridan Hill were gathered all those who had helped Swanaset to reach the sky. They were listening to Bluejay as he prophesied the arrival of Khaals, who changed them into wren, wolf, fisher, grizzly, black bear, eagle, cougar, deer, and swan. As always, he first returned their souls above. He transformed an old woman into a stump that provided fine weather to those who prayed there for it. Khaals also devised a fish spear.

At Pitt Lake, people spent all their time in the water, so Khaals changed them into seals, including mothers with babies on their backs. Further on, Khaals met very foolish people who did not even have houses.[25] He sent them to live under a lake, where they allowed only locals to drink the water. Foreign drinkers were poisoned and died. As a warning to outsiders, designs about the water were painted on the bluff above the lake. Khaals next met stingy people who would not share; he changed their box of sturgeon eggs into a stone dish filled with sand.

Throughout his efforts, Khaals was just, following the laws given by Lord Above. He sorted the good from the bad and made the world a better place again, allowing those people who showed respect to remain human. When a hunter did not give thanks for the seal he killed, Khaals turned it into stone. Ever since, those who do not pray to Khaals get nothing when they hunt. Finally, Khaals went far away up the Fraser River.

After Khaals left, a man at Pitt Lake was inspired to invent the deer surround technique. His brothers helped to do this, and their sister went along, too. While they butchered the kill, the sister ate a deer heart and her brothers mocked her for this. Angry, she declared that men would never again easily get large numbers of deer in a surround. Then she became the mother of the deer, a remote being rarely seen by hunters and described as having the body of a deer and the head of a girl.

The world continued and the population again increased, resulting in another re-creation. Families settled all over until they overcrowded the world and Lord Above sent a flood. Many people died, but some saved themselves by fleeing to mountain tops so that they could later resettle the land.

Eventually, the world became crowded again. Knowing their past, people grew fearful. That October, snow fell and covered the world. Half of all the people died of starvation.

Yet again, the survivors increased and spread out until the world became crowded. The smoke from their fires filled the Fraser Valley like a dense fog. Too many people were living too close together. Then word came of a great sickness from the east. Smallpox killed many people before Europeans came and pushed native people off their lands. Times became hard, and, ever since, people have had to work for money just to live.

Nuxalk (Bella Coola)

The other well-described system of Salish beliefs — paralleling features of the Lushootseed, Katzie, and others — comes from the Nuxalk (misknown as Bella Coola, McIlwraith 1948, xx, 23, 32), the most northern of the Salishans, surrounded by Wakashan Southern Kwakiutlan speakers.

Using Chinook jargon, the Northwest trade pidgin, Thomas McIlwraith (1948, viii) lived intermittently at Bella Coola during 1922–24, recording in the tradition of British social anthropology these "interwoven social, religious, and folk-lore concepts of a people, the sum-total of their mental life, collected by one man at one time" from wise elders such as Joshua Moody, Jim Pollard, Mrs. Webber, and Captain Schooner, who adopted him as a son before dying in the summer of 1923. In consequence, McIlwraith assumed many of Schooner's former responsibilities during the winter ceremonials of 1923–24, joining the ranks of the aged officials, who seem to have staged more events that year under such encouragement. Thus, rather than producing memory ethnography, McIlwraith was fully involved in the intellectual, ritual, and public life of this community, assuring high quality for this information.[26]

The Nuxalk world was created by a high god known as A⅃quntam, who made four immortal carpenters and set them to work with crews to manufacture everything in existence. Like any other chief, however, A⅃quntam was neither all-knowing nor all-powerful. He could be gullible and he did make mistakes. He has, as the Bella Coola say, the virtues and vices of any man.

Covering the earth was the huge dome of the sky, which was clear to allow the sun to shine through.[27] The top of the dome was another flat land where the creator lived in an enormous house called Nusmatta, which had many rooms. His carved seat rested behind the central fire in this home. He was closely associated with the sun, which he used like a canoe. When he traveled, he wore a cloak lined with salmon, which, when reversed inside out, caused salmon runs to start in the rivers of earth.

The world itself was a round, flat island held in place by a being named Sninia, who lived in the icy north holding a rope that kept the world tight against his outstretched feet. Whenever he adjusted this rope, an earthquake resulted. The undersea was controlled by a leader called Qomoqʷa, who lived in a huge house with all other marine beings. This wealthy chief always wore a large hat to shield his face, which was painted black and covered with eagle down. Humans visited him in the past to receive power, and he himself sometimes visited Nusmatta.

Under the earth was at least one subterranean world, where the ghosts lived and shamans often visited. Everything there, such as tides, seasons, day, and night, was the reverse of how it was on the earth surface, as Lushootseeds also believed. Its river flowed from west to east and was the source for all the springs in this world (McIlwraith 1948, 497). What would be cottonwood fluff on earth was snow there. Ghosts themselves had green faces and weird actions, speaking with sounds humans heard as whistling or gurgling.

Along the inside walls of Nusmatta hung the cloaks of many species, especially ravens, eagles, whales, grizzlies, black bears, and seabirds. To start human society, the creator asked those dwelling in his house to choose a cloak and put it on, so as to transform immediately into that animal or bird. The creator then entrusted each of them with hereditary names, tools, houses, clothing, and foods in compressed form. He sent them to earth as Nuxalk founders, with groups and couples landing on particular mountain peaks. From there, each removed cloak floated back up to the creator. These ancestors, returned to human form, came down from the mountain and founded various of the forty-five or so Nuxalk towns. Other ancestors came directly to earth in human form because they climbed down the pillars between sky and earth.

These first beings were the origin for the ancestral families (*minmints*), which were basic units of Nuxalk society. Each one guarded the privileges of its ancestors, especially knowledge of the names, the species cloak, the place where they landed, and the crest (or emblematic representation) representing these claims. Since a Nuxalk belonged to all the ancestral families of both of his parents, he or she represented these memberships with tattoos. For example, a design representing the primary family of the father, whose ancestor wore a Raven cloak, adorned the right breast, while the eagle cloak worn by the mother's ancestor was on the left side. Similar designs were painted on the prow of a canoe or the front of the house.

The more details known about these privileges, the more noble the family. When a Nuxalk died, he or she went back through the line of ancestors to the original mountain top and ascended to live in Nusmatta.

Every winter solstice, the creator entered his house and his heat was so intense that all the immortals living there fled except for three, who then conferred with Him about the fates of humans during the coming year. Births, deaths, and initiations were arranged, with the creator having final approval. Dreams sometimes forewarned humans of what their coming destinies would hold.

The animals and plants made by the carpenters' crews had human forms and minds, and lived in plank houses, but humans, because they were usually impure, rarely saw these dwellings as they really are. For example, some mountains were the homes of mountain goats, though humans did not realize they were hollow until a goat befriended a lone hunter and took him home. All species were given fire by the creator, with the color of their smoke being the same as that of their covering. Thus, the smoke from a mountain goat home was white, that from a beaver's was black, smoke from a squirrel's was reddish, and that from wolves' homes was gray. Species lived much as humans did, with health and illness treated by Grizzlies and Wolverines, who were the animals' shamans.

Each of these species was also said to have a Mother, much as the earth itself was regarded as the Mother nourishing the lives of all those who dwelt with her. Nothing was said of a Father, but the logical surmise would be that he was the creator himself, who ordered the world.

In addition to the bonds connecting ancestors, animals, and humans, twins and salmon shared a common link. Since twins had a dual (two-in-one) existence, literally seeming to be in two places at once, like the salmon who died and returned each year, twins could understand the speech of fish, animals, and birds.[28]

Humans maintained good relations with spirits and deities by fasting, praying, sacrificing, and observing "ceremonial chastity." These acts made the person pure and able to succeed at hunting, raiding, questing, gambling, building a salmon weir, or hosting a potlatch. In the most intense form, a set number of days of chastity (in multiples of +4 such as 4, 8, 12, 16) ended with private intercourse with a woman acting in a ritualized role to curb the accumulation of power. While all skilled hunters engaged in this duty, those few women who assumed the avowedly male hunting role had to hire a man other than their husbands to conclude their chaste intervals (cf. Miller 1997, 171, note 8).

In the beginning, the creator gave to every Nuxalk three spiritual aspects: a spirit in the body, along with a tally post and a water basin set up at Nus-matta (1948, 94–104). Though every person was said to have a post and basin, these probably represented fixed names, which were both immortal and hereditary, passed down through individuals of a family. Each post was decorated with the crest (species cloak) of the first ancestor and it leaned over when its person became ill. During a cure, shamans went above to try to set it upright. When it fell over, the person died, so shamans could estimate the likely duration of a patient's life from its angle of incline. A shaman diagnosed by consulting the curing power that lived in his or her wrist, using its strength to reverse the post's decline.

The creator set up an enormous wash basin, with a section for every one of the named Nuxalk individuals. During cures, shamans washed a patient to improve the quality of this water in the basin.

The person's spirit resided at the back of the neck in a thin, palmate (maple leaf–shaped) bone, which trembled to increase wealth or remained inert with misfortune. Associated with the spirit, somehow, were mentality and vitality. Mentality provided awareness and was localized in the heart, while vitality stretched as a force field between the little fingers and little toes of a person. Any damage to these circuits was often fatal.

At death, the person divided into a corpse, shadow, and ghost. The spirit became a ghost, who traveled back through generations of his or her ancestors to the family mountain peak, donned the cloak of the ancestral species, and ascended to Nusmatta. Existence above was like that on earth, except that all personal skills and abilities were enhanced.

According to more personal beliefs, the vitality at the feet stayed with the corpse and disintegrated along with it, provided that a nose ring was fastened through the septum; vitality at the legs became a wolf; and that at the throat-voice became an owl, which lived in a gigantic tree near Nusmatta. The shadow went to the land of the dead under the Bella Coola Valley. After a long time there, it died again to be reborn as a human infant. Food was scarce in the land of the dead, so offerings were much desired. Proper kinspeople burned food for the dead in the section of the house fire toward the door. From there, it went directly below. In legend, cemeteries provided another entry to this land (1948, 587).

At death, the corpse was washed by someone of the same sex and folded into a coffin box (1948, 436). People visited to bid farewell during the wake, which lasted between one and four days, its length and elaboration reflecting the social rank of the deceased. For a member of a secret society, a drama was enacted to make it appear as though the body was carried away through the smokehole by the major ancestral crest.

After the wake, the coffin box was taken out through a front corner of the house, behind a woman with a burning cedar taper. Mourners followed, with women keening, to the town cemetery behind the row of houses. The grave, generally near those of close kin, was not dug until the body arrived. Four times, an elderly man touched the sides of the hole with a spruce bough to protect those who had dug the grave from joining the dead.[29] Then the bough was tossed westward. The box was lowered so that the corpse faced east. Planks were placed over it, then stones and fill. Posts might be set up in the corners and a cedarbark rope strung along the east and west sides to trap the shadow inside.

A fire was kindled from the woman's taper and clothes and other possessions were burned for the shadow to take below. On the way back to the village, four spruce saplings were laid across the trail to block any of the dead from returning to the house. Four days later, more of the possessions were burned near the grave. The widow(er) was led through bent spruce saplings four times to deter any attempts by the deceased spouse to force a fatal reunion. During the following year of mourning, he or she had short hair, wore a special hat, and rubbed ashes on the face (1948, 457). During mourning, a widow(er) could not go near the river, so each village had a special rock near the shore where mourners could enter canoes for sea voyages.

In ancient times, Nuxalk cremated their dead, except for twins, who were placed in trees (1948, 450). Burials began after a shaman preached that wolves and other predators were taking too many bodies from the scaffolds holding grave boxes.

The dead were never far from the minds and deeds of the living. Indeed, the hallmark of the Nuxalk potlatch, setting it apart from those of their neighbors, was the dramatic enactment of the return of a deceased relative in the guise of a crest (1948, 458). Unlike their neighbors, moreover, Nuxalk sang but did not dance during their gift give-away feasts (1948, 470).

In sum, these coherent belief systems of Katzie and Nuxalk provide insight and context for other Salishan and Northwest religions. Throughout the Americas, European diseases and dislocations shattered any orderly transmission of native traditions, particularly when these involved fragile links between older and younger family members. In some cases, crucial knowledge of awesome import could only be held by a single person in a community, to safeguard its proper use, and, accordingly, it had to be passed on from a death bed. Sudden epidemics left heirs without fundamental understandings and survivors without an integrated outlook, further increasing their overwhelming sense of frustration and despair.

Certainly, shamans shared basic information about the way of the world and its animating principles, but these were not common knowledge, nor have they appeared in the printed record. Therefore, to fill such gaps and to regain a consistent overview, comparative data from other Salishans and more distant cultures must be consulted. A remote common ancestry makes Katzie and Nuxalk data readily relevant for grasping aspects of Lushootseed culture, as do the beliefs of their Nooksak neighbors on the slopes of Mount Baker.

OVERLAPPING SYSTEMS

Pamela Amoss (1978, 43) observed that modern Nooksak employ four semi-autonomous expressions of religion. These systems are the guardian spirit complex, the ghost complex, the magic complex, and the high god complex. She also noted that these modern complexes were simplified from the ancient religion, which she suspected was closer to that already described for the Katzie. Further, a variety of past religious specialists (mediums, priests, ritualists) have been subsumed by shamans fulfilling such formerly distinct roles.[30]

In modern beliefs about guardian spirits, that power attaches itself to a person at birth but only reveals its presence at puberty. "It" (as natives most frequently call their own power) has at least two aspects, a being and a song, although a third term used to refer to it seems to personify the vision itself. Some or all of these aspects "travel" during the year and only join together during the winter when the person becomes "possessed" (united, joined) by his or her spirit partner.

The song, at least, comes from the east in the fall, moves slowly westward during the winter, and, in late April or so, heads east again. As a group, powers come each year to the Nooksak before they reach Vancouver Island, where they linger until spring. In contrast to these career powers, curing powers are available at all times. According to Joyce Wike (1941), while the song traveled, the spirit itself stayed close to the human partner. Fierce black paint spirits traveled more widely than did those of red paint, who stayed nearby and could be used to cure or help others.

During the day, spirits also move around. Vi Hilbert said that they hover in the air (rather than tread on the ground) and are lower in the early morning than later in the afternoon. They are constantly aware of human actions and will leave if their partner becomes ritually impure or disrespectful. Then the spirit is said to "lift off" until it can be coaxed back by a shaman. Spirits are attracted to the warmth of daylight but, lacking form or substance, they are truly ethereal. Smith (1940, 57) reported that spirits had the most nebulous of existences, with their appetites and pleasures supplied vicariously through their links with humans.

A woman's spirit power is regarded as a personal friend, while for men it is an impersonal force that infuses his entire body when it returns (Amoss 1978, 51).

The ghost system had to do with the souls of the dead, who were tormented by hunger, loneliness, and nostalgia for their possessions and relatives (Amoss 1978, 73). They lived in a land of the dead, which often had two separate removals. After death, souls became ghosts who went to a land where they were still remembered by the living, who kept them fed and clothed. After a time, however, they faded from human memory and entered a second land of the dead where they had less contact with the living. Sometimes, they were reborn in babies from this second land, although there are also indications of even more remote lands of the dead, where they faded further into oblivion—somewhat like the half-life of a radioactive element.

Those ghosts who were still in contact with the living roamed the earth between about 3:00 P.M. and 3:00 A.M. Ghosts were especially attracted by human gatherings, especially when people were eating. In particular, a ghost was closest of all when its name was being inherited by a descendant.

In the ancient religion, certain humans acted as mediums because they had a special relationship with a ghost who came unsought or who was initially contacted by sleeping in a cemetery or near a gravebox. Such a medium learned from the ghost if some calamity was due to happen, and could thereby avert it, or conducted rituals in which food and clothes were burned in a fire to send them to the dead. Such burnings for the dead still precede all important Lushootseed events and follow special funerals, but they are performed now by shamans who have taken on the role of medium. While such burnings were once held separately, they have become the first event at modern power displays and potlatches.

In some instances of soul loss, a medium could send a ghost partner to retrieve a missing entity. In addition, Joyce Wike (1952) argued that it was ghosts, rather than immortals, who upheld the social order because they could take revenge on the living for a lack of respect or generosity. Yet they were, by and large, not expressions of a thorough-going ethical system because, for example, ghosts did not avenge their own murders.

What Amoss (1978, 78) called the magic system is properly a set of enchantments (incantations, formulae, dicta) for influencing the world and its inhabitants. These spells were passed down family lines and, at least in the Star Child epic, were given by the twins while they were redistributing the ashes from their burning of the earth.[31] These incantations used special terms that controlled the minds and hearts of all living things. Often the terms were paired into male and female versions to influence affections. In this way were wayward spouses returned or lovers attracted.

Curtis (1913, 111–12) provided the best Lushootseed examples of such evocations. A warrior in the midst of a fierce fight would pause to slap his thighs, arms, chest, and head while naming each one with so-called "charm words" to renew the strength and stamina of each section of anatomy. When a storm began to swamp a canoe, a paddler would slap the sides and call them by special terms to keep the vessel strong and steady. Such spells could be purchased at the cost of canoes, slaves, and hundreds of dollars' worth of goods. Lushootseed quester Jacob Wahalchu provided this enchantment (unfortunately only in English), addressed to the elements, for surviving a storm: "Take care of me, O Bright Faced One, the sun! Protect me, water on which I rest, and you, dry land!"

The high god system was fourth (Amoss 1978, 80). In the modern religion, its expressions are the Indian Shaker Church and various Christian fundamental denominations. For some present communities, such as Musqueam in Vancouver (British Columbia), people continue to divide the seasons such that they participate in winter dances to manifest their power at the beginning of the year and devote the summer to active roles in the Shaker Church. Initially, however, Shakers regarded themselves as distinct from the ancient forms of native religion. Since their spirit partners usually also decided to convert at the same time as humans did, both became new Shakers simultaneously.

Yet, as Old Pierre and other native intellectuals insisted, belief in an ultimate power was ancient in the region. Often termed *xa'xa*—which means anything sacred and holy as well as forbidden, taboo—this deification of power was the cap for the entire religion. Belief in the high god, who was somehow equated with the sun before the arrival of Christianity, integrated all of the other systems, although Amoss instead treated each as if it were semiseparate.[32]

Miller (1988, 151) noted that while Amoss denied that power had a single source, this belief in a high god logically indicates that this deity was both source and summary for the flow of power in the universe. As the most important spirit, as the deciding factor in the incarnation of souls, and as the primary referent for the working of enchantments, the high god, known best to elite families and their shamans rather than to most members of society, was the cosmic nexus for the entire system of existence. Among the Nuxalk, as noted, he lived in a house which was synonymous with their universe.[33]

4 HOUSES

DWELLINGS

American expansion into the Northwest brought logging tools and saw-mills. Natives themselves desired milled planks in place of the more labor-intensive wedged and adzed ones of their past, and they wanted, of course, to use such boards for multifamily houses. Americans, however, exerted great pressure upon Lushootseeds and other native peoples to abandon communal housing in favor of single family homes, ideally with clapboard sides and gingerbread detailing painted in tasteful colors. Native plank houses in villages at West Seattle, Port Townsend, Sauk Prairie, and Minter Creek were burned to the ground so that settlers could claim these as "un-occupied" lands and force resident natives onto reservations or into poorer locations.

Originally windowless with dirt floors, communal houses became "death traps" (White 1980, 28) where germs thrived, infecting everyone inside. Sharing food, utensils, and space contributed to the devastation. By the 1880s, a change to individual family houses, at least outwardly, had been accomplished. The last of the plank houses was the angled Samish refuge on Guemes Island off Anacortes. Such a change of residence, however, was more apparent than real because many family members continued to reside together, several generations and distant kin sharing the same abode.

Inside the house, traditional usages continued, emphasizing cluttered storage and ready access rather than tidy open spaces. Fire hearths were re-placed by iron stoves. Objects in frequent use are kept in view atop various convenient surfaces. Boxes and bags line the walls, providing insulation. Couches are preferred to chairs because each can hold more people and double as a bed, much like the ancient inside platforms.

After Europeans arrived, horses, wagons, trains, ferries, and scheduled shipping also kept native people in steady contact. More recently, phones and vans have kept family members in touch even if they cannot live

together. In place of canoes, modern paved roads, a summer circuit of re-
vivals, powwows, and rodeos, a winter round of smokehouses, and larger
vehicles have helped, not hindered, native interactions along very traditional
patterns.

PLANK HOUSES

Like other native inhabitants of the Northwest Coast, Lushootseeds built
large houses of cedar posts and planks, which also provided a metaphor for
the corporate ancestral family.[1] Each ancestral house (*gʷədˀaltxʷ*) was associated with a building, a place, a resource, and a stock of honored names that
defined its membership over many generations. Each river had its own style
of house construction, but the regional architectural pattern was largely
consistent.

As Suttles (1991) noted in his masterful summary, the slope-pitched shed
house was aptly suited to the flexibility of Coast Salish and Lushootseed
society because it could be expanded at either end as needed. More than a
home, the building also functioned as a food-processing and storage plant,
workshop, recreation center, theater, fortress, and temple.

Because the house was enclosed, warm, and dry, many winter activities
took place there, even the sewing of cattail mats, which took up considerable
floor space. In the evenings and during lulls, games were played and stories
were told. Singing, dancing, and dramatic retellings of personal events were
staged in the house, generally after it had been cleaned and cleared of bulky
objects like boxes and stockpiled wood. Before the adoption of buckskin-
covered drums, the musical accompaniment at these events was provided by
long poles pounded against the roof. Houses were fortified against outside
attack by cramped doorways, blind passages, emergency escapes, trapdoors,
and palisades.

The house was also a temple or church where winter rituals were held. In
addition, each region had a town containing an extremely large building,
often called a potlatch house, where huge gatherings were held, particularly
during winter when religious rituals drew people together. After the death
of the owner or sponsor of a potlatch house, the building remained standing
but unused as a memorial to his fame.

Roofs

The style of roof was the most distinctive feature of Lushootseed architec-
ture. Most houses had a shed or single-slope roof, but gabled and hip (gam-

brel, mansard) roofs were also built. While the shed was most common, gables were used for the homes of the rich. The mansard house was little known, consisting of a central square covered with planks and four lean-tos with mat roofs and plank walls. Two were side compartments where people lived, while the two end ones were used for storage (Suttles 1991, 220).

According to Marian Smith (1940, 281), the Puyallup, Nisqually, and Chehalis had gables; the Sahewamish built both gables and hips; the Steilacoom and Squaxon used both gabled and shed roofs; and the Suquamish, Duwamish, and people on the salt water at Gig Harbor and Carr Inlet had shed roofs. Waterman and Greiner (1921, 49) reported that the Salishan shed-roof house spread to the Nootkans, Makah, Chimakum, and Quileute, interrupting an almost continuous distribution of the gabled house along the Pacific coast from Alaska to California.

A long rectangular house was built parallel to the river, with doors at each end. Pairs of support posts were placed along the sides, then covered with overlapping planks along the walls and roof. Vertical planks were the easiest to attach to the frame, but when rot began at the bottom, every board had to be replaced. Thus, horizontally planked houses, each plank tied on to the supports, were easier to maintain because only the bottom one had to be replaced when there was rot. Roof planks were made with either deep or shallow troughs to alternate so that deep ones, which carried off the rain, were linked by inverted shallow ones (Waterman and Greiner 1921, 30). Each plank was carefully prepared and treasured, finished in rippling adze marks, and taken with the family whenever they moved to other camps, resorts, or houses.

An old-style Stillaguamish house had "walls of wide boards laid overlapping horizontally, like cedar siding, tied at corners and door posts with cedar bark. . . . The walls were supported by several cedar posts with short pegs in them on which baskets and clothing were hung. From the ridge pole hung bundles of smoked salmon and other foods" (Bruseth 1950, 9).[2]

Since they were loosely attached, wall and roof planks served as resonators, pounded with poles, during rituals. Some mornings, to rouse children in training, an old man struck the walls with a switch, calling for everyone to rush down to the stream to bathe.[3]

Inside, double wooden platforms ran along the sides, an outer one that was a yard above the ground and an inner one that was half as high.[4] The inner one was used for sitting and storage, and the upper one for sleeping. Firewood was stored under the platform, storage boxes were set along the outer wall, and preserved food was placed on an overhead shelf and drying racks. Most of the dirt floor was excavated except under the platforms, which rose from ground level. Fires burned along the sides in front of the section between support posts occupied by a family. Only during public ceremonies and gatherings were large fires built along the middle of the house.

In cold weather, cattail mats were hung along the inner walls for insulation. In frigid conditions, mat tents were built around the family area to keep it warm.

According to Waterman and Greiner (1921, 38), "From the native standpoint the center and soul of the house was a great rack for drying fish" that hung from the roof in the middle of the house. Presumably, this claim was based on the ostentation provided by a full rack of hanging fish.

The decorated house posts and the central fire, however, had better claim for being the heart and soul of the house. Every family had its own fire along the side, where each wife prepared meals for her own family, although fresh game, porpoise, or fish was shared with other fires. The main meal came in the late afternoon, much of it consisting of foods taken from storage (Smith 1940, 228). If an honored guest were present, special foods were served on a fresh mat of sword fern fronds (Smith 1940, 229). Guests were also given food to take home with them. For example, Smith (1940, 243) provided a delightful image of visiting Sahaptins heading inland from Nisqually villages while munching on necklaces formed of dried clams.[5]

OWNERS

Each house was owned by a group of siblings amassing the wealth, resources, and status needed to coordinate the labor to build such an imposing structure. The location used was a hereditary site belonging to that family, usually at a productive fishery. The most famous of leading families indicated their high rank by having several such houses, each built at the location of an important resource that they controlled—in the sense of acting as host for the harvesting and dispersal of that bounty. In addition, a famous leader arranged for the building of an especially large house in his town, called a potlatch house in English, where public events took place and out of town guests could stay. It was this ability to accommodate a large influx of people that defined a town.

The senior brother or man considered the owner of the house and his family seems to have lived in the right corner of the house,[6] with less prestigious or younger families on the left. Slaves might sleep on the lower platform if there was room; otherwise they had to find whatever sleeping place they could. Unlike other tribes to the north, such as the Nuuchahnulth,

Kwakwaka'wakw, and Tsimshian, places—called "seats"—within the house do not seem to have been strictly ranked.

The owners of a house lauded themselves by carving and painting the houseposts located in the center or at the outer corners of the house.[7] Though never as explicit as the carved totems of the matrilineal north, each painted post represented a spirit partner of the owner and was, therefore, his claim to a special relationship with specific land.[8] Before the Change, a being who became an immortal had occupied that place and, over the generations, shared its resources with members of the leading family. Among the Twana and Songhees (Suttles 1991, 218), these decorated posts were kept draped or covered most of the time, only being unveiled at a potlatch or other social event, when the owner wished to show by this evocative depiction that he had a spiritual helper without being more specific.

While northerners lavishly decorated the outside of their houses, along with the rear inside screen that sheltered the hereditary treasures of the house, Salishans displayed their rights on the inside of the house. A few painted housefronts are reported, particularly one at Tolt (now Carnation) among the Snoqualmi, but these probably derived from northern styles to add exotic prestige.

Painted houseposts were the rule, and carved ones were the exception. Describing a potlatch house, Frank Le Clair (Haeberlin 1917, notebook 4, 8) said that two of the posts were painted with a wide black band as background for two stacked horizontal white crescents or half moons.

John Fornsby (Collins 1949, 296, 326) said that his own grandfather kʷaskedəb had a potlatch house above Skagit City, with the house posts at each end painted to represent his powers. His children also became famous, notably Sneatlam, a Lower Skagit leader who was an important middleman in the fur trade at Fort Nisqually. A daughter married among the Chehalis. When the grandfather died, he was laid in "the middle back of the house." As children, John and his friends were shocked to find the skeleton still there. Eventually, the skeleton was buried at Swinomish; the house later washed away in a flood. When one of the houseposts was found downriver at La Conner, John held a potlatch to set it up on his own behalf. In this way, he both honored his ancestor and enhanced himself, presumably inheriting the power represented on the pole at the same time.

Kate Mount (Haeberlin 1917, notebook 41, 4) said that a house was burned or given away if its owner died inside it, but otherwise it was only vacated for a few months after the owner died. Henry Sicade (Haeberlin 1917, notebook 28, 19, 31) added that ownership of the house followed a set order of succession. A son had first claim, then a wife, and subsequently other family members. Daughters, since they commonly lived with their husbands, gained rights through their brothers, unless there were only sisters, who unquestionably inherited the home.

When houses were huge, they had several doorways leading into separate family compartments divided off by plank walls. Oleman House, the communal longhouse at Suquamish (associated with Chief Seattle's father and uncle, then himself) was built in this manner.[9] For the Upper Skagit, Collins (1974, 7) mentioned both the decorated houseposts and wooden figures set up in and near a house. Huge Skagit houses served special functions at several towns. The prophet who centralized the Upper Skagit lived at Rocky Creek in a house that was 120 feet long and 40 feet wide. All of the Upper Skagits gathered inside for meetings, for modified Christian prayer services in summer, and for traditional winter dances during the winter. A house the same size was located at Marblemount and was occupied by twenty families. Another huge house at the confluence of the Sauk and the Skagit was used for meetings of all the people living along the Sauk.[10]

While inland towns were scattered along a waterway with neighborhoods having one or more houses, dwellings along the salt water were often clustered together within a palisade for defense. The Upper Skagit town at Concrete was also palisaded because these people had frequent downriver contacts and made saltwater canoes for sale (Collins 1974, 13). A Skagit warrior who moved to Quartermaster Harbor in southern Puget Sound build a fortified and palisaded town from which he led attacks on the Duwamish. When he became old and feeble, his village joined the people at Gig Harbor (Smith 1940, 11). A Suquamish warrior married to a Duhlelap Twana woman had a palisaded home on the south arm of Hood Canal (Elmendorf 1960, 169).

In some cases, communal settlements were actually forts, such as that of Samish on Guemes Island. Lahalbid, a prophet, and his family were the lone survivors of a smallpox epidemic that breached a fort on Sullivan Slough among the Swinomish (Roberts 1975, 49, 56).

Klallam forts guarded their colonies at Sehome and Toanichum (Ebey's Prairie), as well as home turf at Dungeness, visited by Paul Kane (1925, 159; Harper 1971) on 9 May 1847: "Evening reached I-eh-nus, a Clallum village or fort . . . composed of a double row of strong pickets, the outer ones about twenty feet high, and the inner row about five feet, enclosing a space of 150 feet square. The whole of this inner space is roofed in, and divided into small compartments, or pens, for the use of each separate family. There were 200 of the tribe in the fort at the time of my arrival. Their chief, Yates-sut-soot, received me with great cordiality."[11]

Just southeast of Stanwood in northern Puget Sound, the Stillaguamish had a Treasure (or Strong) House, a fortified dwelling, under the care of a famous warrior, Tsalbit (Bruseth 1950, 13). It was built of "big logs set on end, a roof of heavy cedar slabs," and surrounded by a concealed moat with sharpened stakes set along the bottom; the door could be entered only by knowing where to step safely. Both sturdy and safe, the house provided many Stillaguamish families with haven and storage for their most prized items.

Communal effort implied that laborers shared use rights, in some sense, if not quasi-ownership. For example, everyone who worked on a house had the right to live in it when and if they chose to do so. Similarly, everyone who worked on building a fish weir could take fish from it. In this way, voluntary and cooperative labor served both public good and personal advantage.

Yet the ownership of more limited and valued resources was controlled by families. Houses, as noted, were built at the best fishing sites and were occupied by siblings, often brothers and their wives. Women, by comparison, inherited root-digging plots in the great prairies of the region. Among the Upper Skagit, plots of tiger lilies and wild carrots at Sauk and German prairies passed from mother to daughter (Collins 1974, 55). Among Swinomish, camas and horse clam beds were owned and inherited as private property (Roberts 1975, 88).

Now, as in the past, along each river, communities intensely identified with their particular locale as saltwater, delta, inland, upriver, or mountainous, with relatively less movement among these habitats farther upriver. People on the salt water traveled much more than people upriver, so there was a kind of urban/rural split, according to some sources. For example, though the Puyallup River was only fifteen miles long, there were upriver people who had never been more than a few miles from their home and expressed no desire to visit the sound (Smith 1940, 41). Nevertheless, every region was valued for its specialties, which were gladly received as trade or gifts in other places.

The more outgoing and better-traveled people were those near the river mouths with trade and ceremonial routes along and across salt water. Leaders and families were famous mainly to the extent that their names were known in other communities. Although Smith (1940, 48) insisted for the Puyallup and Nisqually that women could not obtain prestige because they were excluded from these public events, her assertion is not borne out. While few women dominated public events, those who did, generally the daughters of famous chiefs, showed that women could indeed become famous on an intertribal scale.[12]

In addition to the prestige that came from building a potlatch house for use during his celebrations, a leader was expected to be generous at all times. As an indication of this willingness to share, he should always have over a hundred carved wooden spoons available for use at his feasts (Smith 1940, 274).

HOUSEHOLDS

Smith (1940, 37) suggested that the average size of a family was about five people, and that villages had between twenty and fifty members. Towns had as many as seventy-five residents, gathered around a famous family with a huge home.

According to her reconstruction of one Nisqually village about 1870–75, two longhouses were located on either side of the river (Smith 1940, 37–39). The house on the north bank was occupied by the leader, who was the oldest male. On the south bank, the house was larger and owned by a famous shaman, who was related to the leader, perhaps his nephew. Shamans usually had their own homes because their continuous contact with spirits and vulnerability to attack by other shamans made them dangerous to live with. The practicalities of performing cures and conducting public rituals also required that they have their own space. In modern times, shamans have often had a separate building behind their single-family home to use as a doctor's office and clinic.

The Nisqually leader's house on the north bank had six fires, each associated with a family. The leader lived in the right-hand corner of the downriver end with his remaining wife, who was so crippled that he carried her everywhere; with his youngest son and daughter; and with a daughter by another wife and her half-Hawaiian child. On the right-hand upriver corner was the oldest daughter with three children from a prior marriage and children from her present husband, who was also married to one of her daughters. In the middle of the right side lived another daughter with her husband and a forty-year-old son who never married. Nothing is known of the family in the downriver left corner. At the left center fire was Yelm Jim, the leader's brother's son, and his much older wife.[13] In the left upriver corner lived the son of Yelm Jim's wife, whose own father was probably a relative of the leader.

In the shaman's house on the south bank, the owner also lived in the downstream right side corner with his mother, his wife and children, and his wife's sister and her children. In all probability, both sisters were his wives. Other occupants of the house are not known, but both houses together had almost forty children.

By the late 1800s, impelled relocations onto the reservation doubled the number of houses, with two on the north bank and two on the south one. When the Puyallup Reservation was allotted, each family took a homestead and lived individually, as their descendants continue to do.

Smith (1940, 39–40) also included data, from after the reservation was established, on a four-fire Puyallup house located far upriver. The leader lived in the downriver right corner with his four children, his half sister with her husband and children, and a bachelor brother who spent most of his time in the mountains, probably hunting. The half sister was there to mother the younger children of the leader, their own mother having died when her fourth child was born. Another man with a wife and son lived in the downriver left corner, but when they were away, the half sister's family stayed there. In the right upriver corner lived a couple with two children. In the left upriver corner lived an older pair with a female slave.

The relationships within this Puyallup household were not well known. The men in the downriver corners were from the mountainous divide between the Snoqualmi and Kittitas near modern Ellensberg, where their Pshwanwapam Sahaptin connections seem to have been stronger than their Salishan ones. When the reservation was allotted, the families each took a separate homestead, and the communal house was claimed by a man who was probably a brother of the leader.

Along the Skagit River, six houses at *slox* are well reported.[14] Located between modern Lyman and Hamilton, the best known of these houses (that of Vi Hilbert's father's father) was eighty feet long and fifty feet wide, with six to eight fires. The site included an important fishery, for both salmon and trout, where people used dip nets, spears, and hooks but no weir. Every day, those who fished shared their catch with everyone in the house.

Owners of this house were four brothers and a sister, with their families, at five fires. One of the brothers was the father of Charlie Anderson, whose own sister and her husband had a sixth fire. The other two fires were occupied by the families of other grown children of the brothers. These first cousins were regarded as siblings in the native terminology, so the household consisted of parents and their children, who regarded each other as brothers and sisters.

Indeed, this house provides the clearest illustration of the link between siblings (family core), house, and place. Each year to this day, the salmon fishing season begins with a blessing of the Upper Skagit fleet at *slox* as a reminder that the man appointed by the Skagit Prophet to be head fisherman for the river always belonged to that community.

SETTLEMENTS

Instead of graded chiefly rankings, as to the north, Lushootseeds speak of entire villages as having been either high or low class. High class towns, which were the rule, had wealthy leaders and a variety of specialists who were famous in the intertribal network. Low class communities, which were located in exposed positions with few resources, lacked such nobility and probably were formed either by slaves, marginals, or outcasts; by refugees from another area driven away by warfare or natural disaster; or by remnants of a decimated town who had yet to recoup their losses (cf. Collins 1974, 129).

While few in number, these settlements of "nothings, no goods" were clearly remembered because they served to set the nobility off in high relief. They were the negative examples of what not to be or to do for the vast majority of other Salishans. Sometimes, these marginals, who were tactfully and politely called "little younger siblings" lived at one or both vulnerable ends of a town, but more often they lived apart.

At the Skagit village at Sneatlum Point, a palisade surrounded a long house with three segments of high class families, while the "no accounts" lived outside the walls and were not allowed inside (Suttles 1978, 5).[15] In villages at Saanich on Brentwood Bay of southern Vancouver Island and at Sechelt on the lower mainland, members of the upper class lived in the middle and those of the lower class were at each end (Barnett 1955, 23, Suttles 1987, 5). Both the Klallam and Snohomish had separate villages of inferiors.

Conflicts sometimes developed because of the strained relations between the two classes. At Oak Harbor on Whidbey Island, classes came to blows. Since only the nobility included warriors, inferiors were at a distinct disadvantage because they lacked protectors of their own.

Sally Snyder (1964) suggested a complex dynamic among the Lower Skagit in which populations increased, class distinctions became emphasized, and class conflicts festered. Then the settlement would split and the new settlements began their own separate sets of stratifications. In time, the leaders of the new communities gained sufficient status to intermarry with the established elite and win intertribal prestige, assuring high rank to their descendants.

Some villages were described as occupied by vassals of more important settlements. While the meaning of this status is not clear, some kind of tribute was involved. For example, the people on Dugualla Bay had to bring firewood to the Swinomish during the coldest periods of winter. North of Nanaimo on Vancouver Island, the marginal Nanoose could only marry among themselves or, more distantly in the lower Fraser River, among Coquitlams subject to neighboring Kwantlens who had saved them from famine (Duff 1952, 27). An interesting implication of these Nanoose-Coquitlam intermarriages is that people only took strength from their homeplace if they were autonomous; otherwise its powers were apparently siphoned off to their superiors.

While it is now difficult to understand how such drains on a society worked, the motivation was religious, as in so much else. For natives, industry and generosity were basic assumptions. Doing otherwise was a selfish expression of personal whim or malevolent influences. "To be completely without allegiance, marital stability and economic usefulness was so difficult that it was thought to indicate an amount of determination which might at any moment shift into more usual channels" (Smith 1940, 52).

Much of the suspicion that characterized dealings with those outside the family was similarly motivated. Since spirits could impulsively accept or reject a person, shifting loyalties overnight in the balance of powers, it was best to be circumspect, polite, and wary in all interpersonal dealings. While the highest and lowest statuses were stable, those in the middle range apparently could and did fluctuate widely.

HOUSING GROUPINGS

As noted, all valued life among Lushootseeds was communal. No healthy, normal person was ever entirely alone, as long as people had their spirit partner(s). Ever aware of other intelligences, any mortal was surrounded by a sentient crowd. Yet within these masses were internal rules and units that served to organize the entire world.

Classes

In the classic discussion of human social classes and ranks among the Coast Salishans, Wayne Suttles (1987, 3–14) has argued for a model of this society as an inverted pear because the majority of people considered themselves to be noble and respectable. The narrow bottom of the pear was occupied by the low class, and the very base by a small number of slaves. Usually, these memberships are called the upper class, the lower class, and slavery, but these terms obscure degrees of rank within the upper class. Indeed, while most people had only a class identity, members of elite families always held names that had long been famous intertribally. Thus, while houses and towns might be attributed to a social class on a local basis, rank was a matter of regional recognition.

In reality, kinship links through both father and mother aligned Lushootseeds into discrete kindreds—bilateral descent groupings associated with households. In most cases, each formed a "nodal kindred," where the node was a bond of parent and children or, after those antecedents' deaths, of siblings, often brothers. For most families, a kindred had cohesion only as long as it had a dominant node, sometimes expressed as attenuated family prestige.

Of particular note, however, was the permanent node provided by an elite name, the basis for a "stem kindred" that had continuity over time because succession to that name stemmed across generations. Since the system was and is bilateral, the actual inheritance of that name was optional, to some extent, passed to the kinsperson with the best success in upholding overall kindred honor, prestige, and generosity.

Based on present-day patterns, every region had and has certain families, those with honored names, that clearly stand out from the other nobles. These families were the obvious elite and they passed on names that were well known in the international network. They were the equivalent of a Roosevelt, Kennedy, or Astor, rather than a Jones, Smith, or Miller.[16]

Collins (1966) has distinguished these titles as "renowned names," and it was the holders of such names who owned several big houses in various endowed locales. Indeed, in Lushootseed, such a person or family is called *hikʷ siʔab*, in the sense of a grandee, "big" in terms of authority, respect, and ability.[17] In a few instances, such an owner might have several large houses, each located near an important resource. That he (or they) could coordinate the building of more than one large home further spoke to his (their) leadership abilities.

Also, based on observations at modern reservations, where some families are still called "low class" behind their backs, the distinguishing characteristic of such people is that they cannot be relied upon always to behave well at public gatherings or to help out in times of need.[18] Some families are simply called lazy, but others are even more frustrating because they vacillate across the spectrum of good and bad behaviors. Their position is so unsure that sometimes they devote considerable time and effort to putting on a good front, and sometimes they appear drunk or unruly at gatherings, where they are quietly but grudgingly tolerated. High class Lushootseeds realize that the undistinguished have a "tough" life, but good people and families are expected to uphold "pluck" and rise above uncertainties and momentary hardships.

Now as in the past, there are families who are famous and elite, others who are respected, others who are stolid, and others who are looked down upon. Similarly, in certain contexts, reservations and communities are also graded. Those placed on reservations with a full complement of rights from the treaties of 1855, conferring full federal recognition, sometimes slight leaders whose reservations were established by presidential decree since these people have a more confused relationship with the federal government. Lastly, those few tribes who are described as landless—lacking treaty rights, federal recognition, or trust land—sometimes meet with open hostility from the leaders of treaty tribes, both at native gatherings and in the U.S. district courts. These attitudes seem to be carried over from the expressions for relationships between the classes and among the ranking families. Houses and towns that appeared prosperous always received more respect and attention. The basis for this prosperity, according to the Salish, was continuous relations between the leading family and local immortals. In the most successful of families, these relations were intentionally so diverse that their households were filled with a range of specialists—in crafts, medicine, command, management, and religion—who were vital to the intertribal network of trade, ceremonies, and hospitality.

Other expressions of rank were the private ownership of desired resources, such as fisheries and trade items; strict rules of inheritance, particularly from father to the oldest son and from mother to the oldest daughter; the ownership of houses and slaves; and the possession of family wisdom (x^wdik^w). While some of the details of this wisdom—in addition to family history, complex genealogies, gossip about other families, and full accounts of spirit quests by ancestors—expressed many aspects of the Golden Rule and Ten Commandments, these practicalities were complemented by a range of esoteric knowledge, from prayers used during life cycle events of family members to a special set of enchantments to control the minds of all intelligent life forms, ranging from animals and weather spirits to humans.

Often these enchantments, sometimes called magic spells or formulae, were associated with the houses of particular leaders and were passed on to descendants of families who had been resident there. Bits of these formulae might also be sold to a person outside the family for a high price. Though these have often been regarded by scholars as a separate religious system, the foregoing discussion (ch. 1) has indicated how these phrases were given to the family by the high god, either directly or through the efforts of the changers who did His bidding and prepared the world before human arrival.

For the neighboring Twana, hallmarks of nobility included birth, wealth, personality, and spirit powers (Elmendorf 1960, 322, 327–36). Birth referred to descent from families of good "blood" and reputation who worked diligently to maintain this status by industrious productivity and ambition. Wealth took the tangible form of slaves, canoes, dog or goat wool blankets, fur robes, sea otter pelts, bone war clubs, and dentalium shells — all of which served as currency in the intertribal network of gifts and trade. Personality referred to an even temperament, dignity, regard for others, generosity, industry, self-control, and pride. The greatest of spirit powers were expected to be attracted to the most elite families, conferring wealth, property, progeny, and good fortune.

While a child started with the advantages of a good birth, subsequent training instilled the self-discipline needed to undergo the rigors of spiritual purity. Such training was a determining factor in the molding of personality for the acquisition of powers allowing an adult to enter the ranks of the elite. The entire family took part in this training, although family specialists were usually paid by the parents for taking the time to teach particular lessons, as was the case when three elderly "uncles" taught Old Pierre the Katzie genesis.

At Suquamish, according to Wilson and Ellen George, genealogies were used in arguments about rank. Leaders would indicate places where the blood lines of other families were "weak" because of bad or shameful behavior by an ancestor.[19] A great insult was when a noble spat on his little finger and held it up because this meant that the person he was referring to was of slight consequence.[20]

Although any leader was usually too busy to hunt and fish, his wives harvested roots, berries, and clams. His slaves did the fishing and hunting if they were young; older slaves made canoes and utensils for the family.

While a family might have a slave or two, a chief always had more than two, through purchase, capture, or birth from a slave. Slaves had to do at least as much work as their masters, so most worked long and hard. Master and slave sometimes worked together, but a valued slave always made more effort. If the master got angry, he could beat or kill the slave without consequences. Usually, instead, slaves were scolded or set difficult tasks to punish them. Often, a kind man was asked by slaves to purchase them from a harsh master.

In the plank houses, slaves did all the cleaning and got basic supplies like clams, drinking water, and firewood. In camps, slaves lived in a separate mat hut. Regardless of abode, slaves always ate after everyone else was finished.

Ellen George of Suquamish said her grandmother freed her slaves in response to Lincoln's 1862 Emancipation Proclamation, yet they continued to bring her clams and berries for the rest of their lives. Throughout Washington Territory, however, most slaves had previously been freed under terms of the 1855 treaties. The last slaves at Suquamish were John Kettle and his wife, who, at last benefiting from their own hard work, became prosperous by selling clams in the city of Seattle and never returned to their natal families on Vancouver Island.

Specializations

Just as an English noble house maintained its prestige by sending its children into a wide variety of endeavors, ranging from business, law, and the church to the colonies, so too the most famous Salishan houses encouraged a full complement of specialists. All specializations represented the enhancement of family and personal ability granted by guardian spirits, which thereby provided religious sanction.

Elite status was expressed in terms of successes, bolstering a sense of confidence, competence, and authority. Nobles led by arranging successful group hunts, winter ceremonials, give-aways, elaborate cures, and the building of houses and fish weirs (Collins 1974, 113). A leader's specialty was that he or she was an expert in human psychology (Smith 1940, 49) and was personally characterized by dignity, open-handedness, restraint, wealth, and a knowledge of traditions (Amoss 1978, 10).

Leaders were respected (and perhaps feared for their powers), so that they needed only to suggest what should be done. Then they left it up to others to decide for themselves to do it. For example, the leader merely suggested when it was time to go to a camping place to fish or hunt, allowing everyone else to decide the exact timing of the move. On one occasion, a man decided on his own to remain behind. In response, the leader held a meeting to suggest that they move on, shunning the man. Everyone at the meeting agreed. Alone and unaware, after finishing a new canoe, the man went home to find everyone gone. Chagrined, he searched for and joined them at a later camp, staying close from then on. Thus, his neighbors taught him not to be stubborn or too independent.

Social life was based on consensus, but any person had total freedom to do what he or she thought best, accepting any consequences of this decision. When a hunter killed more than he needed, he gave some meat to the leader to express appreciation for the chief's looking out for everyone's welfare. In turn, the chief gave generously, particularly to people who had little. Whenever someone killed a large animal, such as a deer, elk, seal, or porpoise, the hunter hosted a feast for everyone to share the good fortune. During hard times, as when families were in mourning, people brought them food. The leader might arrange this, or neighbors took it upon themselves to help out.

A leader had to be nice to people. He had "the first say" on things, but he could not order people around. Jim Seattle, that chief's son, lost first place among the Suquamish because of his angry behavior. The aforementioned Jacob Wahalchu was voted into this chiefship because Jim was quick-tempered and easily offended, qualities considered good for a warrior but bad for a chief.

A man from the low class, if he were very smart and good, could become the headman if people liked him. Every village had such a headman, ideally from the same family over generations. He had first say on everything, but afterward, all the others could speak their minds. During war, he decided which warrior would lead in battle.

In addition to local leaders, all the Suquamish were under a single warlord in times of trouble. Before Seattle, this was Kitsap, a man famous for his warrior powers. Seattle himself was chief of both the Suquamish and the Duwamish because these were the tribes of his father and of his mother. He was a great war captain, but in maturity he became a kind and generous chief.

A warrior flaunted a hot temper, stamina, indifference to physical risk, and a willingness to be mean by inflicting pain (Collins 1974, 114). His dagger and club were so closely associated with the killing of men that displaying such weapons at a public event was tantamount to a declaration of war (Smith 1940, 163). A warrior was forceful and aggressive, dominant, imperious, quick-tempered, and implacable, tending toward the despotic (Amoss 1978, 10). According to Smith (1940, 157), Puget tribes engaged in four kinds of warfare, including an organized offense during battle, raids to take booty and slaves, assaults to settle a grievance, and attacks to take revenge. The most famous regional exploit was an expedition (about 1830) made up of warriors from all over Puget Sound to attack native towns along Vancouver Island. While accounts vary, many of the attackers drowned after their lighter canoes were split by heavy Canadian vessels.

Shamans had both career and curing spirits of great power (Collins 1974, 191). Though a shaman often had a separate house, his or her membership in a settlement brought it security from attack by spirits or hostile shamans (Amoss 1978, 20). Shamans also were relied on to explain the cause of hardships, to treat the sick, and to counteract malevolent sorcery. While shamans were generally treated with deference (motivated by a great fear of their power), a shaman who was a family member was the best of allies.

As noted, while shamans still practice among the Salish, many of their curing functions are now shared with members of modern religious sects such as the Indian Shaker Church and Pentecostal Christianity. Indeed, John Fornsby (Collins 1949, 333) said that modern Shakers were like the doctor powers of old and so could recover lost souls and absent powers.

While all men hunted, career hunters were men with talents and powers to harpoon sea mammals or undertake the arduous task of hunting mountain goats. In the southern sound, at least, these special hunters wore clothing and used equipment, such as quivers, made of cougar skin (Smith 1940, 309).

The most specialized of roles throughout this region was that of the prophet, a position that increased in importance with white settlement and forced change.

The most famous example was the prophet known as Captain Campbell (or Camel), who centralized the religion and politics of the Upper Skagit. His father had moved from Nespelem and married a woman from the native town at the mouth of the Snohomish River.[21] As he grew up and returned to visit relatives along the Mid-Columbia, he was introduced to native versions of Catholic rituals, to aspects of the Plateau prophet cult, and eventually to Catholic missionaries like Father Eugene Chirouse, who later founded the mission at Tulalip (Sullivan 1932). Campbell married a woman from Big Lake along the Skagit and settled there. After she died, he married the daughter of Patius, the famous Samish leader from Bayview. Both wives belonged to powerful families who encouraged him. By introducing his own form of the prophet cult, and later serving as the translator for Father Chirouse, he also gained outside authority to abet his centralizing of Upper Skagit religion. Thus, the first salmon caught in the Skagit River each year was brought to him to be welcomed and thanked ritually.

His dynasty continues among the Upper Skagit. After the captain died, the office passed to his son John, then to his daughter, who was remarkably forceful. She had no children, so John's son Joseph inherited the position and passed it to his sons John, then Peter, who died recently.

Genders

Males and females led different but mutually supportive lives among Lushootseeds, yet, unlike in other tribes where male and female roles were mutually exclusive, the same tasks were open to both men and women among the Salishans. While, in fact, men and women led separate lives, their duties were more a matter of frequency than of hard and fast rules. A few women took upon themselves careers that men usually held, and a few men performed jobs usually done by women, but these activities did not compromise their identities as men or women. While berdaches (two spirits) were known for neighboring groups, and some may have occurred among Lushootseeds, these transvestites were accepted on the basis of their self-presentations, although people thought of them in terms of their biological characteristics. Thus, a berdache was always said to be a man acting or "pretending" to be a woman, rather than a third distinct gender (Miller 1982).

For men, careers included those of canoe maker, hunter, storyteller, gambler, harpooner, carpenter, warrior, and ritualist (Smith 1940, 34, 49), while women excelled as midwives, weavers, and basketmakers (Collins 1974, 3).

Men and women expressed a skill in all of its ramifications. For example, a canoe maker also produced paddles. An expert at drying clams also made coarsely woven clam baskets (Smith 1940, 49, 141). Women experts served as cooks at large gatherings, as storytellers, and as midwives (Smith 1940, 140). Other specialties seldom reported in the literature but of great importance for a house and community were those of undertaker, corpse washer, and coffin box maker (Amoss 1978, 17).

For carpenters, as with all specialists, spiritual techniques were learned along with manual skills. While every man could work wood, the building of houses and canoes called for experts. If a leader were not himself a carpenter, he hired one to do his building. While houses were the largest possession, canoes were equally important. As Marian Smith (1940, 144) remarked, "Even when a man was defeated by combat, either in an athletic contest or in a demonstration of power, and forfeited all his possessions, including his wives, his canoe was left to him."

Throughout the Americas, men and women had mutually interdependent careers that functioned at their best in terms of the married couple, since the contributions of husband and wife supplied the full range of needs. Indeed, a person could not properly display his or her spirit power during its annual winter return without the emotional and musical cooperation of a spouse.

As already indicated, men hunted land and sea mammals, gathered fish, and made artifacts from wood, horn, stone, and bone.[22] Woodworking was always important, serving especially for traps, nets, weapons, canoes, and houses (Smith 1940, 139; Collins 1974, 75).

Women took care of the house and family. By season, they gathered roots, berries, and shoots; dried and smoked fish; prepared animal skins, shredded cedarbark for clothing, sewed garments, spun wool, made baskets and weavings; carried wood and water if there were no slaves to do this; and constantly tended children and prepared meals (Collins 1974, 75; Smith 1940, 139). Women became midwives after having numerous healthy children, or they served as baby doctors, able to diagnose physical and spiritual illnesses and to return the lost souls of infants (Collins 1974, 75, 76, 201). In addition, wives and sisters served as adjuncts to male powers by singing for good luck while the man was away hunting, fishing, or raiding (Smith 1940, 165).

Seasons

Families moved with the "moons" to gather and prepare resources to be stored in winter havens (Ballard 1950). Every time and season had its appropriate activity, as can be seen in the following calendar account for the Suquamish. All year long, Suquamish dug clams, harpooned seals and porpoises, and fished by torchlight for flounder. During fall and spring, creeks at Port Orchard Bay provided local salmon runs.

July—Drying clams, catching early salmon, and picking blackberries, blackcaps, red huckleberries, and red elderberries.

August—Drying clams, picking salalberries and storing them in deer intestines, eating fresh summer (dog and humpy) salmon because it was not good for drying, and hunting for fattened deer and ducks.

September—Before the fall salmon runs (of silvers and kings), dams were built at streams so that people could more easily spear the fish, which were split and held open with cedar sticks to be smoke dried. While women were busy drying salmon and collecting and drying clams, men were hunting ducks, which were eaten fresh and not preserved.

October—Huckleberries and dog salmon dried; men fished for smelt until early December.

November—Work was winding down except for duck hunting; spirits began arriving.

December—Sacred season, seasonal games and ceremonies; some clams dug, bottom fish caught from canoes heated by fires.

January–February—Ceremonies and visiting; herring, which started to run in late January and continued into early March, were caught and dried, together with spring salmon.

March—Salmon returned; people started making canoes to be finished by summer.

May—Departure from winter villages to camp near ripe salmonberry sprouts, which were eaten with dried salmon eggs; bottom fish (flounder, sole, and skate) available year around; hunting only bucks since does were pregnant; some camas dug on Smith Island, to be steamed or kept dry in a basket.

June–July—Steelhead (salmon trout) cooked and dried by women, along with drying blackberries, cockles, horse clams, and butter clams; men hunting.

HOUSING EVENTS

Today, families and reservations still gather in gyms, community centers, halls, and smokehouses to host parties, feasts, "work," and "doings" in time-honored fashion. That invitations come by phone, people drive in vans, and the meals are cooked in kitchens merely indicates the versatility and flexibility of living native traditions.

Among Lushootseeds, solidarity of household and family was and is best expressed during public events interweaving economic, social, political, and religious concerns. Such ceremonies included the rituals to welcome the arrival of and thank first (or return) foods; the various economic exchanges epitomized by the potlatch; the growling cult (secret society); the recovery odyssey; and the winter dances when spirits return to their human partners and are welcomed back by singing the song conferred during the initial vision.

Return Foods

The yearly harvest of every new food was consecrated by a ritual of welcome and thanksgiving. In many features, these rituals duplicated the manner in which a leader from another town was welcomed when he or she came to visit.

Of all these food rites, the most famous was that held for the arrival of salmon (Amoss 1987; Gunther 1928), which varied by river. Puyallup and Nisqually held a feast after the first catch was made from the new tripod fish trap (Smith 1940, 101). The salmon was handled carefully, only cut lengthwise, and cooked whole. Every scrap of it was consumed.

Along the Skagit, after the prophet was in command, the first fish caught in the river was taken to him to celebrate their return.

Because the Suquamish had no major rivers in their territory, their salmon ceremony was distinctive. Instead of celebrating the annual returns, they gathered whenever a dog salmon with a deformed jaw, indicating its status as leader, was caught each year.[23] According to Ellen George, little sticks were given to all the children to use as skewers, each roasting a piece cut from that fish while it rested on a special mat. Ordinarily, food was served in large wooden bowls. During the cooking, each child wrapped a mat around his or her waist and went into the water to swim, presumably to represent a bounty of young salmon. Next, all skewers were divided among the children, who feasted. All bones were carefully saved and given to an older boy, who took them into the water where the children had been swimming and left them together at one spot. Holding their sticks, the other children went back into the water and tossed these skewers away. Then they joyfully began to dive, swim, and play. While only children ate this first fish, everyone else was then allowed to catch all the fish they needed.

Exchanges

In our best statement, Smith (1940, 146–47) devoted considerable attention to the varieties of economic exchanges that characterized the southern sound, noting a complex vocabulary that included words meaning to swap, to trade, to hire someone, to pay a shaman, to give a gift, to buy goodwill, to give to affines, and to potlatch (including related terms that meant to scatter, to assist, to invest, and to bet).

Among Nooksaks and other tribes, the sporadic and unpredictable famines that were the result of natural fluctuations in resources were mitigated by three types of feasts, variously involving one tribe hosting another tribe; a family treating a neighborhood; and an invitational potlatch, years in the planning by siblings to "pay off" debts incurred by a father's funeral. In addition, a wealthy man might hold a potlatch every decade to maintain his fame (Amoss 1978, 11–12).

The Upper Skagit held distributions for three purposes: to cement relations among in-laws, to show generosity at the end of a winter spirit dance, and to thank people at a funeral or a memorial for the dead (Collins 1974, 77). In-laws expressed cordial relations by exchanging gifts on a regular basis. In general, people from upriver gave prepared skins, dried venison, mountain goat wool blankets, and coiled baskets in return for smoked clams, oysters, fish, and cattail matting received from downriver. For a winter dance, every dancer brought food and gifts to pile in the center of house (Collins 1974, 184).[24] These gifts, handed out at the end of the night, were mats, baskets, strips of blanket, bundles of wool, and raw material for basketry (Collins 1974, 187). Providing such raw materials encouraged further industry among the guests. A funeral or a memorial was hosted to compensate for services performed for the deceased, to pass on names, and to elevate the status of the family (Collins 1974, 77).

Potlatching

The Upper Skagit held potlatches during September, after people had returned to their winter homes with stores of food and before the spirits returned to their human partners in November (Collins 1974, 131). Traditional gifts were baskets, canoes, prepared cedarbark, unworked cedar and spruce roots (Collins 1974, 139), and mountain goat and dog wool blankets—most prestigious because they enhanced personal warmth. Sometimes, for the fun of it, a joking potlatch was held, the men against the women, each gender trying to embarrass and amuse the other (Collins 1974, 141).

When marine tribes were invited to a potlatch, guests would arrive with their canoes abreast singing a power song to feign an impending attack. These overt displays of aggression were expected and encouraged by the host, who made sure they did not escalate or get out of hand. Such expressive outlets took the edge off any tensions or hostilities deriving from previous breaches, slights, or conflicts (Smith 1940, 108, 114).

For a Suquamish potlatch, Wilson George said that the plank house was divided into sections according to the number of groups coming from different areas. The host sent word to these headmen of different areas, inviting each to come with his people. At the give-away, gifts went to the leaders of these different bands, who then (or later) passed them out among their own people.

When a leader came, he brought his own family to be seated together in a section of the house. The announcer for the host called out the names of people as they came in and ushers showed each group where to sit and with whom to stay overnight. Guests brought food to give to the household who put them up.

Inside a traditional smokehouse, today as well as in the past, members of a tribe or drainage are seated on risers between side posts, ideally occupying the same position in the house as their tribal territory has in the world. Thus, a tribe from the southeast was seated in the southeast of the house. With their physical bodies, these worshipers thereby made one of the house and the world.

When everyone had arrived, the host began to sing his song. Next he spoke to the people, thanking them for coming, and began another song. At the end, he gave gifts in the same order as that in which the tribes had been invited. Anyone else who had joined him in hosting this potlatch then sang his song, finished it, and gave his gifts in the order of his own invitations. Again, only leaders received these goods.

When all the gifts had been given out to the chiefs, there was a feast and a scramble. Proud people did not participate in this grabbing free-for-all because they thought it was crass and undignified, but the young and the poor found it fun and profitable.

For a scramble or "throw," men climbed onto the shed roof, stood on its slope, and threw blankets and other gifts to the crowd below. Everyone tried to grab something without pulling or tearing it. The holder with the firmest grip would claim it, and pay off all others holding on so that they forfeited their share of it. If an old man or woman got hold of a blanket, a strong young man would pull it away from the others until he could give it to the elder, showing respect for age. Poles were also thrown down and each represented a canoe. One person would pay the others for their share if they held the same stick.

A potlatch was held to mark the giving of names, the removal of a stigma (such as when a daughter was sent home by her divorcing husband or a captive was ransomed), or the death of one chief and the elevation of his heir.

According to John Adams of Suquamish, before Chief Seattle held a potlatch at Oleman House in the 1850s, he went to Canada for blankets. Before leaving, he said, "As I come back from Victoria, you will hear Thunder and you will know I am on my way." Indeed, Thunder (his power) announced his return.

Sometimes a chief would deliberately stigmatize himself to have an excuse for a potlatch. Many years ago at Suquamish, the second chief in rank, after old Kitsap and ahead of a young Seattle, deliberately came too close to his hearth so that his blanket would catch fire. When it did, he gave a potlatch to cover the embarrassment and show people he was generous.

Growling Cult

Smith (1940, 92–99) remarked that the Puyallup and Nisqually of her time often confused the growlers with the odyssey because both involved organized bodies of special members performing public cures. Both had lapsed by the time of her research, but details of these ceremonials confirm that they were indeed distinct and separate events.

This "growling cult," a better term than secret society, was an intertribal organization that existed solely to initiate new members from wealthy families, usually during the first days of a large potlatch; as noted elsewhere, the shamanic odyssey served to retrieve a mind, soul, or spirit snatched away by ghosts and taken to the land of the dead.[25] These memberships were mutually exclusive because anyone except shamans could join the growling cult, but only shamans took part in the odyssey enactment. A major point of overlap between these two rituals, however, was that cult members sometimes displayed their power by bringing a baby soul from the land of the dead and placing it in a woman—well past the age of bearing children—who then gave birth to a normal child (Smith 1940, 94).

The cult's patron spirit was available only by initiation into membership and was variously described as a huge black man or a baby covered with blood, who lived in the air and traveled north with ducks. For some groups, it also had aspects of the wolf.[26] Indeed, the name of the spirit, identical with the name of the cult, made reference to "growling."

Tribes who participated in this cult were the Songhees, Lummi, Klallam, Swinomish, Twana, Puyallup, Nisqually, and Suquamish. The remote inspiration for this cult was the dancing societies of the Kwakiutlans, most specifically the Wolf Dances of the Nootkans, who passed them on to speakers of Straits languages, who then initiated Twana and Lushootseed members (Amoss 1978, 72).

For details of this initiation, the best general account referred to the Twana (Elmendorf 1948), and the most detailed to the Klallam (Gunther 1927, 281–88).[27] Lasting from three to eight days, each began with a dance by all the members in a specially prepared house, but the hosting community did not provide other initiators. Rather, each locale brought its own master to oversee the direct transfer of the patron spirit into the bodies of its own new initiates. Again, as always, power depended on place.

During the first night, ducklike wooden rattles were sent flying around the house from one group to another as proof of the cult's powers, and masters indicated their superior possession by vomiting up blood. Klallam members wore carved masks to represent their powers. Some members were so frenzied that they had to be restrained by ropes tied around the waist. Others acted fierce and brandished knives, spears, axes, and clubs.

At Suquamish, according to Wilson George, the cult was known as the Dog Eaters. Meetings were held in the dead of winter solely to initiate new members, who acted "crazy" or "frenzied" when they came under the influence of its patron. If they encountered a dog, they seized it and tore it to pieces like a pack of carnivores. Then they ate it (or gave the impression that they did).

Elite youngsters were initiated when they were about fourteen and acting like "know-it-alls." This kept them humble because they had to listen and learn from older people, but it also gave them access to spirit powers at a young age.

Winter Dances

At Suquamish, according to Wilson George, about November, when all of the dog salmon were gone and what had been caught was dried, the spirits acquired by young men would return for the first time since they met. For this debut, people were invited by the boy's father to help to sing.

The father did the inviting because the son was so overcome by the power ("sick to sing") that he could do nothing except deal with his own spirit. He was unable to talk or engage in regular activities. When guests came, the father seated them according to their locales and statuses.

When the spirit power came, the man had to sing his song to remain healthy. The first time the boy sang, certain people who knew about powers came to help out. The young man could not start to sing until someone else sang his song to loosen his mouth. Hearing the song, the spirit forced its way out of the man's chest and emerged as song.

Long ago, a boy was going from house to house in a Suquamish village, pretending to sing just for fun. All of a sudden, of course, his power actually struck him, rendering him helpless. People went to the boy's father and told him to clean up his house. He needed to empty it to make room for a crowd to come and help his son to sing and dance.

The father did not want to do this because his son was joking with power. Since it came when his son was showing disrespect, the father told the people to find another house to use, but they insisted that it was a father's duty to help his son in the winter. Finally, the father agreed and had his house cleaned out for many people to sit on the sleeping benches.

His ill son was brought inside as the father took charge. He had people who knew about power there to help his son. Ushers took care of the guests, showing them where to sit in the house. For four nights, everyone helped this boy, who stayed awake the whole time because his power kept him energized. All night he sang and danced, except for rests in a corner.

First, a man chosen by his father repeated the song that the boy was to sing. Then the song came out of the boy and he sang it. Next, the repeater started it again and everyone joined in so that the boy could dance, until he made a sign for everyone to quit so that he could sing another tune and lyrics. The repeater listened and said these words for all to sing so that the boy could dance the second song. Since only important people had several spirits and songs, the boy was acting dangerously boastful. The same spirit might give several songs, or other spirits might give songs if they liked the child.

Bringing out these songs had to be carefully done, because if they came out in the wrong order or got "twisted up," the boy would become very ill and might die. To prevent a fatality, a shaman was called in to straighten out the songs, placing each in the correct order inside the boy. Then he would be cured to sing an impressive display of power under the protection of his doctors.

On the fourth day, everyone received gifts and departed. The boy ate and slept for a day or so before he went back to work at whatever he had power to do, such as fishing, hunting, or making canoes.

The next year at the same time, the same spirit came back to the son and the father was ready. Later, when the father himself got a spirit, it was up to the son to take charge and choose a song repeater. Every year any human partner understood his or her power better. The repeater only helped for the first year or two, then people could begin singing on their own.

Today, most spirit powers are inherited in families and similarly fixed in a person by a winter-long initiation in one of the smokehouses on a reservation in the northern sound.[28] Every smokehouse includes an experienced shaman or dancer who, helped by his family, "brings out" an initiate's song so that he or she can learn from the power while welcoming it back every year. While black paint powers still spiral the earth during the year, red paint ones seem to remain closer to their human partners, who can and do sing all year long in the quiet of their own homes, until ready for full public expression every winter season.

5 CANOES

Like the famous Viking ships of their European homelands, rowed boats with lapboard sides—preferred by settlers because they rely more on brute strength than on detailed knowledge of a waterway—eventually replaced native canoes throughout the Northwest. After 1821, wherever local conditions made it possible, George Simpson, inland governor of the Hudson's Bay Company, replaced cargo canoes with York boats from the Great Lakes to the Pacific. Designed after Orkney craft, York boats were propelled by oars and constructed of overlapped, nailed, and pitched spruce planks.

Such boat building was a skill among the earliest Oregon and Washington settlers. About 1854, when Robert Espy at Shoalwater Bay needed a lap-struck or clinker-built boat for his oystering, he had one built at a Montesano sawmill (Espey 1977, 60). Enhanced sails and rigging benefited such vessels, although natives probably always had an appreciation for sails of cattail mats. Inboard motors were available by 1900, but reliable outboard motors were not in use until after World War I.[1] By the 1930s at Taholah, Vi Hilbert recalls canoes with the stern cut off and replaced with a flat board to brace such a motor. Similar craft are still in use during annual canoe races along the Quinault River.

Indeed, knowledge of carpentry, engines, and netting became vital to successful commercial fishing. Carpenters were included among employees promised in treaty provisions, while reservation schools often included training classes aimed toward such future employment. In the Treaty of Medicine Creek (Kappler 1904, 663), the first signed and ratified in Puget Sound, article 10 specified twenty years of financial support for "an agricultural and industrial school . . . with a suitable instructor or instructors, and to provide a smithy and carpenter's shop, and furnish them with necessary tools, and employ a blacksmith, carpenter, and farmer . . . to instruct the Indians in their respective occupations."

Famous racing canoe named Question Mark (?), carved by
Charley Anderson and others. (Courtesy of Lushootseed Research)

While providing entrance into settler society, carpentry also augmented
native traditions, which had long included woodworking power, so that a
carpenter could and did as easily make a stairway or closet as provide a coffin
box, shamanic effigy, a rattle, or power boards. Similarly, factory-made
paints and laundry bluing were given a distinctively native purpose by using
them to decorate such objects.

Then as now, such subversive crossing over enabled natives to construct
their end of the bridgework allowing intercultural negotiation with settlers,
officials, and "others."

TRANSPORT

Waterways defined larger identities throughout the Americas, and Lu-
shootseeds relied on canoes for all manner of activities (Waterman and
Coffin 1920, Carlson and Hess 1971, Lincoln 1991, Roberts 1975, 30). Today,
the continuing importance of canoes and canoe lore among natives of the
Northwest has been underscored by the "Paddle to Seattle" for the 1989
Washington State Centennial, the 1993 Qatuwas Festival drawing canoes to
Bella Bella (with the motto "a stroke towards indigenous unity"), and the
1997 paddle to La Push hosted by Quileute.

Among northern nations like Tsimshians, hereditary houses include a stock of canoe names, still given to power boats, and they assign seats in a canoe on the basis of the same status as the all-important "seats" in a house. Rituals to launch, christen, or empower a new canoe are also performed, indicating that a canoe is a living, named being.

Lushootseed specialist beliefs are less detailed, and, before being "brought out" (returned to public knowledge) by recent flotilla festivals, were regarded as lost. Since any new canoe is called a "baby," it presumably had a "sense of being" derived from its parents, the canoe maker and his wife. During manufacture, the carver did not comb his hair so that the wood would not split apart, avoided his wife, and used enchantments that were gender specific to the wood, manly for course grained and womanly for fine grained.

A canoe had both a heart and a hearth. "The heart of the tree ran only slightly lower than the center of the finished canoe" (Smith 1940, 289). Moreover, while we lack a specific Lushootseed reference, one from a Yurok of northern California can probably be extended north (cf. Elmendorf 1960). "In making a canoe, the Indians always leave in the bottom and some two feet back from the front or bow a knob some three inches across and about two inches high, with a hole about one-inch deep dug into it; and this they call the heart of the canoe, and without this the canoe would be dead and unsafe" (Thompson 1991, 34).

For the hearth, during dark or cold, "fishing canoes were fitted with a plank, laid across the canoe about midships and covered with a thick coating of dirt, on which was made a fire of pitchwood" (Smith 1940, 253). Moving along the shore, such lighted canoes were also used for night hunting. At other times, people traveled with a punk or smoldering slow match made of dried, shredded, inner cedarbark rolled like a cigar (Elmendorf 1960, 220).

The significance of canoes is indicated by the number of Lushootseed types and terms. In addition to two generic words and a common morpheme, six canoe forms were in use. The generics include *sax^w'ulu+*, meaning "for water travel," and *q'il'bid*, meaning any vehicle of any type, once a canoe most often but now any car, wagon, or craft (Bates, Hess, and Hilbert 1994, 184–86, 203). The morpheme {-*g^wi+*} has an interesting range of meanings including 'vehicle, waterway, narrow passage, throat, body trunk, curved side' further confirming that a canoe was a living body (Bates, Hess, and Hilbert 1994, 103).

The six types of canoe were called river shovelnose, hunting, freight, racing, northern, and Nootkan. Each type could vary greatly in size, though still recognizable by its prow line, although Puyallups, in contrast, emphasized the shapes of the stern (Smith 1940, 288). For each canoe, after a log was thinned and hollowed out, water poured inside was stone boiled to allow the shell to be stretched and shaped before permanent thwarts were fixed inside. Bow and stern pieces were added to the larger vessels.

As an example of the greater diversity among downriver peoples, those upriver had only the shovelnose canoe, ideal for sheltered freshwater, while the downriver and saltwater communities had the full variety of crafts, separate paddle styles for men or women, and a thorough knowledge of the winds and tides to allow them to travel under sail or tidal pull with less effort.

The first four types were indigenous with Lushootseeds, while the last two are derived from styles to the north and were sometimes actually traded from there. The river canoe was the most widespread. More often poled than paddled, it had double flat ends shaped like a square shovel (Bates, Hess, and Hilbert 1994, 153), allowing a man to stand over a fish he was spearing (Waterman and Coffin 1920, 19). The hunting-trolling type, used only by men and especially for ducks, had double pointed and raised ends (Bates, Hess, and Hilbert 1994, 81). The freight canoe, with a even lift at both ends (Bates, Hess, and Hilbert 1994, 226), was often called a women's canoe because it carried families, children, household goods, or if necessary a corpse or grave box. On both the hunting and freight types, "the tip of the prow is shaped into a 'notch' resembling an open mouth" (Waterman and Coffin 1920, 17).

The racing canoe is thin and sleek, holding a crew of eleven, and seems derived from the ancient war canoe (Bates, Hess, and Hilbert 1994, 267). During the summer, intertribal races are held at Suquamish, Lummi, and off other beaches throughout Washington and British Columbia, making this elongated style widely familiar (Roberts 1975, 259), both atop vans and in the water.

Two types have been introduced. The northern, sometimes called the Alaskan, canoe, the name of which seems to be derived from the Stikine River, was large and double ended (Bates, Hess, and Hilbert 1994, 239). The Nootkan, also called the Chinook, had an animal head on the prow (Bates, Hess, and Hilbert 1994, 9). Since Nootkan words form a large part of Chinook jargon, the Northwest trade language, the two names for this same canoe are the result of extensive trade contacts and its own seaworthiness between the west coast of Vancouver Island and the lower Columbia River.

Lushootseed has borrowed the Nootkan word for this craft, which means "holder for pursuit," specifically of California gray whales, because hunting them was a privilege of Nuuchahnulth chiefs along the "outside" of Vancouver Island. Across the Strait of Juan de Fuca, on the coast of Washington, whaling was also done by leaders of the Nootkan Makah and their nearest neighbors, such as the Chemakuan Quileute and the Salishan Quinault.

Wilson Duff (1981, 206) traced some uncanny resemblances between this whaling canoe and the umiak used by Alaskan Eskimos (Inuit) to hunt the same whales, including ritual acts concentrating on etched lines inside the wooden canoe in the exact location of the lashings of the skin boat. Moreover, Ahousat canoe makers assured him that the animal-head-like bow was indeed a Wolf, although this was a "secret" known only among certain families. Throughout the Northwest, both wolves and orca killer whales were regarded as the same being, taking the shapes of a pack on land or a pod in the sea. Since both species are social carnivores, this astute equation enabled such a canoe to partake of the power of wolf + orca when in pursuit of whales. Interestingly, since Nuuchahnulth believe that whales have keen eyesight, designs to give added power to a vessel were hidden under a black overpainting.

In the same way, the specialized carpentry power given by a being like Woodpecker or Cedar to a canoe maker was also conveyed, to some extent, to the finished craft during rituals to enliven it, if not also name it.

Made of local timber by a resident specialist, all canoes were the means of transport to other regions, where local abilities were stretched and enhanced in intertribal contexts. Finally, after death, members of the elite were placed in a single canoe, sometimes with a second one overturned on top, lodged in a tree. Holes were bored into the bottom to allow rain to run out until the body and canoe decomposed together. During his quest, Jacob Wahalchu tried to float a crumbling grave canoe, but it was much too old. Today near his grave is that of Chief Seattle, marked by a sculpture of canoes set high on posts.

ACROSS SPACE AND TIME

For all these reasons, the vehicle used to transport shamans to the land of the dead to recover lost vitalities was called a *q'il'bid*, the most generic and useful form of any transport.

6 BODY

Although birthdays, weddings, anniversaries, and funerals are now celebrated by Lushootseeds in recognizably American fashion with cake and flowers, members of the winter smokehouse religion (*siyowin*) continue to observe traditional rituals enhancing spiritual aspects of a person. Each dancer regards his or her day of initiation as another (sometime more significant) birthday to be observed with traditional foods and festivities. The virtues of age and family have kept their ancient emphasis, as has the transmission of inherited wisdom. While tape recorders, cameras, and videos have helped to promote these values, the most important information remains the most private and hard earned.

Personhood

While any flesh and blood body served as a vessel for a "being," its actions could have far-reaching consequences, as when a shaman closed his or her eyes in the crook of the right arm to "see" into a disorder. Similarly, the thoughts or gestures of a high god or creator or changer served to change the world forever. Among the Katzie, as noted, the sloughs along Pitt Meadow were first drawn by Khaals on his own face.

The various parts of a Lushootseed person were a body, soul, mind, and spirit ally. The source for the body was not reported, although the Tillamook, the southernmost Coast Salishans living south of the Columbia River in Oregon, believed in a special land of babies who provided the template for a fetus (Miller 1988, 108). To this body were added a soul, closely associated with breath, and a mind, located at the heart, and, according to Katzie belief, instilled by the high god when the infant uttered its first cry.

The spirit was an immortal who attached itself to the infant, after it came unsought during childhood, was actively acquired by questing, or, in the best cases, was attracted by prior ties with the family. A spirit partner or partners stayed near a person during life, guaranteeing success and a healthy family. Though the spirits were private knowledge during young adulthood, at maturity, a person participated in the winter dances that publicly displayed such links with immortals. Just before death, these spirits left the person and sought another, younger human ally, often in the same family. As a prelude to death, the soul wandered the path to the land of the dead, where it became a ghost. At death, the mind faded away, perhaps returning to the creator or high god, although this was not stated. In the Robe Boy instance, in which brains were created from Skagit soil, memories obviously returned into the ground.

Since the soul is described as light and insubstantial, like a feather, in the image of the person, it was gender specific, while the mind seems to have been largely the same for men and women (Amoss 1978, 44) and was therefore a common link across life forms, susceptible to the use of enchantments, which themselves had gender-specific expressions.[1]

Puberty

While a boy's coming of age was marked by changes in his voice and body, the onset of puberty mostly provided the occasion for the climax of his training to acquire guardian spirits. For girls, however, more specialized restrictions were observed.

As described at Suquamish by Ellen George, a girl who began to menstruate was placed in seclusion. Most girls had a hut built for them in the woods, but sometimes a noble girl stayed in a curtained off corner of her house. Her bed was made of fir boughs because they smelled so fresh. Every night, she left her hut to go to a creek to bathe and scrub with a sponge made of rotten cedar to make herself clean. During the day, she kept very busy, weaving mats or blankets, making yarn, or coiling baskets. This effort made her industrious her entire life, indicating that she would be a good wife.

If it was ripe berry season, a Nisqually or Chehalis first menstruant picked berries with a stick between her teeth (called a "bridle"), which was inspected by older women at the end of each day to see if she had stained it by eating any forbidden berries (Smith 1940, 196).

The second night she also bathed. Throughout, she kept to a strict diet that included food allowed to cool after it was cooked. She ate little, mostly roots, but nothing fresh or warm, and she used special dishes that were destroyed afterward. Fresh and bloody foods were particularly avoided because of her own condition. Toward the end of the month of seclusion, her grandmother invited other old women to sing, dance, and feast to entertain the girl, who could not join in herself because of restrictions designed to prevent her supercharged actions from affecting the world, or aspects of it, fatally. Therefore, she was under strong taboos. She could not look at anyone or they would become sick. She never touched her own hair. Instead, another woman put it up for her by making two tight braids and wrapping a cloth over her head so that none of her hair showed. She used a stick of ironwood to scratch herself if she had an itch.[2]

Every day, the girl was instructed by older women about how to conduct herself when she was married as well as in techniques for drying fish, picking berries, digging clams, and keeping a household. She was told to be good to her mother-in-law, other affines, and all elders while showing kindness and compassion to everyone.

At the end of her first menstruation, her grandmother gave to the other women who had helped a piece of the drape that had hidden the girl if she was secluded in a plank house, or part of the matting that had covered her hut. She was now eligible for marriage, but she had to be most circumspect around males, even her own brothers.

Among the Upper Skagit, during a girl's puberty seclusion, she was regarded as dark or light according to the phases of the moon for six weeks. On dark days, when the moon waned, her face was painted red, and on light days, when the moon waxed, she was visited by other women (Collins 1974, 226).

Marriage

Marriages were arranged between families and celebrated with an exchange of gifts that continued for the duration of the union.[3] Salish kinship was quite explicit about the obligation of a sibling to marry the surviving spouse. Thus, a sister-in-law was expected to marry the widower (sororate of sisters), and a brother-in-law to marry the widow (levirate of brothers). At the death of a spouse, the in-law terms changed automatically to allow for these marriages, as discussed later under decedence.

An Upper Skagit boy might offer his own marriage proposal by bringing firewood to the girl's house four times. During the first three prior visits, he was ignored, but if he were acknowledged on the fourth trip, he was accepted as a son-in-law. He returned home with the news and a date was set for the wedding. When the groom and his relatives arrived, they danced into the house in single file singing a song composed for the occasion (Collins 1974, 230).[4] They presented gifts to the family of the bride, their quantity proportional to their rank or social class. Later, the bride's family gave gifts to that of the groom, but only about two-thirds as much because they were providing the girl who would be the mother of any children (Smith 1940, 166).

Married women, as a mark of their status, were careful to keep their eyebrows plucked and thin, according to Snoqualmie Jim (Haeberlin 1917, notebook 21, 21).

After marriage, residence was at the choice of the husband, and he usually wanted to live with his family. The couple could choose, however, to affiliate with either of the families traced from any of their great grandparents, which gave them eight options, four sides for each of them. The couple was under the authority of their parents, particularly those of the husband, until the birth of their first child. Regardless of where they lived, if upper class, the alien spouse took his or her children home often so that they could know their relatives and learn the teachings of that family.

Since noble marriages were an alliance between families, divorce was virtually impossible. Enemy tribes could end their hostilities by marrying a son from one to a daughter from the other, just as European noble houses allied. Other people might divorce, however, for barrenness or if the wife was rude or lazy. Sending the wife home was an insult that might lead to fighting unless it was handled very diplomatically.[5] In wealthy families, a potlatch was held to remove any shame for a returned wife, but, even so, it could blemish family honor.

Boys did not marry until they had spirit powers since marital relations (reeking of mortality) repelled the spirits. After marriage, a man could only inherit weak powers; he would never again be able to quest for the strongest ones. At marriage, a boy was usually in his late teens, and a girl slightly younger. Sometimes, a boy was first married to an old woman, and a girl to an old man to gain experience in domestic relations (Jacobs 1958). Later marriages were with age-mate peers.

Child Care

Among the Upper Skagit, a woman delivered her baby squatting over fresh mats and holding on to a housepost (Collins 1974, 217). In this manner, the new life was directly linked with the spirit power of the house owner whose design decorated the post. A woven cedarbark pillow with a protruding knob was sometimes used for a woman to sit upon so that the baby could only use the vaginal opening for birth, with the implication that some infants were so willful that they might find another birth canal.[6]

Once a baby was born, the cord was cut and the afterbirth wrapped up and taken into the woods, where it was either placed in a tree or buried. Along the coast, a newborn was washed in the sound, placed on a cradleboard, and wrapped up. Noble children had a small board bound to their padded heads so they would develop the wide sloping forehead that was a mark of their freeborn status. Only slaves captured from other areas had naturally rounded heads, which were considered ugly along the central coast. Closer to Alaska, however, captured freeborn Salish stood out as slaves because of their shaped heads.

A new mother warmed her breasts for several days, by pressing heated white shells, the color of milk, against them or spending an hour over a steaming basket to increase the flow of milk. The inner bark (called a "skin") of cedar was used for diapers. The father gathered this layer to bring home, where the couple rubbed it between their hands to make it soft, and cut it into blocks large enough for diapers.[7] Larger sheets were used to make a hammock to rock the baby while the mother was busy. Parents also rendered oil from dogfish livers, cooked it, and strained it to use as a baby ointment.

When a woman went into labor, she went off by herself, if possible. She was not supposed to make a fuss, especially not groan, cry, or gasp "to disgrace the family." After hearing the first whimpering of a newborn, her mother, grandmother, mother-in-law, or other older woman went to help her.

Although as noted the afterbirth was usually wrapped up, taken to the woods, and placed high in a tree, some families buried it.[8] The placenta was so closely identified with the infant that it had to be hidden away to prevent its use for sorcery. Tree deposition was safest because the afterbirth decomposed high in the air, while burial, if the spot were not disguised, was more risky for the defenseless infant. Similarly, an infant's waste was saved to prevent its use in sorcery.

The father made a series of graduated cradleboards, boring holes in the sides to hold leather strings to lace in the baby after he or she was wrapped in cedarskin and a blanket. These baby blankets were made of dog and goat wool mixed with fern fluff or cotton. Like the adult blankets, they were a mark of prestige. The infant was kept in a cradleboard for a year, until learning to walk.

When first born, the baby was rubbed all over with dogfish oil, and some was placed in a clam shell to warm by the fire. A feather was dipped in the warmed oil and used to drop some into the baby's mouth. For several days, this was the baby's food before the mother started to nurse. During infancy, this oil served as a medicine for fevers, colds, burns, and purging.

Once the baby began to nurse, he or she was bathed every day resting on the mother's thighs, being lightly scrubbed with a piece of softened cedar-bark. In the summer, the bath water was warmed in the sunshine, while hot rocks were added in the winter.

Babies were always kept apart because they came into this world speaking a language of their own. Placing babies on the same bed or in the same space gave them a chance to compare how their relatives treated them, causing the baby who felt slighted to choose to die (Amoss 1978, 59).

Babies nursed until they were three or four years old. Sometimes, when there was another baby, older children were allowed to nurse on demand. To encourage weaning, a mother put flounder gall on her nipple to make it taste bad. Solid food was given to infants when they had teeth, beginning with the fat of bear or seal and dried clams soaked in water.

Once the child ate solid food, all the refuse from the diapers, which had been saved to protect it from sorcery, was hidden in some out-of-the-way location. The urine was saved to be used as shampoo by adults.

Children were punished by tapping them with a little stick or denying them food. As toddlers got older, they were given small tasks to do so that they would help out around the house. They were scolded or shamed if they were slow to action. Since the best parts of various foods were reserved for the elderly, children learned reserve and respect at an early age. In addition to physical punishment, children were frightened by tales of wildmen and the basket ogress, which served to keep them at home after dark.

Among Nisqually, if children were not quiet in the house after repeated warnings, someone dressed as the basket ogress terrorized them, wearing a mask made of a whole dog salmon skin painted black and perforated with huge cut-out eyes and a mouth (Smith 1940, 187). This disguised person was draped in a large blanket, carried a clam basket on the back, and hobbled with a cane. Parents and elders made a great pretense of saving their children from this cannibal, but small children were so traumatized by such a visit that they wept until dawn. Generally, one such warning was sufficient to maintain the necessary quiet of a household for months.[9]

From the time they were toddlers, boys were given toy tools such as bows, arrows, slings, and carving knives to undertake the practice of adult careers. As they got older, the toys got larger. Girls were given toy needles, awls, and cooking utensils to play at weaving and keeping house. In theory, a girl's first complete basket was made during her puberty seclusion.

Children were known by kin terms and nicknames until they were about twelve and received an ancestral family name. Of course, in elite families, children were named at an earlier age, and each acquired a series of names over his or her life. Names could come through the father or the mother, but the father usually suggested the first one.

After someone died, that name was not used for a year or so as a sign of respect. Mentioning it might also call someone back from the land of the dead and cause harm to the living. At the gathering when the name was next bestowed, a cherished possession of the previous holder was displayed and then burned in the fire. This special offering pleased the deceased person and protected the newly named child.

Important families celebrated the name bestowal with a potlatch, with the quantity of distributed gifts equal to the prestige of the name and the families involved. Today, names are often shared across generations so that a grandfather and grandson might have the same name for a while until the elder died.

When his or her baby teeth fell out, a child was told to discard them carefully with a prayer to a particular animal known for its strong teeth. According to Frank Le Clair and William Shelton (Haeberlin 1917, notebook 4, 5), the first one to come out was thrown into the river with a prayer to dog salmon, the second into the water for beaver, and the third into the woods for deer. Le Clair specified that his own adult canines were a gift from dog salmon, his lower incisors from beaver, and his upper incisors from deer.

Education

As children approached their teenage years, they were entrusted to trainers who prepared them for undertaking quests. Parents never interfered with the trainer because he or she became the focus for any resentment by their child, thus sparing parents from resentment or estrangement. Boys were subjected to rigorous discipline, sometimes beginning as early as six years of age. Parents would leave small children on the edge of berry patches or activity areas, out of sight but not hearing so that they could learn to be solitary.[10] Later, boys were encouraged to go out alone or in pairs to hunt and fish away from settlements.

Children from elite families were singled out for extra attention in terms of harsher and stricter discipline and more arduous exposure. They were sent longer distances to more remote areas. After every bath, the trainer would rub them over with a stick or stone to "toughen them up."[11]

About 1872, the Nisqually village at Muck Creek had about thirty-five children under the supervision of two trainers (Smith 1940, 189), senior men with proven powers. They awakened the trainees before dawn each day, and any slugabeds were struck with a switch made from a bundle of eight vine maple branches. The children were taken to the creek and, in turn, told to walk in and squat down so that the water was up to their necks. Discipline was most severe during the winter, when a trainer had to break the ice covering the stream. Children stayed in the water until they were numb, about ten minutes. When they came out, they rubbed their bodies briskly with a smooth stick, stone, or bundle of yew twigs until the skin was "red and prickly." Then they submerged again and ran home to the waiting fire.

This bathing was intended to remove human and mortal odors, such as sweat and house smoke (Amoss 1978, 13). Fasting and emetics cleansed the inside of the body.

While all boys were actively sent on quests, girls undertook them on personal or family initiative because females had the advantage of being susceptible to spirit encounters just after menarche and during pregnancy. Because males were courageous enough to travel to the remote places inhabited by the most powerful spirits, men usually had stronger spirits than women. Exceptions were those few girls who went to these places and acquired curing powers. Elite families encouraged this female initiative, using their resources to provide hidden protectors to watch secretly and safeguard the girl in such remote terrain.

Either men or women could receive spirits later in life if they suffered from a near-fatal fright or traumatic event that caused the powers to pity them. Such near-death experiences often gave survivors new or renewed powers.

After training for a year or two, a child was given a stick and told to leave it at some named location, often one famous in legend, during the dark of the night. Later, a trainer would visit that place to make sure the stick was there.

During severe storms, older children were told to run naked into the bitter wind because this would enable them to face anything when they grew up. By showing bravery, they would never be afraid, nervous, anxious, or excited. If someone spoke harshly to them or acted "mean," they would not be upset.

Just before puberty, this supervised training climaxed with a quest over a five- to ten-day period. Though children had long been preparing for it, the risks were very real. Stories were passed down about a few boys who had frozen to death while out on quests. Lack of food, sleep, and comfort encouraged a vision. A successful child, as were most, returned exhausted and slept for a day or so and then was fed clear broth to build up strength before beginning to eat regularly again. Nothing was said about the spirit ally for years, although the child was said to have "graduated." Its existence remained the private knowledge of the child until he or she became a responsible and prosperous adult. Then, in maturity, as indicated by the birth of grandchildren, he or she took part in the winter dances.

Spirits were strictly localized. For example, though he was born a Duwamish, John Curly acquired Rattlesnake power in the Okanogan region of eastern Washington. While visiting there, he misbehaved and was spanked by his mother. Upset, he went crying into the mountains. There, Rattler appeared to make him feel better. When he danced, the spirit came from eastern Washington to be with him. Such highly specific anchoring provided each immortal with a home and terrain from which to radiate by making contact with other beings, including mortals, both close and distant. What the Curly experience illustrates so well, moreover, is that all such contacts begin close and intimate, and then, only afterward, can they be "taken away" or extended to more remote locations. Once forged and effectively maintained, therefore, a bond exists regardless of distances until the mortal dies.

Maturity

Throughout Puget Sound, men and women dressed differently. Women wore two braids, with the hair evenly parted in the middle. Men wore their hair long, loose to the shoulders.

As noted, women had responsibility for drying berries, shellfish, meat, and fish; all the cooking; and weaving dog wool blankets, cattail mats, and baskets, including gathering the necessary materials of cedar boughs, bark, grasses, and roots. Men made the open-work clamming baskets, canoes, tools, and houses, and did all the hunting and fishing. Both men and women were adept at fishing and paddling a variety of canoes.

In addition, men built the smokehouses for curing meat and fish, constructed the hearths, made cradleboards, did the woodwork on carvings and multipurpose planks, got the firewood (if no children or slaves were available), made long wooden needles for mats, and prepared the ironwood (syringa) stakes for cooking salmon and clams.

Women made clothing and rain gear from shredded cedarbark, which invigorated the wearer because it lightly chafed the skin during activities. These clothes were much more effective at shedding rain and keeping the body warm than the European (wool) clothing that replaced them, but buying cloth clothing was much easier than giving time and effort to gather, prepare, soften, and weave cedarbark. In upriver and mountainous regions, leather clothes were worn, and leggings were worn by both men and women throughout the region when walking overland, as protection from brush and thorny undergrowth.

Couples cooperated in endeavors, even as they observed sexual continence or chastity, which was required for hunters before a hunt, shamans before a cure, and warriors before a battle (Amoss 1978, 57). While the husband was engaged in this task, the wife prayed and sang to help him, as did his sisters, lying inert to incapacitate the prey similarly.

Death

When someone died, closely related women keened. Snohomish believed that a person died at the same time of the day as he or she had been born, adding a daily cycle to the human one. The body was washed by undertakers possessing this specific power, and prepared for burial. Word was sent to nearby communities to announce the date of the funeral. More people attended a service for someone who held an honored name and was well liked than for a commoner. All attenders were feasted and given those possessions of the deceased which were not placed with the body or burned. Keeping heirlooms in the family was a reminder of their grief but also a link with the dead that might bring them harm. Only a particularly cherished item or a masterpiece made by the deceased was kept by the family for later use when that name was again passed on.

Mourners judged the life of the deceased, particularly evaluating the manner of death and omens at the funeral. A quiet death was a sign of a good life, but a tormented passing might indicate bad intent. At the 1995 funeral of a famous shaman, mourners filing out of the building looked up to see an eagle atop a tree, which was universally regarded as a final visit by one of his spirits in testimony to his power and ability.

Before the recent use of burial coffins, a body was wrapped in mats and placed high up in a tree until it decomposed and a reburial potlatch was held to bury what remained. Nobles were placed in a canoe, with holes bored into the bottom as drains; this craft was believed to take them across a river to the land of the dead. Important elite people had a second canoe placed upside down over the first. A surviving spouse would visit the grave to cry, but women did this longer than men did. Sometimes, the seemingly dead person revived and these visits by a mourner helped to rescue him or her from the bindings that held the mat coverings in place.

The Swinomish and Lummi held periodic feasts for the dead under the direction of shamans. People brought cooked foods intended for the dead, placed these dishes in the center of house, and then hid under mats along the side bunks of the house until the dead left (Collins 1974, 236).

Souls became ghosts that went to the land of the dead, which was "on the other side" of that of the living. People had different opinions as to where this was. Most thought it was underground, but some thought it was far away on the edge (horizon) of the earth. There, the dead lived in plank houses and towns in mirror image to those of the living. Every river had such an inverted afterworld occupied by the ghosts of its mortal residents. The parallel world of the dead kept pace with that of the living so that frame houses, cars, and mechanics have been reported from the Quileute and Twana beyonds (Elmendorf 1960, 519; Miller 1988, 108).

Mention of ghosts was used to frighten children so that they would not stay outside after dark. Toys and clothes were always taken inside at night because otherwise the ghosts could steal the "warmth" (vitality) of their owners, who then sickened and died.

Two paths led to the land of the dead, one short and one circuitous. Those who were killed or died suddenly took the short one from which there was no return. The long route allowed shamans time possibly to retrieve the soul before it became a ghost. This long path was taken by the shamans during the odyssey, but they often returned via the short one.

The soul of a living person might start on the long path if someone hurt that person's feelings so badly that he or she wanted to die. Mourners were also in danger of having their souls wander after a loved one or go so far astray that they could be snatched by the dead. Therefore the surviving spouse and other close members of the family observed strict rules during the period of mourning. Afterward, the spouse was obligated to marry a sibling of the deceased, unless, by mutual agreement between families, the widow(er) were released from the intention and free to chose another partner.

This requirement to remarry into the family of the deceased was reflected in the kinship system, which included a special set of decedence terms that changed at the death of a linking relative.

KINSHIP WITH THE DEAD

All-pervasive expressions of respect, a mark of highest rank, required knowing how to relate to others—human, biotic, and spiritual kin. While the northern Northwest Coast was distinctly matrilineal, tracing kinship through the mother, Lushootseed kinship explicitly recognized equal contributions from both parents, both living and dead extending far into the past through inherited names.

Unlike other areas of Native North America, where "the terminologies for American Indian cultures are rarely complete with respect to the relationships brought about by death of a relative or by death and remarriage" (Edmonson 1958, 13), Salishan, including Lushootseed, terminologies have been well reported, although given little if any cultural context.

Overall, distinctive features of the Lushootseed kinship system were that it was descriptive, bilateral, and took into consideration the factors of generation, gender, age, and decedence (Collins 1974, 86). While the other criteria were common among all human societies, decedence, a change of kin terms precipitated at the death of a linking relative, was rare. This particular term (as a substitute for "condition of life," the last of eight principles listed by Alfred Kroeber in 1909) was introduced by George Peter Murdock (1949, 101) as a possible feature of classificatory kinship systems—generation, sex, affinity, collaterality, bifurcation, polarity, relative age, speaker's sex, and decedence: "the last and least important of the nine, based on the biological fact of death" (1949, 106). While kinship always involves the cultural recognition of biology, mostly in terms of age and gender, Lushootseed adds this concern with death itself.

Decedence

In most societies, death called for circumlocutions and polite forms, rather than the use of separate kin terms. Often, these consisted of adding tags, lexicals phrased as "the late," or actual necronyms (death names) for defining classes of people who are mourning specific types of relatives (cf. Buchler and Selby 1968, 170). In most cases where decedence occurred, it was a reflex of the marital alliances between families, moving a former affine into the category of "potential spouse" in anticipation of the levirate or sororate.

Throughout the world, polite concern for ways to refer to the dead, for the welfare of children, and for remarriages were expressed by kin term usages, but only in the Northwest was particular importance attached to a corporate "ancestral house." Therefore, elsewhere in North America where decedence also occurred, it derived from other factors (Drucker 1937), such as in native California, where it was so common in the north and south that the Huchinom felt called upon to explain why they did not use it. Everywhere else, "the continued use of the terms [for parent and collaterals] is said to be 'on account of the ch[ildren]'" (Gifford 1922, 119, 257). After a mother died, her children were "fed" by her parents and brothers, in addition to their own father. The implication, then, was that the families stayed in contact for the benefit of their children.

Yet, for fifteen Californian "tribes" listed (Gifford 1922, 17, 33, 36, 56, 60, 68, 70, 71, 77, 115), almost all of the decedence terms involved only affines. For example, among the Karuk, "for all terms of affinity following the death of the connecting relative the term *gardim* is used." Only the Tolowa specified terms for parental siblings: *trinxne* for deceased parent's sister and *trine* for deceased parent's brother, both of which were related to *trinxne*, meaning 'ghost, spirit' (Gifford 1922, 17, 33). In addition, they applied *tamage* to all affines after the death of the linking relative. Such data confirm the link between decedence and ongoing marital alliances through the sororate and levirate.

Among the Salish, decedence was such a prominent and wide-ranging feature that it was applied to both affinals (in-laws) and collaterals ("blood" kin on the sides). While the requirements of remarriage explain the affinal shifts, terms for collaterals appear problematic because they involved surviving siblings (aunts and uncles) and their "niblings" (nieces and nephews), the children of the deceased.

The few explanations proposed for decedence note its involvements with entitlements, with responsibilities, or with custodianship of family resources.

In general, Goodenough (1970, 90–93), who found decedence "of considerable interest," suggested that it represented how the "entitlements" of kin relationship were transferred at death.

More specifically, Galloway (1977, 530), who worked among the Fraser River Sta:lo (Upriver Halkomelem Salish), suggested that their decedence terms indicated a shifting of "responsibilities" to the survivors. Among his examples were two terms that meant deceased person (other than a parent) responsible for Ego, such as uncle, aunt, and grandmother. He concluded, "The Stalo way of viewing . . . these terms is that you are related to a person who dies or you are related to a person through another person who dies. These terms are looked at as a process."

Thus, for much of your life you were supposed to be the responsibility of your parents, and, secondarily, of other adult members of your family. Then, with the death of your own parents, you became a primary responsibility of these other surviving adults.

Modern Lushootseed elders explain that decedence terms were adopted "for the sake of the children," but not because they became orphans. While there was indeed a word for "orphan," the whole point of changing terms was to prevent young children from being regarded as lacking close kin.

The full explanation, therefore, involved general considerations of family honor and traditions. Indeed, decedence was invoked for the sake of the "family," the broad bilateral kindred holding corporate rights to traditions and resources—most particularly the inherited ancestral wisdom sometimes called "advice," described earlier. Moreover, since children were the epitome of the family, its hope and pride for the future, special care had to be taken to give them continued access to family teachings, which were put at risk by the death of a parent.

Among Lushootseeds, the four terms reflecting decedence are *yəlab*, *sqəla(y)jut*, *sbalutsid*, and **tsəɬbaskayu*, first discussed by Arthur Ballard (1935, 111).[12]

According to Hess (1976, 631.1–3), *yəlab* is "either parent's sibling of either sex when the parent is deceased." The term *yəl-* means 'both, pair' and *-ab* is a suffix that extends a meaning. Thus, the designation seems to mean 'embracing both sides.' Of related interest is the use of the term *yəlyəlab* to mean 'ancestors.' Skagit speakers explicitly recognized such collateral ties when speaking English, remarking that their genealogies traced the "fathers of our uncles."

The term *sqəla(y)jut* has been translated as "nephew/niece when sibling link is deceased, reciprocal of *yəlab*" (Hess 1976, 375.2). It is based on the term *qəl* meaning 'bad' and may mean 'badly off, unfortunate.' Also, there was some dialectical variation in the suffixes applied to it. While Ballard used {-əɬ}, the term in Suquamish as spoken by the late Lawrence Webster had {-ut}.

The third term (*sbalutsid*) has been translated as "in-law when link is deceased" (Hess 1976, 18.3), although the verbal form means "court a girl, be going after someone." Related words include *balbal* 'confused, mistaken' and *-utsid* "lexical suffix 'gap, opening' and 'mouth, language, door, river'" (Hess 1976, 17.3, 541.5). The whole word seems to mean 'to cover a mistake (or embarrassment),' giving added credence to the observation by Ruth Underhill (1965, 69) that in the Northwest "death was an insult that had to be wiped out, not by avoidance of the dead but by glorifying them." As applied to actual situations, the term connotes 'intended spouse,' much as English refers to betrothed individuals as 'intended' for each other.

As diagramed by Hess (1976, 383), during the lifetime of a parent, a *yəlab* was known as either aunt (*'əpus*) or uncle (*qəsi*), and the nibling was called *staləɬ*. In the southern dialects, *pus* was the term for aunt. The vital link of such kin with living traditions was shown by the fact that, after their own deaths, parents' siblings were again called 'aunt' and 'uncle,' fitted back into their former genealogical role within the family.

The last term included reference to the dead: *skayu* 'corpse, ghost' and used the productive prefix of {tseɬ-} 'make, build' (Hess 1976, 95, 232.1), which indicated step-relationships when applied to kin terms. Thus, the term for a stepfather meant 'made a father.' The term under consideration seems to mean 'created by death.' Other dialects used other prefixes. At least some of the southern dialects used {tsiⱡ-} (cf. Ballard 1935 and Hess 1976, 52.2).

The medial -b- may refer to repetition and thus mean 'made again by death,' but it may also derive from -ab- 'belonging to,' applying to in-laws, especially parents-in-law, who were called skʷʔalwas during life (Hess 1976, 254.6, 261.1). The term kʷʔaⱡiwʔ now means to change residence at marriage, to go to the home of in-laws.

While the other three terms are known and used by present speakers, this fourth term is not, although its meaning makes transparent reference to the dead. Present confusion about this term may be due to the fact that it severed a relationship rather than created a new one (Ballard 1935, 112–13), suggesting that it might actually be more in the nature of an anti-kinship term, as with the English prefix ex- for relationships that have been denied or legally severed.

According to responses by elders, modern Lushootseed speakers are particularly insightful with regard to the collateral terms but less clear on the affinal ones. For yəlab, people said that it signified that "someone became like a mother or a father," a living aunt or uncle; while a sqəla(y)jut "became like a son or daughter." The implication was that the shift to these terms moved the kinspeople closer together.

Similarly, sbalutsid was said to indicate "the person you're going to marry" or "the person you're next in line to marry." Of course, given the levirate and sororate, when someone died, the surviving spouse became "intended" for another sibling.

In her rigorous treatment of Skagit (Northern Lushootseed) terminology, June Collins (1974, 83–110) gave careful attention to important features of this system. What she wrote about this specific instance has direct bearing on more general conclusions. Collins confirmed the fundamental importance of siblingship for understanding the system, regarding it as "the most tightly knit, firmest bond in the society." When siblings died, their children became the concern of surviving brothers and sisters, who argued for levirate or sororate marriages out of "fear of unkind treatment by unrelated stepparents" (Collins 1974, 91, 94, 102).

Among the Skagit and other Lushootseeds, divorce was infrequent among good families, particularly because "both parents had to give up the children because of the fear already discussed of allowing the children to live with stepparents. Parents could not dispose of a child as they wished. . . . Both families had to agree to the child's residence" (Collins 1974, 105).

Other reasons against divorce included an unwillingness to return any of the gifts and property exchanged, along with possible dangers that might befall a lone woman making a journey back to her parents (Collins 1974, 105). The only acceptable grounds for divorce were a barren wife, adultery, or excessive cruelty. Even after marriages were ended by the death of a spouse, everyone in the immediate blood line had a say in the care of any underage children.

In all, then, the feature of decedence among the Skagit and other Lushoot-seeds revolved around a concern for young children, not for general family alliances, as was the case when decedence applied to affinal terms. The effect of the terminological changes was "closing ranks" to look after the welfare of younger heirs. This tightening was also consistent with the manner in which kinship was traced by the Salish.

By a process of overlapping kindred families, people adopt a kin claim to someone on the basis of a relationship that has already been acknowledged by a linking relative. Thus, a person might say, "I call that person 'nephew' because he calls my close cousin 'aunt.'" Obversely, someone laying claim to a relationship might find the statement rejected or acted upon coolly because that person and family were not highly regarded. The rebuff often took the form, she or he is "the only one I ever heard about that connection from."

Other societies acknowledge such kin realignments in other ways, so the explanation for the Lushootseed system must be found internally. The tight bond among siblings and kindreds among the Salish rests firmly upon a belief in "family wisdom." The all-pervasive significance of these inherited teachings gave the Northwest much of its distinctiveness, providing the basis for distinguishing a variety of corporate groups localized within households.

In the north, these corporations were characterized by matrilineal sentiments, establishing clear channels of responsibility within matrilines (Durlach 1928), themselves regarded as impervious to death because immortal names were inherited across generations.

Among the Salish and others of the central coast, these kindreds were ambilateral (had many-sided options) and localized in households. While the system itself recognized open bilateral components, actual choices were limited to the eight households of acknowledged great grandparents. In practice, households included three generations of actual residents, along with at least a fourth generation recalled through hereditary names (Amoss 1981, 237).

Among Lushootseeds, every individual represented the conjunction of several of these "ancestral families" (kindreds). In addition to the term for ancestors based on collaterals, Lushootseed also used *st'ax*ʷ*shəd* meaning "root (especially cedar root), ancestors (figurative)" (Hess 1976, 531.3).

Cedar roots were widely used for basketry and bindings, so they were much in evidence. Also, they grew in every direction away from the tree, sending tendrils throughout the landscape. Lushootseeds recognized that like a network of roots, an individual represented a 'coming together and stretching out' of links from many different places. As a tree fed from diverse roots, so the person came from many sources.[13] Indeed, a tree, person, or culture was regarded as radiating from a fixed anchorage.

Of the eight ancestral possibilities for claiming kin, those of the father and of the mother were most important and were each terminologically distinguished (contra Spier 1925, 74) by terms translating as 'on the entire side of the father' and 'on the entire side of the mother.'[14]

For ranking families, an argument can be made that the transmission process involved fleeting replacements in an immutable position rather than recognized succession by different people to the heirship. In other words, the permanent identity is more important than who has it at any particular time. Names and possessions were defined in terms of the timeless age of epics. Since the universal capsizing prior to the arrival of human beings, people have been periodically re-creating these immortal conditions by "giving people to names."

Reviewing the four Lushootseed terms in the light of wider distributions, two emerge as having the greatest significance for understanding the phenomenon of decedence. The term referring to the dead can be removed from consideration because it has gone out of use. Of the three remaining, that for intended spouse had a broad distribution, presumably reflecting the importance, as noted, of continuing marital alliances to safeguard children. As Sapir (1916, 329) observed, "the levirate itself is known to have been in force among most or all of the tribes of Washington and Oregon." Moreover, Duff (1952, 80) grasped the crux of decedence when he noted that, as a result of such remarriages, "children kept the same grandparents and their education went on without interruption." Though less elaborated than first marriages, these later ceremonies were festive and legally binding.

Most distinctive of the system, therefore, were the two terms for parental siblings and for niblings, which occurred only among the Salish and neighboring Southern Nootkans. Nearby Plateau Sahaptians did not have such terms probably because of the different strategies used by the Salishans and the Sahaptians to encourage intertribal contact.

The Salishans used intertribal gatherings (to dance, visit, gamble, and trade) lasting many days, which also fostered intermarriages, while the Sahaptians sponsored day-long feasts. Since the Salishans, especially of important families, expected to marry among diverse groups, the death of a parent would be more disruptive to the transmission of teachings because of the greater distances and differences involved. As a hedge against this, collaterals changed terms to assume greater closeness, at least when speaking Lushootseed.

Among the Salish, this close/remote relationship pervaded the entire cultural system. In Lushootseed, the term used for close(ness) was $q^{w'}o$ 'gather, collect' (Hess 1976, 432.2), with a range that included "assembly, council, and gathering." Ballard (1935, 112) reported that it signified "join, unite, assemble." Appropriately, today, at large gatherings, individuals still donate money to someone through a speaker, who announces that the offering was intended to show that the donor is claiming the particular person named as a relative. Given the extensive network of kindreds in a bilateral system, such periodic reclaiming of some weakening links served to strengthen the relational ties among elite families, functioning in the present as a reflection of its greater importance in the past.

Similarly, the Thompson Salish have two terms for affines after the death of the linking relative: one for a decedence affine of a close relationship and one for that of a distant relationship (cf. Miller 1985). It was, therefore, logically appropriate and internally consistent for Salishans to invoke this symbolic distinction to "close ranks" and join kinspeople together after the death of a linking relative.

While this solution was distinctly Salishan, it was based on practice that was much more widespread. Fred Eggan (1955, 94) noted the importance given to "brotherhood in Plains and other Native American kinship systems. Among the Numic-speaking Comanche and H3kandika, "the institution of formal friendship among men also entails the use of the brother terminology. The friend . . . takes the status of his brother in the relationship system of his comrade's family, thereby taking over all the privileges and restrictions which go with the new status" (Hoebel 1939, 448). By invoking kin terms and behaviors, friends become kin, intent becomes kinship.

The next step in this process is shown by Nez Perce usage: *yelept* means friend. A man fights in war side by side with his *yelept*. When he dies, his son becomes the survivors' nephew, and the survivor becomes the orphan's paternal uncle (Aoki 1966, 360).

The Nez Perce also have another term for friend (*lawtiwa*) that did not invoke quasi-siblingship. What was notable about *yelept*, of course, was that it moved a quasi-siblinghood into a stronger relationship after the death of the linking man. In motivation and intent it was a weaker form of decedence, closing ranks and strengthening voluntary bonds between participants as collateral uncle and nephew, not as parent and child. Among the Salish, however, the vital store of teachings, class rankings, and family pedigrees of a house were not left to such emotional chance. Hence, the significant role given to decedence in their terminology reflects the greater corporate structuring of their society.

While the Salish are fairly well known ethnographically and very well known linguistically, there has been scant analysis of their greater ramifications although they have been recognized as pivotal for understanding many aspects of Native North America (Miller 1988). Spier (1925, 74) first considered Salish terminology in its own right, and Elmendorf (1961b) studied it in greater detail, tracing its diversification into lineal Coastal and bifurcate collateral Interior forms. While Murdock (1949, 350) derived Salishan structures from the Hawaiian type, he later characterized the Salish system, because it combined bilaterality with a choice of residence options (1965, 31), as the fundamental kinship system of North America.

Because of this great range of relationships and residence flexibility, any Salishan had a vast network of kin to call upon in times of need, whether to host a feast, to care for an orphan, or to arrange for the cure of some persistent illness.

BODILY SICKNESS

Clinics

Today, Lushootseeds recognize two medical systems, their own and that of hospitals and clinics with university-trained physicians and practitioners. The latter has not replaced the former; the two function side by side because each has separate causative agents, either the ill intent of other beings or invasion by germs. Both are willful acts, but their treatments vary according to the attending doctor. More physical hurts are largely handled in the same practical way by both systems.

Medical treatment being guaranteed by treaties, natives have ready access to medicine, albeit as public health. Many of their current medical conditions directly derive from "high rates of alcohol and drug abuse, family dissolution, unemployment, and other effects of long term poverty and discrimination" (Guilmet and Whited 1989, 49). At Puyallup, chemical dependency is regarded as akin to having a spirit partner in that "the power of the alcohol or drugs is [held] responsible for any aberrant behavior" (Guilmet and Whited 1989, 75).

Moreover, while natives remain reluctant around outsiders to mention their resort to native healers, most freely discuss incidents of "ghosting" due to the active role of the dead in their lives and a consequent need for cleansing rites (Guilmet and Whited 1989, 120). It was and is just such visits from the dead that once motivated the shamanic odyssey, and that now are factored into various curing strategies used by modern natives deciding among treatments by allopathic physicians, Pentecostals, Shakers, or smokehouse adherents (Guilmet and Whited 1989, 52).

Cures

Health and well-being remain a constant concern among Lushootseed adults, expressed in terms of the integrity of a body and upheld by ritual purifications and heartwarming acts of kindness and regard. Like any house, the body should be kept in good repair, just as the spirits within should be nurtured and protected. Any breach of this integrity, whether by personal loss, displacement, boundary transgression, or outside attack, resulted in disease. For the most severe of such breaches, the ultimate outcome was death.

Lushootseeds say that sickness could afflict any and all aspects of a person, with effective treatments ranging from home remedies for minor skin disorders to cures involving specialists qualified for this by transferred spiritual and hereditary abilities, and sicknesses due to the mortal dangers of shaman attack and soul loss.[15]

To cure internal complaints, sucking shamans had extraction powers from Leech, Eel, Mosquito, or other appropriate animals. They specialized in treating symptoms like bleeding, stiffness, infected cuts, and congested lungs or head. In the most extreme cases, they removed a magical weapon or probe shot into the patient by another shaman to cause a painful death after long suffering.

While a mind could be driven insane by fearful monsters, ghosts, and spirits or could temporarily be removed to another realm, these disasters could only happen if the soul was already in peril (Kew and Kew 1981).

Souls could be lost by a sudden fright or by a strong attraction to a person, place, or thing. They could also be stolen by a hostile shaman or snatched away by a ghost or the dead in general. In all of these instances, the result was that the person began to wither, weaken, and languish, sleeping all the time and becoming colder and colder. Friends and family noticed a growing lethargy that soon became total unless desperate measures were taken and a specialist was consulted. Everyone knew that untreated soul loss was fatal.

In ancient times, this diagnostician was either a shaman with the ability to see into other realms or a medium with ghost power. For the past century, members of the Indian Shaker Church have performed this function, seeing the soul as a tiny transparent replica of that individual (Amoss 1978, 44). For several decades, Pentecostals have also recovered souls by prayer alone, without gestures or ritual.

If the soul was attached to a place or thing, a shaman or Shakers intervened to break this link. The soul was "taken off" whatever held it and returned to its owner, who improved immediately.

If sadness, hopelessness, depression, anger, a sense of unworthiness, or hurt had started a soul on the long path to the land of the dead, a shaman went after it and brought it back. Once it had arrived in a village of the dead, however, only the full scale odyssey by several shamans could bring it back.

If a soul was snatched by a ghost, a shaman could send his power after it. A medium was able either to persuade (or trick) the dead to return the vitality or to have his or her own ghost helper snatch it back. Since ghosts were dull witted, two mediums could work together to lure the ghost holding that soul into their own world. While one medium called the dead and offered each one a plate of food, the other one grabbed the soul from that ghost when it let go to reach for food (Amoss 1978, 84).

Cooperation among curers was taken for granted by Lushootseeds, unlike in other regions where a shaman worked alone and was hostile to (and jealous of) all others in their common profession, at least in public.[16] While there were bitter power contests, as discussed later, joint curings did occur. Smith (1940, 81) noted that when two shamans worked together, they alternated so that one sang while the other dealt with the patient. This cooperation lasted only for a single cure and had nothing to do with having the same spirit, home village, common kinship, or mutual respect. Still, in difficult cases, the feeling was that having more shamans involved improved the chance of a successful cure.

Possession

Salishans recognized three kinds of possession. The first was the unwanted attachment of the soul of someone else who was overly fond of the victim. Once a shaman identified a soul's rightful owner, it was returned. If this other soul remained away, its owner died and the unintended host became ill, but not fatally. The second possession type was the return visit by a guardian spirit to its mature human partner, who was cured of being "sick to sing" by expressing their alliance at a public winter dance. The third type was a shaman attack, occurring when a hostile doctor sent one of his spirits to invade and kill a person. As the person died, he or she gave vent to this fatal intrusion by gloating in the voice of the invasive shaman (Amoss 1978, 122). Sometimes, the voice boasted of the victimizer by name. Smith (1940, 61), though this is an overstatement, described these deathbed outbursts as leading to "an orgy of accusal," which in the worse cases resulted in the killing of the accused shaman by the relatives of the deceased, as in the 1874 Fisk trial.

In its intensity, shaman attack was at one extreme of the constant struggles among powers that were and are pervasive in Salishan life (Smith 1940, 61). Every seeming accident or misfortune is evaluated in terms of such power contests between those with career or curing spirits, although only shamans are locked in the fiercest of competitions. Since doctors provide their own protection for self and family, these struggles often are believed to cost the lives of the most defenseless, namely the children of these rival families. Other people who were vulnerable to shaman attack were the aged and fatigued, especially when they were away from the safety of their home town (Smith 1940, 86).[17] In other words, being out of place, in any sense, was a spiritual hazard.

Shamans diagnosed any ailment with a distinctive gesture. The right arm was bent at the elbow so that it covered the eyes (Smith 1940, 78). Only by losing mortal sight could a shaman "see" into other realms. In addition, placing the wrist near the forehead or ear allowed the spirit who lived inside the crooked arm to converse with the shaman, aiding his or her determination.

Once the cure began, only the shaman but not his or her human helpers could see the offending agents, whether ghosts, spirits, or other shamans. Yet a shaman's (tunnel) vision was highly localized, with the outer edges blurred. As the shaman closed in on "it," the room was filled by a deafening noise as everyone beat and sang to a crescendo.

Once the shaman had it cupped between the hands, he or she asked the crowd what to do with it. Options were to send it back to its shaman owner, to hide it away in the mountains where it could no longer be used, or to kill, maim, or cripple it. If the latter, the shaman stacked one fist above the other so as to twist his hands, crushing the intruder. Shortly after, the suspected shaman died.

If a shaman arrived too late to perform a cure, he prevented the hostile shaman from achieving final victory by binding up the patient with cattail fiber twine. This kept the possessing spirit from escaping, consigning it to the grave with the body. As a result, the hostile shaman shortly after joined the dead (Smith 1940, 82).

Though slighted in the published literature, each of these spirits, shamans, and cures had artifact correlates, like those for the odyssey, as noted by Smith (1940, 99): "Since carved wooden figures were used in the *spadak* [odyssey] as other power objects were used in other demonstrations of power, and, since not all powers had such figures connected with them, only certain shamans could take part in the *spadak*." She reversed the native argument, however, since it was partnership with an immortal Little Earth that provided this ability, not possession of the wooden effigy, which was a mere token manifestation of the greater bond.

These other power objects included painted houseposts, canoe prows, ten-foot drumming poles, a seal-shaped buoy, carved torsos about a yard high, and a square-topped board, five by two and a half feet, painted by Nisqually shamans and placed against the outer wall of their bed platform, presumably to protect them during sleep.

In addition, all winter long, Nisqually and Puyallup towns along the salt water placed carved torsos near the doors of their houses to protected themselves against soul thefts by ghosts, who were most active during their own summer (Smith 1940, 115).

While all shamans had carved icons of their powers, ranging from the power boards and poles to special rattles, the most awesome figures of all were wooden Little Earths. These figures were best known for their active role during the odyssey, but shamans also brought them out for other cures. At Suquamish, Ellen George vividly recalled that some Little Earths came out of a house corner during a cure and danced around the fire. Then they went back to the corner and sat like wooden figures again. Even while dormant, they protected the house because they would bump and rustle if some unfriendly person tried to hurt an inhabitant or steal something.

Ordinary people were fearful of these carvings, understandably, so the shaman usually kept them out in the woods in a hollow tree stump until they were needed for a cure or odyssey. Yet, like any other power object, they were probably brought into the house occasionally to be fed, clothed, and tended. During the winter ceremonial season, they were so often in demand that they probably "lived" in a corner of the shaman's house, vastly expanding the range of persons and people who were members and protectors of that household.

Throughout Puget Sound, relying on the remarkable cooperation of shamans with this special power, specific accounts of the odyssey rite exist from the Skagit, Swinomish, Snohomish, Snoqualmi, Duwamish, Suquamish, Puyallup, and Nisqually, along with versions from the neighboring Lummi, Klallam, Twana, and Chehalis.[1] While Miller (1988) considered these in some detail, overall synthesis was delayed until now to allow for over a decade of mature consideration.

This retrieval rite, for all its importance for comparative religion, also brought together every aspect of Lushootseed culture. For the duration of the ceremony, realms of spirits and ghosts, efforts by shamans, and complexities of a person's life (and death) were drawn together inside a house, which was decorated with specialized artifacts.

A plank house was used for the rite, either one owned by the patient or one borrowed for the occasion. Its floor space was cleared so that paired planks could be stood up and carved effigies of each shaman's Little Earth placed in a row down the middle.

What was unique about this enactment was that although doctors usually worked alone, here several shamans worked in unison to mime a journey to the land of the dead, a confrontation to regain some spiritual aspect of a person, and a hasty return to put the lost vitality back into the patient.[2]

Along the way, central concerns of Lushootseed culture were epitomized and validated in a public community setting during the coldest, wettest months of the year. To balance the depicted vehicle, an even number of shamans, usually four or six, co-officiated during the rite, although one of them took the lead. Along with their power from Little Earths, their other spirit allies were called upon periodically to help so that the shamans could safely go to the afterworld and return. As already noted, the Little Earths were synonymous "owners" of the earth itself and so could draw the shamans back home. Almost all of the shamans were men. Women were not prohibited from joining the rite, but few female shamans had the necessary spirit helpers.[3]

The shamans went at midwinter because everything in the afterworld was the reverse of their own. When snow covered the ground here, there it was summer with warm, flower-lined trails. Similarly, our day was their night, our high tide was their low one, and objects broken here were whole there.

Everyone in the community was involved in the preparations. Women cooked food and cleaned the house, while men hunted and helped out as needed. Children gathered nearby, ready to run errands and carry messages. A sense of place was so profound that every odyssey enactment was customized specifically to the locale and people involved. In other words, specific features of that place and population were explicit in that version of the rite, with the local graveyard doubling as the land of the dead.

Meanwhile, the shamans, or that shaman associated with the house, went into the woods and selected a large cedar tree, which was hauled or floated to a convenient location near the community. There it was split into planks, each to be shaped into a particular form, with an arched top, snout, or disk.[4] Every drainage had its own style of plank. For example, the Snohomish cut out a snout because they traced descent from a legendary marine mammal.[5]

Each plank was coated with a chalky white layer of paint to provide a background before thick black outlines were drawn along the edges. The day before the ceremony, each shaman was assigned a plank where he painted an image of his primary power in the very center, colored in combinations of red, white, and black. Sometimes, dots in red or black surrounded the figure to represent the song that linked shaman and spirit. Since humans were alien in the afterworld, shamans felt as though they were traveling through an engulfing viscosity. Whenever they sang or talked, their breath escaped as bubbles, represented as painted dots, moving through the thickness.

Poles were also made for or by the shamans to serve multiple purposes during the rite—as bows, punts, probes, spears, paddles, or place markers.

Every shaman kept a carved humanoid figure about a yard high representing his Little Earth. Before an odyssey, this figure was repainted and dressed, as appropriate, to look its best. When the Little Earths, primordial male and female spirits who lived in forest marshes, heard the shamans singing as they departed for the afterworld, they rushed into the house to help out by lodging in their carved effigies.[6] According to common belief, these earthlings actually made the voyage that their shamans merely depicted.

During the arrival and setting up of the objects for the ritual, spectators had to keep very still and silent since these actions were fraught with danger. The membrane between worlds was being thinned or breached and much could go wrong that could lead to fatal consequences. Ghosts might be attracted to vulnerable spectators, or shamans might decide to steal souls and hide them in the other world. Other supernatural beings might be unleashed because of a miscue or a wrong move at a crucial moment.

When all was prepared, spectators sat quietly near the walls of the house. Meanwhile, the shamans and their human helpers lined up outside, ready to march in and set up the paraphernalia so that they could start their odyssey.

Surrounded by drumming and singing, the procession entered the house. The shamans were wearing special cedarbark headbands and painted faces. Sometimes, long strips of woven cedarbark were draped around the neck. Each curer carried his Little Earth, with an assistant carrying the painted plank. Sometimes, the planks were held so that they appeared to peek inside the door, making their power seem more lifelike. The shamans placed their figurines in a line down the center of the house and sat down on the sidelines. Helpers arranged the planks in pairs so that each shaman faced an image of his own spirit power painted on the middle of the plank ahead of him. The boards at thè ends were painted on only one side, while those in the middle were painted on both. In this manner, the images looked at each other and provided protection for the shaman both front and back. When the schematic vehicle had been constructed in the middle of the floor, the shamans returned to stand in the enclosed spaces between boards. Then they acted as if departing.

They had to hurry because, in Lushootseed belief, any illness was a prelude to death (Collins 1974, 206), not a temporary disability. Their patient was wasting away without any obvious cause because the dead were sapping his or her vitality. During the entire ritual, the victim rested unobtrusively on a cedar mat at the rear of the house.

Along the way, the voyagers made routine stops to gather power, influence the future, and collect information with great caution and circumspection. For example, a shaman used his cedarbark scarf to wipe off sweat and other body secretions so that they could not be used against him by ghosts and other doctors. Lost souls and images of other objects from the land of the dead were also brought back entangled in its weave.

At the first stop, shamans visited a land filled with the spirits of artifacts, each of which sang its song. Moving among them, the healers learned and repeated these songs since knowing them would help people to use tools more efficiently. Artifacts themselves represented the full cooperation of natural products, human resourcefulness, and spiritual inspiration. The manufacture of useful items required supernatural assistance because career powers enhanced any personal abilities. Melville Jacobs (1958, 85) noted that

Musical transcriptions by Dr. Christopher Kauffman of two songs used by the doctors on the odyssey. While most such songs, like the upper one (Recording 3), include only vocables (burden sounds with occasional esoteric meaning), the recognizable phrase in the lower song (Recording 9), probably sung on the return, is *ʼa dᶻal gʷaləb* ("You folks turn back"). Sung by Jack Stillman for Arthur Ballard on 19 June 1938 in Auburn, Washington, these historic tapes are stored in the Melvile Jacobs Collection (#14550), University of Washington Libraries.

principal foods and major tools were regarded throughout the region as akin to "spirit-powers, kindred, or co-villagers. Foods and tools themselves wanted relationships with people just as spirit-powers and kin yearned for their relatives. All must help and lean upon one another."

Since this was the initial encounter with the "other side," everyone was reminded that it was the spiritual aspects of existence that were the most important, a logical beginning place for any such journey, and for life in general. Tools and other artifacts often served as appropriate "houses" for spirits, contacted through song.

After some time, the trip continued until they got to a berry thicket, which was also spiritual because the berries were the size of birds, hopping about in the shape of human babies. Since everything was believed to have an essential human form under the cloak of its species or appearance, this visit was a reminder of the common humanity of all life. Shamans tried to pluck a berry or two with their poles, and their clumsy antics created much humor for the audience. If they managed to get just one, there would be a plentiful berry harvest the next fall.

The Nuxalk had a similar belief that berries in their true forms looked like goggle-eyed little boys (McIlwraith 1948, 691). Among the Katzie, berries and mollusks were primordial foods, available from creation and later augmented by foods provided by beings transformed into modern species.

Continuing on the journey, the shamans next came to a lake where their vehicle was reconfigured into a flat-water canoe. Since deep lakes were and are the abodes of powerful spirits, this place was a particularly important source of power. Indeed, a shaman with a lake-dwelling spirit like Otter called out its name to speed the canoe across the water. In addition, lakes and marshes provided a wide variety of foods, which were also being celebrated at this stop.

Next, they came to a wide prairie where the shamans used their poles as bows and seemed to hunt meat. If they were successful, then there would be plenty of game in the fall. Those crews who used planks carved with snouts took time to offer pieces of meat to each mouth in a symbolic feeding gesture.

Fifth, they came to Mosquito Place where they were attacked by such insects the size of birds. They fought these off with their poles, being careful not to be stung for that would be fatal. Since Mosquitoes were shamans in the spirit world because their ability to suck blood was useful in curing, this encounter was a test of shamanic ability.

Moving on, the doctors came to Beaver Den, where they hunted using their poles as spears. If they killed a beaver, furs would be of high quality the next year.

Afterward, the shamans went on to meet the Dawn after they had been traveling most of the night. The appearance of light added to the heaviness of their thick surroundings, so the curers had to pause to "lift the daylight" by passing their poles over their heads.[7] Because Dawn had different intensities, they had to lift it five times, the sacred pattern number for southern Lushootseeds, to move safely underneath and beyond this light. What was dawn for the shamans was sunset for the ghosts.

After their exertion, the shamans rested all day long, since it was night in the land of the dead; they prepared to resume the next evening. Sometimes, the lead shaman, if he had great power, would take time to make a quick trip to the land of the dead to plan the final assault better.

The next day, once the journey resumed, the major difficulty was a raging river with collapsing banks and on-rushing boulders. The shamans held a quick conference and decided to tip up one end of a plain cedar plank as a ramp to help them jump across the river, using their poles to vault. A shaman was most vulnerable at the moment when he was suspended in the air supported only by his spirits. If his spirits were weak or another shaman held a lingering grudge, that shaman would lose his balance. If a shaman slipped or fell, he was expected to die within the year.

By now the crew was close to the town of the dead, whose physical surroundings looked like the location of the nearest human graveyard, customizing the rite according to the characteristics of the participating shamans, the tribe and family of the patient, and the locale where the ceremony was held.

Near the ghosts' town, the vehicle was beached. While a few shamans reversed the planks and figures so that they could head back home, the rest went along the trail to the town. There they sometimes encountered a ghost, played by a member of the audience, out picking berries. They knew it was a ghost because he or she walked by crossing and recrossing the feet. Pretending that they too were ghosts, they asked for news and learned the quality and name of the newest occupant and where it dwelled. This newcomer was the soul, mind, or spirit of the patient.

Once informed, the shamans quickly killed the ghost and buried it in a shallow grave. Such murder was possible because there were at least two lands of the dead. The first, where they were, was inhabited by people who were still remembered by the living. When all memory of them was gone, they died again and passed to the second land of the dead. From there, according to some shamans, they were reborn into a descendant to begin living again. The cycle, in theory, was endless, either through rebirth or through increasingly remote abodes of unremembered dead.

By learning from the ghost what they were after, the shamans planned a strategy for when they got to the town. Sometimes, they created a diversion by having one of their spirit powers appear in front of the town as an elk, deer, or beaver.[8] When everyone rushed to the river to hunt that animal, the houses were left deserted. Then, acting like a ghost, the most powerful shaman entered the house where the patient's vitality was, quietly leading it away. Outside, other shamans joined them to protect the retreat as they rushed to the vehicle. Once they had boarded and pushed off, a shaman "threw his meanness" at the ghosts, who swarmed from the town. Apparently, by successfully fighting for the lost spirit, shamans were able, in fairness, to keep it. If they merely lured it away, the ghosts could take it back.

In some towns, this final battle was enacted with long flaming splinters shot at the shamans by youngsters acting the part of the ghosts. If a shaman were hit or burned, he died within the year. Since the enactment took place at night, often inside a house, these flames were both dramatic and fraught with danger because of hazardous, old, wooden buildings.

Having made their escape, the shamans paddled hard, with their Little Earths providing protection on the way home. Sometimes, they took a shortcut used by those who died suddenly, which brought them back in a few hours instead of days.

The patient was still lying quietly on a mat in the back of the house when the shamans arrived, each quivering with power.[9] Their leader came forward with the missing vitality and acted as though he was pouring it into the head of the invalid. Slowly at first, then with renewed vigor, the victim began to sing his or her power song.

Sometimes, shamans saw in the land of the dead the souls of other people, seemingly well but soon to sicken, and these too were brought back, carried in a shredded cedar scarf or warmed in the skin crease between neck and shoulder, and restored to the owner. These patients liberally compensated their healer.

Among Twana, before the doctors returned, the patient and spectators were protected by a rope barricade. "Those people inside the rope are all the souls that are coming back from the ghost land. The sick man will be singing too now, shaking his head. And they keep pulling them all toward the sunrise" (Elmendorf 1993, 231).

Once the vessel returned safely, everyone in the house heard about future conditions. Any artifacts, berries, or meat brought back were given out to families who might need them. Usually, berries went to a woman since picking was her job. At least once, a baby was brought back to a childless woman, who gave birth nine months later.[10] Other predictions were also made, either to delight or to warn everyone.

Though doctors might rest briefly, the used paraphernalia had to be dismantled quickly to close off the route to the afterworld. Planks were taken into a remote area of the woods to rot, returning to their elements. Only in the most dire of circumstances could boards be reused for an immediate return to the land of the dead, always accompanied by special songs. The only reason for such reuse was to enable a crew that had gone to the wrong town to embark immediately on the correct route to the other abode of the captured entity. Any delay gave the ghosts time to pass on word ("telephone") that the shamans were coming and allowed them to hide the spirit away so that the patient would die. Having made the journey once, the planks were contaminated and unsafe.

The poles may also have been abandoned, but some seem to have been reused in later rites. Kept for a lifetime, Little Earth figurines were carefully washed, losing much of their paint, and hidden in special places in the woods, often in hollow trees.[11] There each awaited the next ceremonial use by its shaman partner. Only after the shaman died was the Little Earth left forever in the forest.

Though these are not well reported, a counter attack by ghosts was described by Jerry Kanim, a Snoqualmi leader (Miller 1988, 33). They came late at night, their day, and spat down the smokehole at individuals, who became comatose and foamed at the mouth. While relatives attended them, shamans rushed down the trail to the land of the dead. They did not pause to set up effigies or grab paraphernalia. By starting specific songs, they alerted the Little Earths, who rushed on to slow down the ghosts by engaging them in conversation. When the shamans caught up, they killed a ghost, took back the souls, and immediately restored to health the stricken individuals.

Great urgency was required because if the ghosts got to a particular place on the trail, probably the sticky lake, then the souls stayed in their keeping until the shamans mounted a full odyssey and fought to get them back. Though this attack was revenge for the killing of ghosts during a final fight, the victims were not shamans but those with less spiritual protection.

In Puget Sound, intertribal contacts were long an aspect of the local social, political, and religious complexity. Important leaders fostered these interchanges at their feasts, namings, marriages, funerals, cult initiations, and winter dances. These activities in turn had repercussions throughout the larger environment and enabled spiritual connections to be made that facilitated the complex cultural elaboration that was the shamanic odyssey.

CONCLUSIONS

In its full complexities, the shamanic odyssey involved all of the institutions of Lushootseed society, ranging through technology, economy, polity, kinship, religion, and language. Each will now be considered in turn.

Technological relations with the environment were at the forefront of the rite. Every enactment was customized to reflect local terrain, materials, and conditions. In addition, specialists like carpenters worked to make the various artifacts used in the ceremony, if the shaman himself or herself did not have this ability. Trees were cut down and floated to a secluded place near a town, where they were made into planks. The Little Earths had been long carved and ready for each occasion, as were the poles, but, sometimes, new ones were made.[1] For every appearance, these objects were carefully cleaned and painted to look their best.

In terms of economy, an entire community, now viewed as members of a reservation, amassed food for all those who attended, seriously depleting their stores in some cases. Once the odyssey was effective, moreover, the patient was expected to give most or all of his or her property to the shamans to pay for the cure of this life-threatening illness. Sponsoring the rite, therefore, was a heavy financial burden on the patient, his or her family, their house, and the locality—although their generosity in undertaking to share with outsiders added luster to themselves and their own community. Large gatherings, however, provided anonymity to conceal any harmful acts by some shamans. In consequence, attending an event in another community bespoke a certain trust in an ability to protect oneself. Generally the rule of personal survival was never to eat where one was unsure of the intentions of the host or the quality of the food.

As with any other gathering, leaders of the polity increased their prestige by becoming better known in the intertribal network. For the odyssey this status particularly involved successful shamans, but public speeches and generous gifts of food and treasures permitted hosting chiefs and other leaders to stand out at the public events during interludes in the rite.

Through this retrieval journey, kinship drew relatives together to help one of their own. If the patient were poor, a wealthy relative volunteered the use of his or her house for the ceremony, and all relations, whether close or distant, gave generously toward the payment of the shamans and the feeding of the guests.

The full range of spirits, both career and curing, were involved in this religious rite. Shamans called upon all of their spiritual allies to produce a successful cure. While their Little Earths and curing spirits effected the healing, their career powers also went along to help with the hunting, gathering, transporting, and decoying needed during the trek.

Lastly, special linguistic features were involved. Esoteric vocabulary and phrasings were probably used by the shamans during the rite. Everywhere else in Native America, shamans had an arcane language that they used during ceremonies and with one another. Sometimes it was a subdialect, sometimes a set of metaphors expanding the meanings of ordinary words. Now that there are few shamans, knowledge of this language has faded. In addition, the special language used for the family-owned enchantments was probably also invoked during the journey, if only to protect some of the shamans from hostile actions by other doctors.

TODAY'S SOUL LOSS

Although the odyssey has lapsed among Lushootseeds, soul loss continues to be a medical and spiritual problem for natives and is treated today by Shakers, shamans, and charismatic Christians on a more modest scale. The urgency that brought people together in the winter to cure one of their own threatened by the dead has now found other outlets. In addition, the inter-tribal visiting that such events encouraged has now been facilitated even more by the use of vans and telephones to keep in touch with kin and friends over a vast region.

The elitism (with potential jealousy, revenge, and spiritual danger) of the shamanic rite has now been replaced by a more democratic and fluid response to soul loss, a solution nevertheless in keeping with the ancient values and traditions of Lushootseed culture.

In all, therefore, Lushootseed culture has remained centered in religion, emphasizing conceptions about powers, persons, presents, and respect. Powers have been immortal since the beginning of the world, each localized and personified at a cataclysmic moment when the world changed, sometimes capsizing like a canoe.

While they were shape shifters during primordial eons, their forms are essentially human under the cloak of their species, space, or attribute. As such, they appear as humans to child supplicants before bestowing the gift of power as a personal present. Only as they turn to depart do questers get a glimpse of their species counterpart.

Among Lushootseeds, trembling has long manifested possession of and by such powers. When sacred objects such as power boards and effigies began "of themselves to quiver . . . the man holding them was thrown into a tremble. . . . Shamans would shake and tremble in every limb. Here we see, therefore, in ancient times, almost the exact counterpart of the modern Shaker exercise; the patient helpless, with the operators gathered around him all shaking and quivering. Nowadays they are, of course, trying to get the sin *out*, instead of putting a soul *in*. The ideas have shifted, but the performance remains the same" (Waterman 1924, 505).

In all cases, such power transfers and bestowals rely on the careful observance of respect, a distinct regard for highly localized boundaries with unbreached integrity. Since all flowings of power depend on place, these discrete separations allowed famous families to expand their horizons by interacting with other tribes and regions, to act local and think global. By drawing on a local power uniquely their own, each elite family could call upon their own reserves in an intertribal situation. For this very reason, the greatest Snohomish curing spirit lived in a house surrounded by a fence, as did the Skagit warrior on Gig Harbor; similarly enclosed were several Klallam forts, the frame house visited by John Slocum in death, and homes of many of the entrenched "old families."

Hoarding served no useful purpose, so all advantages had to be shared. The goal of individuals and communities was and is to "connect" by sharing with others. A natural attraction was and is believed to exist throughout the world, holding everything together. More than a scientific notion of gravity, this attraction binds together spirits, foods, tools, and all variety of persons, only some of them human.

Integrity meant vitality, especially as warmth generated by gifts of food, dog or goat wool blankets, and by winter ceremonials bringing people together. Such continuity provided the means for resilience.

Damage to self and to others came from breaches across such barriers, as with the woman spirit who casts diseases over the wall beyond the seas surrounding the Lushootseed world. People away from home were vulnerable to any number of diseases because they were less secure. Yet, at home, they were also subject to magical probes and other invasions of their bodies. Unless a shaman removed them, using greater power than the sender's, the person died. A rim, gunnel, skin, or wall that had been breached needed repairs. Vigilance and rituals were the best promise for continuing security.

At all times, it was best to present oneself as humble in outlook, leaving to others the precaution that things were and are never what they seemed. Even babies had a language of their own that excluded adult understanding except in special cases, such as a native woman who specialized as a baby doctor to communicate with infants.

Powers were proportional. Patkanim, a Snoqualmi leader, had Mountain Goat, whose power was increased by the bulk of its house—a mountain in the Cascade Range. Chief Seattle's Thunder power was enhanced by its home in the sky.

For the most powerful individuals, their personal actions could affect the world. Thus, Swanaset made the Pitt Meadow sloughs by first painting them over his own face, the Nuxalk creator caused salmon runs by reversing his cloak, and Lushootseed shamans grabbing a berry during their odyssey guaranteed abundant fall picking. Sometimes an entire being was transformed, as the Pitt Lake sister became the mother of deer, a daughter became sturgeon, and changers decreed modern species.

Today, as in the past, Lushootseed culture is highly satisfying because it remains well placed and spacious, with ample room for all. A family no longer has to share a house to remain close—phones, cameras, roads, and home videos now bring members together. In the past, place meant a communal plank house, the residents of which were anchored there as a prelude to its elite radiating outward to connect with others of the upper class holding famous names.

For over two hundred years, Lushootseed responses to Euro-American interference has been highly creative. Outboard motors have been attached to canoes, bright pieces of alarm clocks have been put to better use as fish lures, and, most especially, religion has more old and new outlets, especially as the Indian Shaker Church, Lushootseeds' very own response to this alien presence.

In all, Lushootseeds aptly distill all of these old and new traditions by continuing to say, "The biggest tree has the deepest roots."

NOTES

INTRODUCTION

1 The classic 1930 booklet on Puget Salish (Lushootseed) by Erna Gunther translated and amplified Hermann Haeberlin's posthumous 1924 German summary, using his forty-two notebooks from 1916–17, which Franz Boas entrusted to her when founding anthropology at the University of Washington in Seattle. In the aftermath of the famous Gunther-Spier contractual marriage, Leslie Spier gave them in 1927 to what became the National Anthropological Archives in Washington DC. Letters between Haeberlin, his most promising student, and Boas are archived in the American Philosophical Society Library in Philadelphia. Most are in English; in German, as poignantly translated with Astrida Onat, he chronicles his fatal diabetes, just before insulin was discovered.

2 Miller also supplied free translations of "Fly," pp. 33–41, and "Moose," pp. 145–49; verse translation of "Boil and Hammer," appendix 1, pp. 169–78; text data, appendix 2, pp. 179–82; and bibliography, pp. 183–204.

3 A clear contrast between historical and ethnographic sources is presented in the roll of landless tribes, where "Edward Davis claimed membership in the Snoqualmie Tribe through his mother's father, even though he identified both his parents and his birth community as Duwamish" (Harmon 1995, 496). The Duwamish had no land base at the time, while the Snoqualmi did, providing a basis for their 1997 federal recognition, to which Davis contributed greatly.

4 The bailing out of a canoe in this equation of renewals is confirmed by Elmendorf (1993, 209).

5 No source is adequate for Lushootseed potlatching, feasting, give-aways (Smith 1940, 146–50; Collins 1974, 131–43; Snyder 1975; Bates, Hess, and Hilbert 1994, 2, 4, 19, 102, 247, 251), and all (even dictionaries) are overly biased toward American ideals of economic, boastful, and self-centered stereotypes. Concerted efforts and much questioning of elders at events themselves, there in the midst, provided me with four key terms, all expressive of etiquette, respect, thanks, honor, and precision indicative of "knowing the rules" in the cosmic terms of a well-ordered world. For generalized gifting, Lushootseeds use the Chinook trade jargon *paɬach*, derived from Nootkan meaning "to give." It does not appear in dictionaries because of its foreign origins, yet, by usage, it belongs in the language. Finer distinctions are based on function, "honoring and

thanking" those coming to an event involved with naming, memorial, gratitude, prestige, or removing stigma. Attendees include living, dead, spirits, and the Creator, with the bond of antecedents and descendants strongest during these festivities.

Key terms are *xʷəsalikʷ*, *s'abalikʷ*, *'ixʷ('əxʷ)*, and *sgʷigʷi*. The first pair end in *-alikʷ* for "repeated, patterned, creative, well-ordered activity," plus either *xʷəsh*, "to potlatch, apportion, seed by hand"—indicating its personalized, nurturing intensity—or *-'ab*, "to reach, extend arms or legs, radiate." The term most often reported for potlatching, *sgʷigʷi*, merely means "to be invited, invitational" for all such gestures.

Most spiritual of giving is *-'ixʷ* (*-'exʷ*), when pleasing gifts were exhibited in public to be admired by immortals before guests selected one or more of them to take home. Its spirituality derives from the close identity among spirit, host, powers, and offerings. The only two Miller ever saw were hosted by shamans, one after his own funeral and the other when a pair of powers were upgraded from bark to wood to strengthen that doctor's own legs.

By contrast, more crass terms indicate gift tossing or scrambling, and impersonal distributions such as *washəb*, "to dole, hand out" goods at a treaty.

6 Lushootseed and other native languages use "real" when immortals are forcefully involved. Similarly, siyowin smokehouse initiates refer to a spirit partner as their "Indian."

7 As regards ritual words, among the Gulf of Georgia Coast Salish, Siwin involved "word formulas, gestures, acts, and objects (principally eagle down and red ocher)" secretly passed from father to son, mother to daughter, and distinct from the "prescriptions and behaviors enjoined by individual guardian spirits" (Barnett 1955, 129).

8 During my dissertation research on Keresan Pueblos of New Mexico, I came to admire the ability of Curtis and his staff to get significant details missing from more academic accounts. Incidents he reported for Keres towns were subsequently confirmed by researchers and by models designed to characterize their overall culture. While Curtis indeed had a flair for the dramatic and photogenic, he could and did publish vital data from Native America, such as those used herein for Jacob Wahalchu's questings and Lummi replacement of the Stockaders (in ch. 1).

9 Churning up the surface of the earth to "break through" to another dimension was the first act of the Twana shamanic odyssey (Miller 1988, 2) and of the Cheyenne ritual called Massaum (Schlesier 1987, 6, 91).

1   PANORAMA

1 Lushootseed derives from the word stem *ləsh-*, meaning specifically the sheltered salt water of Puget Sound, with *-utsid* for 'river, mouth, language.'

2 Though the seasonal distinction between towns and camps is ingrained in the literature, elders speak of traditional summer camps as more like resorts. Of course, this may be more a reflection of their youth, when hard work was done by adults, but the image is telling. Similarly, native settlements themselves require more varied and suitable English terms such as hamlet, haven, or town.

3 By an irony of history, a writer at Fort Langley on the Fraser River noted the arrival of

Suquamish with salmon in their canoe, which allowed U.S. Federal Judge George Boldt (Finding of Fact #5, Order of 18 April 1975) to decree to their descendants such fishing rights in Canadian waters, though these are unenforceable. Acknowledging this one instance because it was written denied all the others known to have occurred without documentation.

4 Since a standard argument for taking native homelands was that settlers worked better to "improve the land by conquering nature," it is significant that scholars have only recently begun paying attention, first in native California and the Great Plains, to elders explaining how fire was used to maintain open grasslands, hunting grounds, and berry patches. As Walter Crockett, an early settler on Whidbey Island, wrote in 1853, the primary goal of pioneer farming was "to get the land subdued and the wilde nature out of it" (White 1980, 35).

5 Barnett (1955, 13) attributed the invention of reef netting techniques to Straits appreciation of available ocean shoals in compensation for a lack of local salmon streams.

6 A Lummi perspective on these events, now largely self-suppressed to forge unity within the modern reservation community, is provided in "How the Lummi People Came to Their Present Location and How They Got Their Name" by Al Charles (Charles, Demers, and Bowman 1978).

7 Variant English spellings of the same word, both Duhlelap and Tulalip mean "the end far away."

8 Smith (1941) revised this model to include the pasture meadows so important for Nisqually horses, but this need does not reflect aboriginal conditions. As Gibbs (1877, 169) sagely noted, Nisqually fondness for horses created "an exception to the otherwise universal aquatic life of the coast region."

9 These five salmon species can be confusing because of a great variety of local names. All belong to the genus called *Oncorhynchus*, further designated by versions of Kamchatka native names for these species:

O. tshawytscha (chinook, king, spring, quinnat), up to 80 pounds, spawns in large streams or rivers, sometimes with spring and fall subspecies.

O. kisutch (silver), usually 6–12 pounds, up to 30 pounds, runs in early fall but may not spawn until late fall, in smaller streams far from the sea.

O. gorbuscha (pink), 3–10 pounds, spawns early fall, in smaller streams near the sea.

O. keta (chum, dog), 8–18 pounds, spawns late fall, in smaller streams near the sea; flesh is lean and smokes well.

O. nerka (sockeye), usually a few pounds, fattest species, spawns upriver in lakes; when landlocked, known as kokanee.

In addition, steelhead (*Salmo gairdneri*) is a sea-run rainbow trout of up to 36 pounds that, like Atlantic salmon, spawns and returns to the sea. Pacific salmon spawn and die, nourishing local carnivores and enriching poor soil (Suttles 1990, 24–25).

10 Not eating with someone indicates hostility, suspicion, or sorcery. Native children, in particular, are told never to eat with strangers.

11 While Suttles (1987, 187) concluded that "Lord Above" was historically introduced, amplifying a prior belief in a sky or daylight deity, he did not consider that belief in a high god was a guarded privilege of the elite, as among the Calusa of Florida and Yurok of northern California (Miller 1980).

12 Bates, Hess, and Hilbert (1994, 77) suggest derivations of *dxʷda'əb* from either *da'a* 'call, name' or *da'* 'support.'

13 Of all the discussions in this volume, Vi Hilbert had most to say about this section, insisting that I repeatedly rethink and rewrite. While the published literature makes much of this down-/upriver distinction, treating it like an urban/rural one and disparaging those inland as hicks, Hilbert always denied any such contrast, insisting that the riverway was itself a unit.

14 In a fascinating study of such sharing among Tsimshians, greatest prestige in potlatching comes from gifting totally unrelated guests (Dunn 1984).

15 John Slocum and Mary Thompson came from prominent families. John's brothers were Jack and Tom, his father was Old Slocum, and his grandfather Old Chouse, a chief who died in the 1860s at great age. "The Shake" came first to Mary, who I suspect was already an odyssey doctor (Miller 1988, 17).

16 Shaker conversion is all inclusive because when a person becomes a Shaker, all of his or her property and possessions also convert, including spirit helpers. However, ever in command, any spirits who do not want to join the Shaker Church simply leave their human ally.

Nonetheless, another active belief insists on the antagonism between ancient spirits and those of Shakers. Ed Davis said that when he became a Shaker, he turned his back on all the old ways, and a Twana Shaker minister refused to tell Elmendorf traditions he knew well. A woman in the southern part of the sound shriveled up and wasted away because, as a Shaker (Smith 1940, 64), she refused a ghost power that made her "sick to sing"; yet it is unclear if her death was the result of the spirit's own intent, her refusal as a faithful Shaker, or her inability because "she could not talk" to ask for help from other Shakers.

Older Shakers distinctly kept their own spirit help apart from those of the smoke-house church, but this no longer seems to be the case, a wise tolerance helping to protect native beliefs from attack by white officials.

17 The larger implications of the heart = hearth = fire = sun equation are explored in Miller (1980, 1981).

18 Miller once saw a water-filled plastic bowl used to drown a "bad" spirit who had been sent to harm a young boy. The precaution had as much to do with the tender age of the victim as with the strength of the intruder.

2 ETHNOHISTORY

1 As an apt example of how closely Lushootseed identified with their own home villages, the first American sailors on the coast were called Bostons (*pastəd* in Lushootseed) because that was their home port. By contrast, the English were called Kinchachman for "King George's Man."

2 Harmon's own route toward academic history, after fifteen years as a reservation law-yer, is also worth noting since it well illustrates the strains between native, popular, and scholarly concerns. A bogus need for courtroom certainties, shifting native identities, and a desire for personal satisfactions led her to trace through the documentary record

the "image of the Indian" in Puget Sound. In law, this was the process by which modern reservations became "successors in interest" to the native villages and towns along the waterways of the region; in reality, the result was marginality yet resilience.

3 Henry Sicade, the source for this observation, was a Puyallup who was among eighteen students taken in 1880 to form the first class of the Indian Industrial School at Forest Grove, Oregon. When he later expressed interest in furthering his education, Henry Minthorn, Quaker doctor in charge, threw him out and threatened to beat him up if he returned (Reddick 1996). Instead, Sicade graduated from Tualatin Academy and Pacific University before becoming a successful farmer at home and a source for Hermann Haeberlin. In 1885, this industrial school became Chemawa Indian School near Salem, Oregon, still operated by the federal government.

4 The theological basis for these missions responding to a Macedonian call from the Plateau had to do with recruiting numbers for a coming millennium, but when natives did not convert wholesale, missionaries judged them "selfish." Rather than try to understand such cultural differences, they viewed proud intransigence as uncompromising personal obstinacy (C. Miller 1985).

5 Named for the major river off Mount Baker, Nooksak, once a distinct Coast Salishan language, has been replaced by Halkomelem (Fraser River Coast Salish) and by English, while surviving downriver Stockaders have mingled with Straits Salishan Lummi, as described in chapter 1.

6 Many aspects of these early missions also reinforced native beliefs that religious leadership ran along family lines and that shamanism included both curing and schooling. For example, at least three Blanchet brothers served among Catholic clergy (Francis, Bishop of Oregon City; Augustine, Bishop of Walla Walla; and Georges, an Oblate), while the sons of Cushing Eells, Congregationalist missionary among the Spokan, were Myron, missionary at Skokomish, and Edwin, federal Indian agent for the southern sound. The elderly Chirouse—reassigned to the Canadian Fraser in 1878 before he died in 1892 and was buried at Mission—was joined in 1879 by a Oblate nephew of the same name.

Further, in terms of native regard for the spiritual abilities of women, in 1856, at Fort Vancouver, Mother Joseph and the Sisters of Charity established both the first hospital and the first school in Washington state.

7 Father Bolduc actually wrote of Netlan, chief of the Skadjats.

8 After hostilities, the Diocese of Walla Walla was suppressed in favor of that of Nisqually, which, in 1909, became the Diocese of Seattle, from which that of Spokane separated in 1913 (Sullivan 1932, 17). Regional Oblate headquarters moved from the interior to Budd Inlet near Olympia in 1848, before relocating to Esquimalt near Victoria, BC, in 1857.

9 The Durieu system, implemented when he became Bishop of New Westminster in 1875, relied on appointed chiefs and subchiefs to lead by example and keep out undesirable whites such as bootleggers; one or two watchmen to report on moral lapses; soldiers (police) to collect fines, to punish, and to oversee penances; catechists to instruct members in prayers, liturgy, and dogma; and bell ringers ("la cloche," "ting ting" men) to summon everyone to services thrice a day (Whitehead 1981, 18–19). A Eucharist chief worked closely with the local priest, whose overall authority derived from the bishop,

safeguarding spiritual matters. Novenas, processions, and passion plays involved everyone in church pageantry (Duff 1964, 91) to appeal to a "highly developed appreciation of symbolism, mysticism, and solemnity, and Catholic ceremonials were steeped in centuries-old traditions, highly symbolic of past history" (Whitehead 1981, 93). In particular, the community-wide rituals involved in the consecration of a new church had many parallels with the banned potlatch.

10 At Fort Nisqually on 29 July 1837, trader William Kittson gave smallpox inoculations to twenty Nisqually, Snohomish, and Suquamish (Harmon 1995, 110).

11 For a decade after 1869, John Pinnell's famous Seattle brothels such as the Illahee prostituted native girls (Speidel 1967, 113).

12 These are Chinook jargon words, *illahee* meaning "country" and *tillicum* meaning "people, friend, relative."

13 Other denominations arriving in Washington were Disciples of Christ (1855), Baptists (1859), Methodists (1859), Episcopals (1860), and Presbyterians (1853) (Bruege and Rochester 1988, 95). Several early Shakers, particularly Mud Bay Louis Yowaluch, had honed their organizational skills as Presbyterian elders (Ruby and Brown 1996, 118).

3 COSMOS

1 Farther north, the matrilineal nations also believed that the surface of the earth was a round disk, but it rested upon a pole held on the chest of an immortal being, known to the Tsimshian as Smokehole. When he moved the pole, an earthquake resulted. Compare the Nuxalk belief (discussed later in this chapter) about the outstretched rope holding the earth and causing earthquakes when it slackened.

2 Similarly, along the Klamath River, as noted by one of their own, members of the Yurok elite "possessed in their secret breasts the true name of God" (Thompson 1991, 73).

3 This mountain was "broken off" afterward, but Swinomish locate it as the hill where Pioneer Park is now located, near the Rainbow Bridge to La Conner. As confirmation, from the flatness of the Skagit delta, this elevation still stands out on the horizon.

4 According to Dr. Brian Compton (pers. comm.) this bird is probably Swanson's thrush. A thousand miles north, Tsimshian say this bird sings to ripen salmonberries.

5 Given the link between mind and heart as the core of being, the creation of brains from the very soil of that locale, conferring abilities of articulate speech, is an extremely potent reminder of the power of place for a sense of being in these and all other native communities. For example, while Lushootseed located the "mind" at the heart of a person, "thoughts" were also stored in the head, so thought, language, and land were one.

6 The intent of this enchantment was to keep Grizzly from fully concentrating and thus lessening her effectiveness, both physically and spiritually.

7 This hill is across from Big Rock gas station on Highway 9 in the Skagit River valley.

8 Herein, my Star Child (Hilbert 1979) is based on that of Aunt Susie Sampson Peter with her full listing of Skagit place names (Lushootseed Press 1995a) augmented by that of Dora Solomon and a composite in English only (Miller and Hilbert 1996).

9 These first four house support posts were living trees, making an animate equation among all such limbs in the images of body, house and world.

10 This prelude to Star Child appears in Thelma Adamson (1934, 379–84) and was called to my attention by Dale Kinkade. The mother is variously Earthquake or Pheasant, both associated with rumbling or "drumming," while the grandmother is variously Hell Diver, Inch Worm, or Marsh, to fold up the earth to shorten distances.

11 Though this is unstated, she probably became the first nurse log, a term for a fallen tree trunk nourishing seedlings. In 1975, Dora Solomon insisted that by kicking the grandmother back into a log, the older sister thereby kept everyone from reaching ripe old age. Because of her angry act, some people now die before their time.

12 Known as *xachadad*, this mind control concentrated all intelligence. Its strongest form was called *siyu'id*, derived from the high god, and very exclusive. Some epics have two versions, an innocuous story and an esoteric formula with symbolic force. In a familiar story of Coyote trapped in a cave, he takes himself apart and reassembles his body outside. In the esoteric version, he named his pieces with special enchantments which enabled them to remain alive. Such practices resonate around the world, as when Tibetan monks meditate in graveyards to overcome a sense of limited mortality.

13 In a similar Tsimshian account involving Saaban, a chiefly name of the Raven crest, a European longboat is mistaken for a water spider filled with hairy beings (Miller, 1997, 131).

14 Suttles (1951, 357) is confirmed by Amoss (1978, 64).

15 Significantly, while John Slocum was dead the first time, he visited a house with a fenced yard (Ruby and Brown 1996, 4). Entering the open door, he went from room to room until he received a message from God.

16 Because Marian Smith was crippled, native people were very kind in providing her with data not generally shared. The other early monograph to begin with religion was McIlwraith (1948), composed in 1926.

17 As Thom Hess (Amoss 1978, 70) noted, this term has an etymology only in Lushootseed, indicating its origins there, meaning "the thing that bends down over to protect."

18 These wild men ("bigfoot, sasquatch") are known as *ts'yatkʷo*.

19 Among Lushootseeds, such a "leader of the earth" would be a dwarf Little Earth who gave shamans the ability to journey to the afterworld.

20 There is also the possibility that the heart functioned more like a battery, photoelectric cell, or combustion chamber, storing heat for the body, as with heated rocks for stone boiling, sweat bathing, or steaming planks to make bentwood containers.

21 Duff (1952, 85) noted that Franz Boas, Diamond Jenness, and Charles Hill-Tout were also told these traditions, but each received another set of names for these first ancestors. The wonderful thing about such private knowledge was that variants existed side by side among families and neighbors, with each able to glorify its own.

22 Such references to two-headed snakes coincide with the known distribution of the Pacific rubber boa, which does indeed taper at both ends (York, Daly, and Arnett 1993, 273, note 45). Barnett (1955, 158) listed Gulf "swaihwe masks" as beaver, sawbill duck, raven, owl, and spring salmon. Each dancer was protected by family-owned enchantments recited as paint was applied to his toes, hands, and face.

23 According to Dr. Brian Compton, consumption plant is *Lomatium nudicaule*.

24 Many such humanoid stone sculptures have been found around Vancouver (Duff 1975).

25 Note that the universality of houses was so taken for granted that any lack of dwellings was remarkable.

26 This Nuxalk study, filling over seven hundred pages, avoids regional comparisons and theoretical debates. Delayed twenty years, in part for its discussion of ceremonial chastity, it remains our most detailed account of a North Pacific cosmology.

27 The first dome that the carpenters constructed collapsed because it had no supports, so the second one was built with pillars, which were later removed.

28 Tsimshian also make this same connection: their very word for twins means "lots of fish." Other Salishans, however, seem to regard the birth of twins as a sign of divine disfavor, calamity, or disaster (Elmendorf 1960, 421). Twins were elsewhere regarded with fear and disgust, considered too much like an animal litter and thus inhuman.

29 Known as the "sharp against" motif in European peasant folklore, such prickly brushes served to keep dimensions apart. Among the Arrow Lakes Salish of the Plateau, a wild rose branch is used to sweep out freshly dug graves for the same reason, according to elder Charlie Quintasket.

30 Suttles (1977) also listed four systems of power for the Coast Salish: vision quest, ritual words, ancestors, and wealth. Focusing on the Fraser River Sta:lo, Suttles's treatment applied only to some of the traditional beliefs. For Stalo, incantations dominated the other systems, and Duff (1952, 102) suggested that the inheritance of these enchantments was so beneficial that few people went to the trouble to quest for power. Since Suttles's four categories provide only partial coverage, Amoss's four systems are the focus for my discussion because they are more exhaustive.

31 Katzie, as noted, received these secret enchantments from their Creator.

32 Similarly, a deity (high god) forms the nexus (apex?) of the Katzie and Nuxalk systems of beliefs.

33 Data suggest that other Nuxalk worlds also had their own houses, such as that of the Qomoqʷa, lord of the undersea.

4 HOUSES

1 While the plank house was the most usual dwelling, other habitations in the region included pit houses found throughout the Plateau as well as along Fraser River and among Nooksaks (Amoss 1978, 8), where these semi-subterranean houses were ideal for the winter cold on the slopes of Mount Baker. Absolutely unique was a single plank house with a V-shaped roof, to trap rain water, built along the Fraser by a remarkable leader whose name was passed down through six generations (Duff 1952, 44).

2 This Stillaguamish house stood at the confluence of South and Koch sloughs, south of Silvana, Washington. A potlatch house at Trafton contained "pictures carved and painted on wood hung on the walls" which related to "stories" (Bruseth 1950, 10, 11). By analogy with modern practice, these stories probably related to family ancestors.

3 In the Gulf of Georgia, women beat on house walls to disorient the enemy during an attack (Barnett 1955, 270).

4 The most elaborate house is being described here, since many had only a single row of bunks along the sides.

5 During Vancouver's survey of Puget Sound, Archibald Menzies saw dried clam necklaces worn by Lushootseed (Barnett 1955, 60).

6 While Marian Smith located the most prestigious fire in the right downriver corner, as indicated by the reconstructed Nisqually and Puyallup households discussed later, northern Lushootseed households favored the right upstream corner, as confirmed by the order of dancing in modern smokehouses at Tulalip and Swinomish.

7 Undecorated houseposts were draped with baskets, traplines, skins, fishing tackle, and other possessions to keep them handy, according to Henry Sicade (Haeberlin 1917, notebook 28, 31). Sicade also said that the owner of a house lived in the center of it, but it is difficult to interpret this phrase in terms of actual living arrangements, unless he meant control of the central fire.

8 These decorated houseposts were powerful in their own right. Vi Hilbert's father had to retrieve and restore a child's soul which had been taken by a such post when the child went too close to it. Among Tsimshians, totem poles are called "deeds" because, like houseposts, they similarly establish claims to particular lands and resources.

9 Oleman (Old Man) House was probably started by Seattle's father and uncles. The name itself comes from Chinook jargon and refers to something "venerable, esteemed, aged," much as a senior corporate executive is called "the old man."

10 In Lushootseed, the same name applied to both the Sauk and Suiattle drainages, although people lived mostly on Sauk Prairie until driven off by American settlers. Chief John Wawetkin tried repeatedly to recover these lands, to no avail. In the 1890s, Wawetkin's brother Jim Brown and t'i'atmus, a brother-in-law known as Captain Moses, led many Sauks to homestead Indian allotments on the Suiattle. After decades, however, the U.S. Forest Service contested these seventy-seven claims on the technicality that they had to be devoted to farming, though they were densely forested and ideal for logging. The stipulation of "agricultural purposes only" was used to drive these natives to yet another location nearby in the 1920s. In time these lands became the nucleus of a reservation when the Sauk were federally recognized in 1972.

11 After his landing party survived warning shots, Kane (1925, 158) made a sketch of this Toanichum fort (Eaton and Urbanek 1995, 106), where Lok-hi-num was chief. Two days later they crossed to I-eh-nus on Dungeness Spit.

12 Sally Snyder (1964, 383, note 9) summarized the career of yagʷaɬo, the daughter of the Skagit prophet and the wife of Patius. Her name was that of a male ancestor, assumed later in life. Her daughter also rose to high position.

13 Yelm Jim was famous for killing Slugia, the nephew who betrayed Leschi into arrest, leading to his two trials (in the first he was defended by Bing Crosby's grandfather), and his railroading to the gallows (Meeker 1980; Smith 1940, 162; Morgan 1971, 49).

14 Both Sally Snyder and June Collins erred in limiting *slox* to a single house, probably because they did not talk to anyone belonging to this family, such as Vi Hilbert. Collins regarded it as the village of the *basla'alox* band, but this term merely describes those living at *slox*.

Of the six houses there at one time, owners are known for four. In addition to that of Charlie Anderson's father (*su'yius*), homes were owned by Dora Solomon's father, Smokey Lyle's grandfather (*hyas slosh*), and a man named Shoemaker. Charlie's sister was the mother of Dewey Mitchell, a famous Swinomish elder, and two daughters.

After the plank houses were abandoned, a European-style house was build at *slox*, where Vi Hilbert lived as a girl. When John Fornsby's daughter-in-law died there of pneumonia, she was buried in a grave behind the house, suggesting a parallel to the final burial of John's grandfather at his potlatch house near Skagit City.

15 George Gibbs (1877, 203) reported that a carved wooden effigy of Sneatlum stood on a high bank on the eastern side of Whidbey Island, "dressed in his usual costume, and wearing the articles of which he was fond."

16 "In the Comox dialect, the superlative term of address for an aristocratic woman was *tihannan*; for the man, it was *tihegus*" (Barnett 1955, 247, note 3). Any influential man of the upper class was called *hegus*, so the high aristocracy was distinguished by this use of *ti-*.

17 In this context *hik*ʷ means "big, high, most, very."

18 In a discussion that deserves to be much better known, Susan Kenyon (1980, 86), a British subject from Wales, described her difficulties in understanding Nuuchahnulth social organization until a Toquaht chief reminded her that the system was much like her own. Members of the elite were careful to trace their descent from illustrious ancestors, famous in their time, while everyone else relied on kinship for tracing interconnections. In other words, nobles relied on both descent and kinship, but commoners traced only kinship.

19 By implication, Lushootseed thought that the common substance shared by family members was "blood," as in popular European notions of kinship. The continuing importance of "bone" in rituals indicates that it too was significant. In many cultures, "blood" comes to a child from the mother, "bone" from the father, and this arrangement may once have been Lushootseed belief.

20 Barnett (1955, 191) confirmed for Gulf of Georgia Salish that holding up a little finger was a way to belittle other families.

21 Located near modern Grand Coulee Dam, Nespelem, now headquarters for the Colville Reservation, is an Interior Salish community along the Columbia River.

22 Ducks were an autumn staple among Lushootseeds, closely associated with the small hunting canoe. Swinomish keenly felt the precipitate loss of local waterfowl in consequence of the 1920s proliferation of elite "gun clubs" along the lower Skagit. Birds were lured with feed and then blasted away merely for sport, until wholesale destruction was prevented by outlawing such clubs a decade later (Roberts 1975, 283).

23 This deformed nose was regarded as equivalent to the flattened forehead of high-born ́ humans, an areal characteristic of rank. Klallam, Songhees, and Upper Chinook survivors along the Columbia River also celebrated the first salmon ceremony by feeding the first catch to children (Gunther 1928; Boyd 1996).

24 The Puyallup and Nisqually stacked these gifts along one wall (Smith 1940, 104).

25 The name of the growling cult has the sense of being on guard, watchful, fearsome, and protective. The best translation is "vigilantes," but that has wrong connotations in English.

26 Indeed, the most direct source for this cult was the Klukwali Wolf Ritual of the

Nuuchahnulth (Nootkan) tribes of the west coast of Vancouver Island. Ultimately, the cult is a southern extreme in the distribution of dancing orders of the Wakashan (Kwakwaka'wakw and Heiltsuk) peoples of the central coast (Drucker 1940), headquartered at Bella Bella.

27 Elmendorf (1993, 59) described hand gestures used by initiates to indicate their spirit powers.

28 Smokehouses have now reappeared in the south sound, the bastion of Shakers.

5   CANOES

1 According to Kenneth Campbell (pers. comm.), Easthope engines were made in Vancouver BC just after World War I.

6   BODY

1 This generalized life cycle presumes normal development. Yet, as in all human societies, individuals could go wrong, as in the epic of perverse Grizzly Wife. More real and chilling was a Fraser River boy who killed his sister's crying baby by throwing the infant and cradleboard into a fire. Thereafter, he preyed upon travelers, killing for pleasure. To shun him, relatives at Agassiz disbanded and scattered along the south side of the river in about 1840 (Duff 1952, 42). From Chehalis in 1927, Thelma Adamson got a semi-legendary story about a sister-killing brother.

2 All these restrictions imposed on a girl at first menstruation are now observed as taboos by new dancers during their winter seclusion.

3 Ed Davis said that children of elite families were expected to stay married for life, under penalty of being fatally set adrift in a canoe if they became incompatible.

4 Such a dancing procession marked the entry of the shamans into the house to begin an odyssey. Potlatches and feasts may also have included these entrances, indicating another way in which the odyssey reflected the culture as a whole.

5 Angeline, daughter of Seattle, had been so pampered, according to one version, that her Skagit husband sent her home, where she then married a Duwamish man.

6 Wrong way birth was a concern among other tribes, as in the Iroquois epic of the first twins.

7 Diaper Boy was wrung from such a sheet of inner bark.

8 Placing the placenta in a tree invoked a special relationship with the spirits, who hovered above the ground, and by circular reasoning, also marked a renewal because the coffin boxes or canoes of the dead were traditionally placed in trees. Later, any remains were reburied at a special potlatch extolling family honor. In Seattle, such tree cemeteries were located at the foot of Seneca Street and on Foster Island until pioneers had them removed for burial.

9 Martin Sampson (in Matson 1968, 103) gave the impression that this was not the only being or legend event to be dramatized on long rainy evenings. Indeed, before television in the wet Northwest, people provided themselves with endless sources of entertainment drawn from their own cultural traditions.

10 The strength of the communal ethic and sense of togetherness is particularly high-lighted by this special practice of forcing a child to be alone. That it was only a visual and not an auditory separation further supports this social value.

11 As noted for the Tlingit (Kan 1989) and Tsimshian (Miller 1996) of the far north, stone represented the ideal of being dry, heavy, and hard. Presumably, among Lushootseed, elite children used stones instead of sticks when rubbing their bodies during purifica-tion. Several Lushootseed towns once had carved boulders used in weight lifting con-tests, linking stone, town, and high ideals. A Snohomish murderer had to go into seclusion for a month, fasting and staying awake by resting on a jagged rock so that he would never be comfortable. Presumably, since "rocks live forever," the murderer needed this reminder of his crime while also hoping for his own longevity, particularly if avengers were stalking him.

12 Ballard's terms have been updated to conform to present spellings. While he listed $k^wə\mathbf{\lambda} iw$ as a kin term, for modern speakers it means "to go and live with an in-law," indicating only a change of residence rather than a type of relative.

13 Indeed, for a clustering of radiating families and kindreds, this tree image can also represent the anchoring "stem" provided by the inheritance of their greatest and most famous names, the basis for their continuity over generations.

14 See Miller (1985) for these terms and their possible relationship with the term for 'born' ($g^wəts$-). One word for house ($g^wəd^zaltx^w$ = ancestral house) derives from the same lexical.

15 In our best summary, Smith (1940, 78) specifically listed eight types of illnesses and their treatments.

16 Sporadic reports of specialized argots and periodic convocations among shamans for both Americas suggest much cooperation behind the scenes (Miller 1992c), despite public stances of hostility.

17 Again, this intensified sense of place has further ramifications, here in terms of greater vulnerability while away from home.

7 ODYSSEY

1 Although the Chehalis are now living in southwestern Washington, their name for themselves indicates that they moved from Mud Bay on the sound, accounting for this parallel with Lushootseed.

2 As Marian Smith (1940, 81) explained, Lushootseed shamans sometimes cooperated for a single cure, but when they did so, they alternated so that one sang while the other worked on the patient. For the odyssey, shamans worked in unison. Only the Midewiwin (Shamans Academy) of the Great Lakes tribes involved a comparable co-operation among shamans. While that tradition is clearly ancient, its modern proce-dures trace to a religious revival about A.D. 1700 at the Ojibwa capital near Ashland, Wisconsin.

3 Chehalis mentioned Queen Susan as a woman shaman with the power to go to the land of the dead and return (Miller 1988, 24). Twana named five men with retrieval power, along with one woman with a Wolf familiar, who could also make two bundles

of cedarbark dance in the air. Most dramatically, when the odyssey vehicle seemed to get to the top of a mountain, her hair blew straight up; then, when coming down, her hair blew back toward the mountain top. At the bottom, she howled like a wolf (Elmendorf 1993, 74, 227, 230).

4 The best evidence that a single log was used to make all the planks is the graduated widths within any single set and identical knotholes in all the boards at the American Museum of Natural History in New York (Miller 1988, 80).

5 Marian Smith (1946, 310, fig. 3) shows five styles of plank tops drawn by a Suquamish, but these have no other documentation.

6 Details of the manufacture of ritual objects are not well known. The only comparable descriptions were provided by John Fornsby (Collins 1949, 297–98) in terms of the making of power boards. Fornsby himself used three power boards, a spirit he inherited from his grandmother's father. Apparently, while a pair "ran" through the house, Fornsby sang behind the third one. These triple boards are pictured in Haeberlin and Gunther (1930, pl. 1B).

7 Gulf of Georgia Salish believed that Dawn had four phases or aspects, each one prayed to while facing east (Barnett 1955, 212, note 20).

8 An account of the rite from Lucy Williams (Collins 1974, 202), in which a shaman assumed the form of his Beaver power to float in the river as a decoy to lure the ghosts out of their homes, was overlooked in Miller (1988).

9 This quivering may survive as the curing mode of the Shakers. Moses (1997) includes an Indian Shaker Song for Soul Loss on his audio tape.

10 The best known instance was Moses Seattle, a dwarf grandchild of the famous chief.

11 As a boy, Mark R. Harrington, later a prolific Americanist, discovered such an effigy hidden in a tree in West Seattle; it was subsequently added to the collection of the Heye Foundation, now the National Museum of the American Indian. I presume it was a casualty of the 1893 burning out of that Duwamish community (Tollefson 1992).

CONCLUSIONS

1 Contemporary Lushootseed shamans sometimes improve (upgrade) their paraphernalia, as when cloth-covered *sgʷədilich* are replaced by carved wooden ones so that they can withstand energetic use. Sometimes, a spirit simply asks a shaman for a "new house" (a new carved form) to renew or intensify an already familiar power.

BIBLIOGRAPHY

General treatments of Lushootseeds include the works of George Gibbs (1877), James Pilling (1893), Edward Curtis (1913), Hermann Haeberlin and Erna Gunther (1930), Joseph Jorgensen (1969), David Horr (1974, land claims testimony), Wayne Suttles and Barbara Lane (1990), and Thomas Waterman (see all).

Salishan languages and linguistics are considered by Barbara Efrat (1979), Thom Hess (see all), Vi Hilbert (see all), Dale Kinkade (see all), James Pilling (1893), Wayne Suttles and William Elmendorf (1963), and Lawrence and Terry Thompson (1971, 1972).

Regional, tribal, and social aspects are treated by Joel Berreman (1937), Charles Buchanan (1916), Kathleen Mooney (1976, 1978), Leslie Spier (1936), Wayne Suttles (see all), Colin Tweddell (1984), Thomas Waterman and Geraldine Coffin (1920), Thomas Waterman and Ruth Greiner (1921), Bruce Miller (1989b), and Thomas Waterman and others (1921).

Oral literature and folklore are presented by Arthur Ballard (1927, 1929), Vi Hilbert (see all), and, dubiously, James Costello (1974). Robert Walls (1987) includes a bibliography.

Traditional and modern economy are discussed by Michael Kew (1976), Rolf Knight (1978), Leland Donald and Donald Mitchell (1975), Wayne Suttles (see all), Nancy Turner (1975), and Ellen Michaud (1977). Gender and modern politics are featured in the work of Bruce Miller (1992, 1994, 1995).

Regional history, from a European perspective, occurs in Clarence Bagley (1915–16), Arthur Denny (1909), Wilson Duff (1964), Mary Gormly (1977), Barbara Lane (1973), Edward Meany (1957), Roberta Watt (1931), and Richard White (1980).

Sources for the various Lushootseed "tribes" are the following, with native authors marked by an asterisk:

Skagit (including the Sauk-Suiattle): Sally Snyder (1964, 1975), June Collins (see all), Vi Hilbert* (see all), Joyce Wike (1941), Frederick Hulse (1955, 1957), Bruce Miller (1989), and Martin Sampson* (1938, 1972).

Swinomish: Natalie Roberts (1975).

Stillaguamish: Nels Bruseth (1950).

Snohomish (including Skykomish): Hermann Haeberlin (1917, 1918, 1924), Thom Hess (see all), William Shelton* (1932), and Colin Tweddell (1974).

Snoqualmi: Thomas Bishop* (1916), Margaret Corliss (1972), Ada Hill (1970), Colin Tweddell (1950), and Kenneth Tollefson (see all).

Duwamish (including Muckleshoot): Duwamish and others (1933), Arthur Ballard (see all), J. P. Harrington (1910, cf. Mills 1981), Jay Ransom (1945), Kenneth Tollefson (1989) and Thomas Waterman (see all).

Puyallup: Marian Smith (1940, 1941, cf. Amoss 1975).

Nisqually: George Gibbs (1970), Marian Smith (1940, 1941) and James Wickersham (1898).

Sahewamish: William Elmendorf (1960), Marian Smith (1940).

Suquamish: Susan Blalock (1979), Hal Kennedy and Karen James (1981), Barbara Lane (1974), Jay Miller and Warren Snyder (ms.), Warren Snyder (1956, 1968), E. E. Riddell (1932), and Suquamish Museum (1985).

For neighboring peoples, sources are the following:

Fraser Halkomelem (Halq'emeylem): Frances Densmore (1943), Wilson Duff (1952), Brent Galloway (1977, 1980), Wolfgang Jilek (1982), Diamond Jenness (1955), Wayne Suttles (1987, 1990), and Oliver Wells (1987).

Lummi (Straits): Bernard Stern (1934) and Wayne Suttles (1951, 1954).

Samish: Kathleen Bishop and Kenneth Hansen* (1978), Charles Roblin (1919), and Suttles (1990).

Klallam: Erna Gunther (1925, 1927, ms.), Laurence and Terry Thompson (1971), Laurence Thompson and Claudine Poggi (ms.).

Nooksak: Paul Fetzer (1951), Allan Richardson (1974), Pamela Amoss (1978).

Twana (including Skokomish): Gaberell Drachman (1969), Myron Eells (see all), William Elmendorf (see all), Barbara Lane (c. 1974), and Robert Lewis* (1942).

Interior Salish Columbians: Dale Kinkade (1981) and Jay Miller (1990).

Sahaptians: Darlene Fitzpatrick (1968), Eugene Hunn (1990), and Melville Jacobs (1932).

Chinook: Melville Jacobs (1959), Verne Ray (1938), Leslie Spier and Edward Sapir (1930), and Jeff Zucker, Kay Hummel, and Bob Hogfoss (1983).

Columbia River Athapaskans (Kwaliokwa, Klatskanie): cf. Wayne Suttles (1990).

Cowlitz: Thelma Adamson (1934).

Chehalis: Thelma Adamson (1934), Dale Kinkade (1963–64), and Katherine Palmer (1925).

Quinault: Ronald Olson (1936), Ram Raj Singh (1966).

Quileute: Manuel Andrade (1931), George Pettitt (1950), Jay Powell and Vickie Jensen (1976), and Jay Powell and Fred Woodruff* (1976).

Makah (including Ozette): Ann Bates (1987), Erna Gunther (1973), James Swan (1971), USA v. Washington State (1981), and Thomas Waterman (1920).

Nootkans (Nuuchanuulth): Eugene Arima (1983), Frances Densmore (1939), Philip Drucker (1951), Barbara Efrat and W. J. Langlois (1978), and Joyce Wike (1958).

Kwakiutlans: Franz Boas (see all, via George Hunt,* Dan Cranmer*), Leland Donald and Donald Mitchell (1975), Irving Goldman (1975), and Stanley Walens (1981).

Nuxalk (Bella Coola): Philip Davis and Ross Saunders (1980, 1997), Thomas McIlwraith (1948), and Stanley Newman (1969).

Abbott, Donald, ed.
   1981 *The World Is as Sharp as a Knife: An Anthology in Honour of Wilson Duff*. Victoria: British Columbia Provincial Museum.
Adamson, Thelma
   1934 *Folktales of the Coast Salish*. Memoirs of the American Folklore Society 27.

Allen, E. J., Jr.

1976 Intergroup Ties and Exogamy among the Northwest Coast Salish. *Northwest Anthropological Research Notes* 10: 161–172.

Allen, Henry

1950 Two Soul Recovery Songs. Recorded by Willard Rhodes in August and September. Reel 16. Bureau of Indian Affairs, Educational Division, American Folklife Center, Library of Congress.

Amoss, Pamela

1975 Catalogue of the Marian Smith Collection of Fieldnotes, Manuscripts, and Photographs in the Library of the Royal Anthropological Institute of Great Britain and Ireland.

1978 *Coast Salish Spirit Dancing: The Survival of an Ancestral Religion*. Seattle: University of Washington Press.

1981 Coast Salish Elders. Pp. 227–61 in *Other Ways of Growing Old*, ed. Pamela Amoss and Steven Harrell. Palo Alto: Stanford University Press.

1982 Resurrection, Healing, and "the Shake": The Story of John and Mary Slocum. Special Issue: *Charisma and Sacred Biography*, ed. Michael Williams. *Journal of the American Academy of Religion, Thematic Studies* 48 (3–4): 87–109.

1987 The Fish God Gave Us: The First Salmon Ceremony Revived. *Arctic Anthropology* 24 (1): 56–66.

Andrade, Manuel

1931 Quileute Texts. Columbia University Contributions to Anthropology 12.

Aoki, Haruo

1966 Nez Perce and Proto-Sahaptian Kinship Terms. *International Journal of American Linguistics* 32 (4): 357–68.

Arima, Eugene

1983 *The West Coast People: The Nootka of Vancouver Island and Cape Flattery*. British Columbia Provincial Museum, Special Publication 6.

Asher, Brad

1995 A Shaman-killing Case on Puget Sound, 1873–1874: American Law and Salish Culture. *Pacific Northwest Quarterly* 86 (1): 17–24.

Bagley, Clarence

1931 Chief Seattle and Angeline. *Washington Historical Quarterly* 22: 243–75.

1980 *In the Beginning: Early Days on Puget Sound*. 1905. Reprint, Everett: Historical Society of Seattle and King County.

Bagley, Clarence, ed.

1915 Journal of Occurrences at Nisqually House, 1833. *Washington Historical Quarterly* 6 (3): 179–97, (4): 264–78.

1916 Journal of Occurrences at Nisqually House. *Washington Historical Quarterly* 7 (1): 59–75, (2): 144–67.

Ballard, Arthur

1927 Some Tales of the Southern Puget Sound Salish. *University of Washington Publications in Anthropology* 2 (3): 57–81.

1929 Mythology of Southern Puget Sound. *University of Washington Publications in Anthropology* 3 (2): 31–150.

1935 Southern Puget Sound Salish Kinship Terms. *American Anthropologist* 37 (1): 111–16.

1950 Calendric Terms of the Southern Puget Sound Salish. *Southwestern Journal of Anthropology* 6 (1): 79–99.

1957 The Salmon-Weir on Green River in Western Washington. *Davidson Journal of Anthropology* 3: 37–53.

Barnett, Homer

   1955 *The Coast Salish of British Columbia*. Studies in Anthropology 4. Eugene: University of Oregon Press.

   1957 *Indian Shakers: A Messianic Cult of the Pacific Northwest*. Carbondale: Southern Illinois University Press.

Barsh, Russell

   1991 Backfire from Boldt: The Judicial Transformation of Coast Salish Proprietary Fisheries into a Commons. Western Legal History 4: 85–102.

Bates, Ann M.

   1987 Affiliation and Differentiation: Intertribal Interactions among the Makah and Ditidaht Indians. Ph.D. dissertation, Indiana University.

Bates, Dawn, Thom Hess, and Vi Hilbert

   1994 *Lushootseed Dictionary*. Seattle: University of Washington Press.

Beckham, Stephen Low

   1969 George Gibbs, 1815–1873: Historian and Anthropologist. Ph.D. dissertation, University of California at Los Angeles.

Bennett, Lee

   1972 Effect of White Contact on the Lower Skagit Indians. Washington Archaeological Society Occasional Papers 3.

Berreman, Joel

   1937 Tribal Distribution in Oregon. Memoirs of the American Anthropological Association 47.

Bierwert, Crisca

   1993 "Poetic Fancy": A Glimpse at the Translative Commentary of Martin J. Sampson. Pp. 529–42 in *New Voices in Native American Literary Criticism*, ed. Arnold Krupat. Washington DC: Smithsonian Institution Press.

Bierwert, Crisca, ed.

   1996 *Lushootseed Texts: An Introduction to Puget Salish Aesthetics*. Translated by Crisca Bierwert, Vi Hilbert, Thomas M. Hess; annotations by Toby C.S. Langen. Lincoln: University of Nebraska Press.

Bishop, Kathleen, and Kenneth Hansen

   1978 The Landless Tribes of Western Washington. *American Indian Journal* 4 (5): 20–31.

Bishop, Thomas

   1916 Applications for Enrollment and Allotment, 1911–17. Records Relating to Enrollment of Washington Indians. Special Agent Charles E. Roblin. National Archives.

Blalock, Susan

   1979 List of Suquamish Settlements. Suquamish Tribal Library and Archives.

Boas, Franz

   1919 Kinship Terms of the Kutenai Indians. *American Anthropologist* 21 (1): 98–101.

1966 *Kwakiutl Ethnography*. Helen Codere, ed. Chicago: University of Chicago Press.

Boas, Franz, and Hermann Haeberlin

1927 Sound Shifts in Salishan Dialects. *International Journal of American Linguistics* 4 (2–4): 117–36.

Bolduc, John

1941 Letter. Pp.79–81 in *Readings in Pacific Northwest History. Washington, 1790–1895*, ed. Charles Marvin Gates. Seattle: University Bookstore.

Boxberger, Daniel, and Bruce Miller

1997 Evolution or History?: A Response to Tollefson. *Ethnohistory* 44 (1): 135–37.

Boyd, Robert

1996 *People of the Dalles: The Indians of Wascopam Mission*. Lincoln: University of Nebraska Press.

Bruege, David, and Junius Rochester

1988 *Roots and Branches: The Religious Heritage of Washington State*. Seattle: Church Council of Greater Seattle.

Bruseth, Nels

1950 *Indian Stories and Legends of the Stillaguamish, Sauks and Allied Tribes*. Arlington (WA) Times Press.

Buchanan, Charles

1916 Rights of the Puget Sound Indians to Game and Fish. *Washington Historical Quarterly* 6 (2): 109–18.

Buchler, Ira, and Henry Selby

1968 *Kinship and Social Organization: An Introduction to Theory and Method*. New York: Macmillan.

Carlson, Barry, and Thom Hess

1971 Canoe Names in the Northwest: An Areal Study. *Anthropological Linguistics* 12 (1): 17–24.

Carlson, Frank

1903 Chief Sealth. University of Washington Bulletin, series 3 (2): 7–35.

Carpenter, Cecelia Svinth

1986 *Fort Nisqually: A Documented History of Indian and British Interaction*. Tacoma: Tahoma Research Service.

1994 *Where the Waters Begin: The Traditional Nisqually Indian History of Mount Rainier*. Seattle: Northwest Interpretive Association.

CARTAH

1997a Nine Categories. Lushootseed CD ROM GNA 220. Seattle: University of Washington Center for Advanced Research Technology in the Arts and Humanities.

1997b Martin Sampson. Lushootseed CD ROM GNA 227. Seattle: University of Washington Center for Advanced Research Technology in the Arts and Humanities.

1997c Charley and Louisa Anderson Perform Indian Songs. Lushootseed CD ROM GNA 246A. Seattle: University of Washington Center for Advanced Research Technology in the Arts and Humanities.

1997d Charley and Louisa Anderson Perform Indian Songs. Lushootseed CD ROM GNA 246B. Seattle: University of Washington Center for Advanced Research Technology in the Arts and Humanities.

1997e Aunt Susie Stories. Lushootseed CD ROM GNA 247A. Seattle: University of Washington Center for Advanced Research Technology in the Arts and Humanities.

1997f Aunt Susie Stories. Lushootseed CD ROM GNA 247B. Seattle: University of Washington Center for Advanced Research Technology in the Arts and Humanities.

Castile, George

    1982 The "Half-Catholic" Movement: Edwin and Myron Eells and the Rise of the Indian Shaker Church. *Pacific Northwest Quarterly* 73: 165–74.

Castile, George, ed.

    1985 *The Indians of Puget Sound: The Notebooks of Myron Eells*. Walla Walla: University of Washington Press for Whitman College.

Chalcraft, Edward

    ms. Autobiography of Edward Chalcraft. Washington State Library, Ms. 039.

Charles, Al, Richard Demers, and Elizabeth Bowman

    1978 Introduction to the Lummi Language. Bellingham WA.

Collins, June

    1949 John Fornsby: The Personal Document of a Coast Salish Indian. Pp. 287–341 in Smith 1949.

    1950a Growth of Class Distinctions and Political Authority among the Skagit Indians During the Contact Period. *American Anthropologist* 52 (3): 331–42.

    1950b The Indian Shaker Church. *Southwestern Journal of Anthropology* 6: 399–411.

    1952a An Interpretation of Skagit Intragroup Conflict during Acculturation. *American Anthropologist* 54: 347–55.

    1952b The Mythological Basis for Attitudes toward Animals among Salish-Speaking Indians. *Journal of American Folklore* 65 (258): 353–59.

    1966 Naming, Continuity, and Social Inheritance among the Coast Salish of Western Washington. *Papers of the Michigan Academy of Science, Arts, and Letters* 51: 425–36.

    1974 *Valley of the Spirits: The Upper Skagit Indians of Western Washington*. Seattle: University of Washington Press.

    1979 Multilineal Descent: A Coast Salish Strategy. Pp. 243–54 in *Currents in Anthropology*, ed. Robert Hinshaw. The Hague: Mouton.

Corliss, Margaret M.

    1972 The Snoqualmie Indians. Ch. 12 in *Fall City in the Valley of the Moon*. University of Washington, Northwest Special Collections.

Costello, James

    1974 *The Siwash: Their Life, Legends, and Tales of Puget Sound and Pacific Northwest*. 1895. Reprint, Everett WA: Paine Field Printers.

Curtis, Edward

    1913 *The North American Indian: Being a Series of Volumes Picturing and Describing the Indians of the United States, the Dominion of Canada, and Alaska*. Written, illustrated, and published by Edward S. Curtis. Frederick Webb Hodge, ed. Vol. 9 of 20.

Davis, Philip, and Ross Saunders

    1980 *Bella Coola Texts*. British Columbia Provincial Museum, Heritage Record 10.

    1997 *A Grammar of Bella Coola*. University of Montana Occasional Papers in Linguistics 13.

Denny, Emily Inez

1894 Types and Characteristics of Puget Sound Indians. *Northwest Magazine* 12: 4–6. September.

1909 *Blazing the Way: True Stories, Songs and Sketches of Puget Sound and Other Pioneers.* Seattle: Rainier Printing Company.

Densmore, Frances

1939 *Nootka and Quileute Music.* Bureau of American Ethnology, Bulletin 124.

1943 *Music of the Indians of British Columbia.* Bureau of American Ethnology, Bulletin 136, Anthropological Paper 27: 1–99.

Donald, Leland, and Donald Mitchell

1975 Some Correlates of Local Group Rank among the Southern Kwakiutl. *Ethnology* 14 (4): 325–46.

Dorsey, George

1898 Accession 660: Salish of Puget Sound and Lake Washington. Chicago: Field Museum # 55848-55960.

1902 "The Duwamish Spirit-Canoe and Its Use." *Bulletin Free Museum of Science and Art,* University of Pennsylvania 3 (4): 227–238.

Drachman, Gaberell

1969 *Twana Phonology.* Working Papers in Linguistics 5. Columbus: Ohio State University.

Drucker, Philip

1937 Diffusion in Northwest Coast Culture in the Light of Some Distributions. Ph.D. dissertation, University of California, Berkeley.

1940 Kwakiutl Dancing Societies. *Anthropological Records* 6 (6): 201–30.

1951 *The Northern and Central Nootkan Tribes.* Bureau of American Ethnology, Bulletin 141.

Duff, Wilson

1952 *The Upper Stalo Indians of the Fraser River of British Columbia.* British Columbia Provincial Museum, Anthropology in British Columbia, Memoir 1.

1964 *The Indian History of British Columbia.* Vol. 1: *The Impact of the White Man.* British Columbia Provincial Museum, Anthropology in British Columbia, Memoir 5.

1975 *Images, Stone, BC: Thirty Centuries of Northwest Coast Indian Sculpture.* Saanichton BC: Hancock House.

1981 Thoughts on the Nootka Canoe. Pp. 201–6 in Abbott 1981.

Dunn, John

1984 Tsimshian Grandchildren. Pp. 36–57 in *The Tsimshian and Their Neighbors of the North Pacific Coast,* ed. Jay Miller and Carol Eastman. Seattle: University of Washington Press.

Durlach, Teresa

1928 *The Relationship Systems of the Tlingit, Haida, and Tsimshian.* American Ethnological Society, vol. 11.

Duwamish and Others

1933 Consolidated Petition in the U.S. Court of Claims. 2 vols.

Eaton, Diane, and Sheila Urbanek

1995 *Paul Kane's Great Nor-West.* Vancouver: University of British Columbia Press.

Edmonson, Munro

1958 *Status Terminology and the Social Structure of North American Indians*. American Ethnological Society, Monograph 30.

Eells, Myron

1884 Census of the Clallam and Twana Indians of Washington Territory. *American Antiquarian* 6: 35–38.

1887 The Indians of Puget Sound. 9 parts. *American Antiquarian* 9.

1889 The Twana, Chemakum, and Klallam Indians of Washington Territory. Pp. 605–81 in Smithsonian Annual Report for 1887.

1985 *The Indians of Puget Sound. The Notebooks of Myron Eells*. Ed. George Pierre Castille. Seattle: University of Washington Press.

Efrat, Barbara

1979 The Victoria Conference on Northwestern Languages. British Columbia Provincial Museum, Heritage Record 4.

Efrat, Barbara, and W. J. Langlois

1978 Nu.tka: The History and Survival of Nootkan Culture. *Sound Heritage* 7 (2): 1–62.

Eggan, Fred

1955 The Cheyenne and Arapaho Kinship System. Pp. 33–95 in *Social Anthropology of North American Tribes*, ed. Fred Eggan. Chicago: University of Chicago Press.

Elmendorf, William

1935 The Soul-Recovery Ceremony among the Indians of the Northwest Coast. M.A. thesis, University of Washington.

1946 Twana Kinship Terminology. *Southwestern Journal of Anthropology* 2: 420–32.

1948 The Cultural Setting of the Twana Secret Society. *American Anthropologist* 50: 625–33.

1960 *The Structure of Twana Culture*. Pullman: Washington State Research Studies, Monographic Supplement 2. (With comparative notes on the structure of Yurok by Alfred Kroeber.)

1961a Skokomish and Other Coast Salish Tales. Washington State University Research Studies 29 (1): 1–37, (2): 84–117, (3): 119–50.

1961b System Change in Salish Kinship Terminologies. *Southwestern Journal of Anthropology* 17 (4): 365–82.

1970 Skokomish Sorcery, Ethics, and Society. Ch. 6 in *Systems of North American Witchcraft and Sorcery*, ed. Deward Walker. Anthropological Monographs of the University of Idaho 1.

1971 Coast Salish Status Ranking and Intergroup Ties. *Southwestern Journal of Anthropology* 27: 353–81.

1982 Deposition of February 25 and 26. Davis, California. Civil # 9213—Phase I.

1993 *Twana Narratives: Native Historical Accounts of a Coast Salish Culture*. Seattle: University of Washington Press.

Ermatinger, F.

1907 Earliest Expedition against Puget Sound Indians. Ed. Eva Emery Dye. *Washington Historical Quarterly* 1: 16–29.

Espey, Willard R.

1977 *Oysterville: Roads to Grandpa's Village*. New York: Clarkson N. Potter.

Farrar, Victor, ed.

1916–17 Diary of Colonel and Mrs. I. N. Ebey. *Pacific Northwest Quarterly* [1916] 7: 307–41; [1917] 8: 40–62, 124–52.

1919–24 Journal of Occurrences at Nisqually House, 1849–1852. *Pacific Northwest Quarterly* [1919] 10: 205–30; [1920] 11: 59–65, 136–49, 218–29, 294–302; [1921] 12: 68–70, 137–48, 219–28, 300–3; [1922] 13: 57–60, 131–41, 225–32, 293–99; [1923] 14: 145–48, 223–34, 299–306; [1924] 15: 63–66, 215–26, 289–98.

Fetzer, Paul

1951 George Swanaset: Narrative of a Personal Document. University of Washington Libraries, Melville Jacobs Collection, accession number 1693-71-13, box 112. 27 pp.

Fitzhugh, William, and Aron Crowell, eds.

1988 *Crossroads of Continents*: Cultures of Siberia and Alaska. Washington: Smithsonian Institution Press.

1993 *Twana Narratives: Native Historical Accounts of a Coast Salish Culture*. Seattle: University of Washington Press.

Fitzpatrick, Darlene

1968 The "Shake": The Indian Shaker Curing Ritual among the Yakima. M.A. thesis, University of Washington.

Galbraith, John S.

1954 The Early History of the Puget's Sound Agricultural Company, 1838–1843. *Washington Historical Quarterly* 55: 234–59.

Galin, Anne

1983 Spatial Organization in Lushootseed Culture, Texts, and Language. Ph.D. dissertation, Columbia University.

Galloway, Brent

1977 A Grammar of Chilliwack Halkomelem. Ph.D. dissertation, University of California, Berkeley.

1980 Upper Halqemeylem Grammatical Sketch and Classified Word List. Sardis BC: Coqualeetza Education Training Centre.

Gellatly, Marjorie Gail

1940 Fourteen Northwest Coast Indian Songs Transcribed into Musical Notation. M.A. thesis, University of Washington.

Gibbs, George

1877 Tribes of Western Washington and Northwestern Oregon. Washington: Department of the Interior, United States Geographical and Geological Survey of the Rocky Mountain Region, part 2: 157–241.

1970 Dictionary of the Niskwalli (Nisqually) Indian Language—Western Washington. Extract from 1877 Contributions to North American Ethnology 1: 285–361. Seattle: Shorey Book Store Facsimile Reproduction.

Gifford, Edward

1922 *Californian Kinship Terminologies*. University of California Publications in American Archaeology and Ethnology 18.

Goldman, Irving

1975 *The Mouth of Heaven: An Introduction to Kwakiutl Religious Thought*. New York: John Wiley and Sons.

Goodenough, Ward

   1970 *Description and Comparison in Cultural Anthropology*. Chicago: Aldine Publishing Co.

Gormly, Mary

   1977 Early Culture Contact on the Northwest Coast, 1774–1795: Analysis of Spanish Sources. *Northwest Anthropological Research Notes* 11 (1): 1–80.

Graburn, Nelson

   1971 *Readings in Kinship and Social Structure*. New York: Harper and Row.

Guilmet, George, and David Whited

   1989 The People Who Give More: Health and Mental Health among the Contemporary Puyallup Indian Tribal Community. *American Indian and Alaska Native Mental Health Research Journal* vol. 2 (winter), Monograph 2: 1–141.

Guilmet, George, Robert Boyd, David Whited, and Nile Thompson

   1991 The Legacy of Introduced Diseases. *American Indian Culture and Research Journal* 15 (4): 1–32.

Gunther, Erna

   ms. Culture Element Distributions: Puget Sound (Duwamish, Skokomish, Klallam, Makah). Berkeley CA: Bancroft Library.

   1925 Klallam Folk Tales. *University of Washington Publications in Anthropology* 1 (4): 113–70.

   1927 Klallam Ethnography. *University of Washington Publications in Anthropology* 1 (5): 171–310.

   1928 A Further Analysis of the First Salmon Ceremony. *University of Washington Publications in Anthropology* 2 (5): 129–73.

   1973 *Ethnobotany of Western Washington: The Knowledge and Use of Indigenous Plants by Native Americans*. Seattle: University of Washington Press.

Haeberlin, Hermann

   1917 Puget Salish, 42 notebooks. National Anthropological Archives. #2965.

   1918 SbEtEtda'q: A Shamanic Performance of the Coast Salish. *American Anthropologist* 20 (3): 249–57.

   1924 Mythology of Puget Sound. *Journal of American Folklore* 37 (143–44): 371–438.

Haeberlin, Hermann, and Erna Gunther

   1930 The Indians Of Puget Sound. *University of Washington Publications in Anthropology* 4 (1): 1–84.

Hallowell, A. Irving

   1992 The Ojibwa of Berens River, Manitoba. Ed. Jennifer S. H. Brown. Case Studies in Cultural Anthropology. Orlando: Harcourt Brace Jovanovich College Publishers.

Harmon, Alexandra

   1995 A Different Kind of Indians: Negotiating the Meanings of "Indian" and "Tribe" in the Puget Sound Region, 1820s–1970s. 2 vols. Ph.D. dissertation, University of Washington.

Harper, J. Russell, ed.

   1971 *Paul Kane's Frontier*. Austin: University of Texas Press.

Harrington, John P.

   1910 Lummi/Duwamish. Microfilm of Fieldnotes. (Cited by frame).

1942 Chemakum/Clallam/Makah/Quileute. Microfilm of Fieldnotes. (Cited by frame).

Harris, Ethel van
1926 Early Historical Incidents of Skagit County. University of Washington, Northwest Special Collections.

Heath, Joseph
1979 *Memoirs of Nisqually*. Fairfield WA: Ye Galleon Press.

Hess, Thom
1971 Prefix Constituent With /xʷ/. Pp. 43–69 in *Studies in Northwest Indian Languages*, ed. James Hoard and Thom Hess. Sacramento Anthropological Society, Paper 11.
1976 *Dictionary of Puget Salish*. Seattle: University of Washington Press.
1977 Lushootseed Dialects. *Anthropological Linguistics* 19 (9): 403–19.

Hilbert, Vi (taqʷsəblu)
1976 Recording in the Native Language. *Sound Heritage* 4 (3–4): 39–42.
1979 *Yehaw*. Privately Printed.
1980a *Huboo*. Privately Printed.
1980b *Ways of the Lushootseed People: Ceremonies and Traditions of the Northern Puget Sound Indians*. Seattle: United Indians of All Tribes Foundation, Daybreak Star Press.
1985 *Haboo: Native American Stories from Puget Sound*. Seattle: University of Washington Press.

Hill, Ada Snyder
1970 *A History of the Snoqualmie Valley*. Reprinted, 1994, North Bend WA: Snoqualmie Valley Historical Museum.

Hoebel, Adamson
1939 Comanche and H3kandika Shoshone Relationship Systems. *American Anthropologist* 41 (3): 440–57.

Horr, David Agee
1974 Coast Salish and Western Washington Indians v. Indian Claims Commission. Findings. New York: Garland Publishing.

Hulse, Frederick
1955 Blood-types and Mating Patterns among Northwest Coast Indians. *Southwestern Journal of Anthropology* 11 (2): 93–104.
1957 Linguistic Barriers to Gene-Flow; The Blood-Groups of the Yakima, Okanagon, and Swinomish Indians." *American Journal of Physical Anthropology* 15 (2): 235–46.

Hunn, Eugene
1990 *Nch'i-wana, "The Big River": Mid-Columbia Indians and Their Land*. Seattle: University of Washington Press.

Indian Claims Commission
1952 Suquamish Tribe of Indians v. United States of America. Docket 132.

Jacobs, Melville
1932 Northern Sahaptin Kinship Terms. *American Anthropologist* 34 (4): 688–93.
1958 The Romantic Role of Older Women in a Culture of the Pacific Northwest Coast. *Kroeber Anthropological Society Papers* 18: 79–85.
1959 *The Content and Style of an Oral Literature*. Viking Fund Publications in Anthropology 26.

Jacobs, Orange.

1909 *Memoirs*. Seattle: Hanford & Lowman.

Jenness, Diamond

1955 *The Faith of a Coast Salish Indian*. British Columbia Provincial Museum, Anthropology in British Columbia, Memoir 3.

Jilek, Wolfgang

1982 *Indian Healing: Shamanic Ceremonialism in the Pacific Northwest Today*. Surrey BC: Hancock House.

Jorgensen, Joseph

1969 *Salish Language and Culture: A Statistical Analysis of Internal Relationships, History, and Evolution*. Bloomington: Indiana University Language Science Monographs 3.

Kan, Sergei

1989 *Symbolic Immortality: The Tlingit Potlatch in the Nineteenth Century*. Washington: Smithsonian Institution Press.

Kane, Paul

1925 *Wanderings of an Artist among the Indians of North America, from Canada to Vancouver's Island and Oregon through the Hudson's Bay Company's Territory, and Back Again*. 1858. Reprint, Toronto: Radisson Society of Canada.

Kappler, Charles

1904 *Indian Affairs 2: Treaties 1778–1883*. Washington: Government Printing Office.

Kennedy, Hal, and Karen James

1981 *Cultural Resource Assessment of the Big Beef Creek Research Facility near Seabeck, Kitsap County, Washington*. University of Washington, Office of Public Archaeology, Reconnaissance Report 37.

Kenyon, Susan

1980 *The Kyuquot Way: A Study of a West Coast (Nootkan) Community*. National Museums of Canada, Mercury Series, Canadian Ethnology Service, Paper 61.

Kew, Michael

1976 Salmon Abundance, Technology and Human Population on the Fraser River Watershed. Paper Delivered at the Northwest Coast Studies Conference, Simon Fraser University.

Kew, Michael, and Della Kew

1981 People Need Friends, It Makes Their Minds Strong: A Coast Salish Curing Rite. Pp. 29–35 in Abbott 1981.

Kinkade, Dale

1963–64 Phonology and Morphology of Upper Chehalis. *International Journal of American Linguistics* 29 (3): 181–95, 29 (4): 345–56, 30 (1): 32–61, 251–60.

1981 *Dictionary of the Moses-Columbia Language*. Nespelem: Colville Confederated Tribes.

1983 Salish Evidence against the Universality of 'Noun' and 'Verb.' *Lingua* 60 (1): 25–40.

Knight, Rolf

1978 *Indians at Work: An Informal History of Native Indian Labour in British Columbia 1858–1930*. Vancouver: New Star Books.

Kroeber, Alfred

1909 Classificatory Systems of Relationships. *Journal of the Royal Anthropological Institute* 39: 77–84.

1960 Comparative Notes on the Structure of Yurok Culture. In Elmendorf 1960.

Lane, Barbara

1973 Political and Economic Aspects of Indian-White Culture Contact in Western Washington in the Mid-19th Century. 10 May. United States v. Washington.

c1974 Anthropological Report on the Identity, Treaty Status, and Fisheries of the Skokomish Tribe of Indians.

1974 Identity, Treaty Status and Fisheries of the Suquamish Tribe of the Port Madison Reservation.

Leechman, John D.

1920 Bibliography of the Anthropology of the Puget Sound Indians. *Washington Historical Quarterly* 11: 266–73.

Lewis, Robert

1942 Affidavit Concerning the Skokomish Indians. In *Report on Source, Nature, and Extent of the Fishing, Hunting, and Miscellaneous Related Rights of Certain Indian Tribes of Washington and Oregon Together with Affidavits Showing Location of a Number of Usual and Accustomed Fishing Grounds and Stations*, by B. G. Swindell. Department of the Interior, Office of Indian Affairs, Division of Forestry and Grazing. Los Angeles CA.

Lincoln, Leslie

1991 *Coast Salish Canoes*. Seattle: Center for Wooden Boats.

Lushootseed Press

1995a *Aunt Susie Sampson Peter: The Wisdom of a Skagit Elder*. Transcribed by Vi Hilbert. Translated by Vi Hilbert and Jay Miller. Recorded by Leon Metcalf. Seattle.

1995b *Gram Ruth Sehome Shelton: The Wisdom of a Tulalip Elder*. Transcribed by Vi Hilbert. Translated by Vi Hilbert and Jay Miller. Recorded by Leon Metcalf. Seattle.

1995c *Petius Isadore Tom: The Wisdom of a Lummi Elder*. Seattle.

1996 *Lady Louse Lived There*. Ed. Janet Yoder. Compiled by Vi Hilbert. Illustrated by Brad Burns. Seattle.

Marino, Cesare

1990 History of Western Washington since 1846. Pp. 169–179 in Suttles 1990.

Matson, Emerson

1968 *Longhouse Legends*. Camden NJ: Thomas Nelson and Sons.

1972 *Legends of the Great Chiefs*. Tacoma: Storypole Press.

McIlwraith, Thomas

1948 *The Bella Coola Indians*. 2 vols. Toronto: University of Toronto Press.

Meany, Edmund

1924 Chief Patkanim. *Washington Historical Quarterly* 15: 187–98.

1957 *Vancouver's Discovery of Puget Sound: Portraits and Biographies of the Men Honored in the Naming of the Geographical Features of Northwestern America*. 1907. Reprint, Portland: Binford and Mort.

Meeker, Ezra

1980 *The Tragedy of Leschi*. 1905. Reprint, Everett WA: Printers.

Michaud, Ellen

1977 *Women of the Puget Sound Coast Salish Indians: An Inquiry into Their Traditional Role in Socialization, Religion, and Economics.* B.A. thesis, University of Washington.

Miles, Charles, and O. B. Sperlin, eds.

1940 *Building a State, 1889–1939.* Tacoma: Washington State Historical Society.

Miller, Bruce G.

1989a After the FAP: Tribal Reorganization after Federal Recognition. *Journal of Ethnic Studies* 17 (2): 89–100.

1989b Centrality and Measurements of Regional Structure in Aboriginal Western Washington. *Ethnology* 28 (3): 265–76.

1992 Women and Politics: Comparative Evidence from the Northwest Coast. *Ethnology* 31 (4): 367–83.

1994 Contemporary Native Women: Role Flexibility and Politics. *Anthropologica* 35 (1): 57–72.

1995 Folk Law and Contemporary Coast Salish Tribal Code. *American Indian Culture and Research Journal* 19 (3): 141–64.

Miller, Bruce, and Daniel Boxberger

1994 Creating Chiefdoms: The Puget Sound Case. *Ethnohistory* 41 (2): 267–93.

Miller, Christopher

1985 *Prophetic Worlds: Indians and Whites on the Columbia Plateau.* New Brunswick: Rutgers University Press.

Miller, Jay

1976 The Northwest Coast of What? Final address at Conference on Northwest Coast Studies. 12–16 May. Simon Fraser University and Canadian National Museum of Man.

1979a A Strucon Model of Delaware Culture and the Positioning of Mediators. *American Ethnologist* 6 (4): 791–802.

1980 High-Minded High Gods in North America. *Anthropos* 75: 916–19.

1981 The Matter of the (Thoughtful) Heart: Centrality, Focality, or Overlap. *Journal of Anthropological Research* 36 (3): 338–42.

1982 People, Berdaches, and Left-Handed Bears: Human Variation in Native North America. *Journal of Anthropological Research* 38 (3): 274–87.

1985a Salish Kinship: Why Decedence? Pp. 213–22 in Proceedings, 20th International Conference on Salish and Neighboring Languages. 15–17 August. University of British Columbia.

1985b Art and Souls: The Puget Sound Salish Journey to the Land of the Dead. In Proceedings, 5th Conference of the National Native American Art Studies Association. 16–19 October. Ann Arbor and Detroit.

1988 *Shamanic Odyssey: The Lushootseed Salish Journey to the Land of the Dead, in Terms of Death, Potency, and Cooperating Shamans in North America.* Menlo Park CA: Ballena Press Anthropological Papers 32.

1992a Native Healing in Puget Sound: Portrayal of Native American Health and Healing. Pp. 1–15 in *Caduceus* (A Museum Journal for the Health Sciences). Springfield IL.

1992b A Kinship of Spirit: Society in the Americas in 1492. Pp. 305–37 in *America in 1492*, ed. Alvin Josephy. New York: Alfred Knopf.

1992c North Pacific Ethno-Astronomy: Tsimshian and Others. Pp. 193–206 in *Earth and Sky: Visions of the Cosmos in Native American Folklore*. Ed. Claire Farrer and Ray Williamson. Albuquerque: University of New Mexico Press.

1992d Society in America in 1492. Pp. 151–69 in *America in 1492: Selected Lectures from the Quincentenary Program, The Newberry Library*, ed. Harvey Markowitz. D'Arcy McNickle Center for the History of the American Indian. Occasional Papers in Curriculum Series 15.

1997 Back to Basics: Chiefdoms in Puget Sound. *Ethnohistory* 44 (2): 375–87.

Miller, Jay, ed.

1990 *Mourning Dove: A Salishan Autobiography*. Lincoln: University of Nebraska Press.

Miller, Jay, and Vi Hilbert

1993 Caring for Control: A Pivot of Salishan Language and Culture. Pp. 237–39 in *American Indian Linguistics and Ethnography in Honor of Laurence C. Thompson*. University of Montana, Occasional Papers in Linguistics 10.

1996 Lushootseed Animal People: Mediation and Transformation from Myth to History. Pp. 138–56 in *Monsters, Tricksters, and Sacred Cows: Animal Tales and American Identities*, ed. A. James Arnold. New World Studies. Charlottesville: University of Virginia Press.

Miller, Jay, and Warren Snyder

ms. Suquamish Ethnographic Notes.

Mills, Elaine, ed.

1981 *The Papers of John Peabody Harrington in the Smithsonian Institution, 1907–1957*. Vol. 1: *A Guide to the Field Notes; Native American History, Language and Culture of Alaska/Northwest Coast*. New York: Kraus International Publications.

Mooney, Kathleen

1976 Social Distance and Exchange: The Coast Salish Case. *Ethnology* 15 (4): 323–46.

1978 The Effects of Rank and Wealth on Exchange among the Coast Salish. *Ethnology* 17 (4): 391–406.

Morgan, Murray

1971 *Skid Road: An Informal Portrait of Seattle*. New York: Ballantine Books.

Moses, Johnny

1997 Healing Breath of Our Ancestors: Sacred Traditions from the Northwest Coast. Boston: Parabola Audio.

Murdock, George Peter

1949 *Social Structure*. New York: Macmillan.

1965 Algonkian Social Organization. Pp. 24–35 in *Context and Meaning in Cultural Anthropology*, ed. Melford Spiro. New York: Free Press.

Nelson, Charles

1990 Prehistory of the Puget Sound Region. Pp. 481–84 in Suttles 1990.

Newman, Stanley

1969 Bella Coola Paradigms. *International Journal of American Linguistics* 35 (4): 175–79.

Olson, Ronald

1936 The Quinault Indians. *University of Washington Publications in Anthropology* 6 (1): 1–190.

Onat, Astrida Blukis

1984 The Interaction of Kin, Class, Marriage, Property Ownership and Residences with Respect to Resource Locations among Coast Salish of the Puget Sound Lowland. *Northwest Anthropological Research Notes* 18: 86–96.

1990 Cultural Resource Inventory of Mt. Loop Highway (Washington Forest Highway 7). BOAS, Inc. for the Mt. Baker–Snoqualmie National Forest.

Palmer, Katherine Van Winkle

1925 *Honne—The Spirit of the Chehalis: The Indian Interpretation of the Origin of The People and Animals.* Geneva NY: Press of W. F. Humphrey.

Parman, Donald

1984 Inconstant Advocacy: The Erosion of Indian Fishing Rights in the Pacific Northwest, 1933–1956. *Pacific Historical Review* 53: 163–89.

Pettitt, George

1950 The Quileute of La Push, 1775–1945. University of California Anthropological Records 14 (1): 1–128.

Pilling, Arnold

1950 The Archaeological Implications of an Annual Coastal Visit for Certain Yokuts Groups. *American Anthropologist* 52 (3): 438–40.

Pilling, James

1893 *Bibliography of the Salishan Languages.* Bureau of American Ethnology, Bulletin 16.

Porter, Frank, III

1992 Without Reservation: Federal Indians Policy and Landless Tribes of Washington. Pp. 110–35 in *State and Reservation*, ed. George Castile and Robert Bee. Tucson: University of Arizona Press.

Powell, J. V., and Vickie Jensen

1976 *Quileute: An Introduction to the Indians of La Push.* Seattle: University of Washington Press.

Powell, J. V., and Fred Woodruff

1976 *Quileute Dictionary.* Northwest Anthropological Research Notes, Memoir 3.

Ransom, Jay Ellis

1945 Notes On Duwamish Phonology and Morphology. *International Journal of American Linguistics* 11 (4): 204–10.

Ray, Verne

1938 Lower Chinook Ethnographic Notes. *University of Washington Publications in Anthropology* 7 (2): 29–165.

Reddick, SuAnn

1996 Chemawa Indian Boarding School: The First Chapter. Ms. on file, Seattle Federal Archives.

Richardson, Allan

1974 Nooksak Tribal Planning Project. Phase 1. Nooksack Tribal Council.

Riddell, E. E.

1932 History of Suquamish. *Kitsap County Herald* (Poulsbo WA), Friday, 14 October.

Riley, Carroll.

1955 The Story of Skalaxt, a Lummi Training Myth. *Davidson Journal of Anthroplogy* 1 (2): 133–40.

Roberts, Helen, and Hermann Haeberlin

1918 Some Songs of the Puget Sound Salish. *Journal of American Folklore* 31 (122): 496–520.

Roberts, Natalie

1975 A History of the Swinomish Tribal Community. Ph.D. dissertation, University of Washington.

Roblin, Charles

1919 31 January Letter to Commissioner of Indian Affairs Summarizing Roll of Landless Indians of Western Washington State. Schedule of Unenrolled Indians. U.S. Department of the Interior, Office of Indian Affairs. National Archives.

Ruby, Robert, and John Brown

1996 *John Slocum and the Indian Shaker Church*. Norman: University of Oklahoma Press.

Rygg, Lawrence Daniel

1977 The Continuation of Upper Class Snohomish Coast Salish Attitudes and Deportment as Seen through the Life History of a Snohomish Coast Salish Woman. M.A. thesis, Western Washington University.

Sampson, Martin

1938 *The Swinomish Totem Pole: Tribal Legends*. Told to Rosalie Whitney. Bellingham WA: Union Printing Company.

1972 *Indians of Skagit County*. Mount Vernon WA: Skagit County Historical Society, Series 2.

Sapir, Edward

1916 Terms of Relationship and the Levirate. *American Anthropologist* 18 (3): 327–37.

Schlesier, Karl

1987 *The Wolves of Heaven: Cheyenne Shamanism, Ceremonies, and Prehistoric Origins*. Norman: University of Oklahoma Press.

Shelton, William

1932 *The Story of the [Everett] Story Pole*. Everett WA: Kane and Harcus.

Sicade, Henry

1940 The Indians' Side of the Story. Pp. 490–503 in Miles and Sperlin, 1990.

Singh, Ram Raj Prasad

1966 Aboriginal Economic System of the Olympic Peninsula Indians. Sacramento Anthropological Society Papers 4.

Smith, Marian

1940 *The Puyallup-Nisqually*. Columbia University Contributions to Anthropology 32.

1941 The Coast Salish of Puget Sound. *American Anthropologist* 43: 197–211.

1946 Petroglyph Complexes in the History of the Columbia-Fraser Region. *Southwestern Journal of Anthropology* 2 (3): 306–22.

Smith, Marian, ed.

1949 *Indians of the Urban Northwest*. Columbia University Contributions to Anthropology 36.

Snyder, Sally

ms. Folktales of the Skagit. Copies at Lushootseed Research and University of Washington Archives.

1964 Skagit Society and Its Existential Basis: An Ethnofolkloristic Reconstruction. Ph.D. dissertation, University of Washington.

1975 Quest for the Sacred in Northern Puget Sound: An Interpretation of Potlatch. *Ethnology* 14 (2): 149–61.

Snyder, Warren

1956 "Old Man House" on Puget Sound. *Washington State University Studies* 24: 17–37.

1968 *Southern Puget Sound Salish: Texts, Place Names, and Dictionary*. Sacramento Anthropological Society, Paper 9.

Speidel, William

1967 *Sons of the Profits, or, There's No Business Like Grow Business!: The Seattle Story, 1851–1901*. Seattle: Nettle Creek Publishing.

Spier, Leslie

1925 The Distribution of Kinship Systems in North America. *University of Washington Publications in Anthropology* 1 (2): 69–88.

1935 The Prophet Dance of the Northwest and Its Derivatives: The Source of the Ghost Dance. American Anthrolopogist, General Series in Anthropology 1.

1936 Tribal Distribution in Washington. American Anthropologist, General Series in Anthropology 3.

Spier, Leslie, and Edward Sapir

1930 Wishram Ethnography. *University of Washington Publications in Anthropology* 3 (3): 151–300.

Stern, Bernhard

1934 *The Lummi Indians of Northwest Washington*. Columbia University Contributions to Anthropology 17.

Stewart, Hilary

1977 *Indian Fishing: Early Methods on the Northwest Coast*. Seattle: University of Washington Press.

1984 *Cedar:. Tree of Life to the Northwest Coast Indians*. Seattle: University of Washington Press.

Sullivan, Nellie [Sister Mary Louise, OP]

1932 Eugene Casimir Chirouse OMI and the Indians of Washington. M.A. thesis, University of Washington.

Suquamish Museum

1985 *Eyes of Chief Seattle*. Suquamish WA.

Suttles, Wayne

1951 Economic Life of the Coast Salish of Haro and Rosario Straits. Ph.D. dissertation, University of Washington.

1954 Post-Contact Culture Change among the Lummi Indians. *British Columbia Historical Quarterly* 18 (1–2): 29–102.

1955 Katzie Ethnographic Notes. British Columbia Provincial Museum, Anthropology in British Columbia, Memoir 2.

1957 The Plateau Prophet Dance among the Coast Salish. *Southwestern Journal of Anthropology* 13 (4): 352–96.

1958 Private Knowledge, Morality, and Social Classes among the Coast Salish. *American Anthropologist* 60: 497–507.

1960 Affinal Ties, Subsistence and Prestige among the Coast Salish. *American Anthropologist* 62 (2): 295–305.

1963 The Persistence of Intervillage Ties among the Coast Salish. *Ethnology* 2 (4): 512–25.

1965 Linguistic Means for Anthropological Ends on the North West Coast. *Canadian Journal of Linguistics* 10: 156–66.

1977 The "Coast Salish" of the Georgia-Puget Basin: Another Look. *Puget Soundings* April: 22–25.

1987 *Coast Salish Essays.* Seattle: University of Washington Press.

1991 The Shed-Roof House. Pp. 212–22 in Wright 1991.

Suttles, Wayne, ed.

1990 *Handbook of North American Indians.* Vol. 7: Northwest Coast. Washington: Smithsonian Institution Press.

Suttles, Wayne, and William Elmendorf

1963 Linguistic Evidence for Salish Prehistory. Pp.41–52 in *Symposium on Language and Culture*, ed. Viola E. Garfield and Wallace Chafe. Proceedings of the 1962 Annual Spring Meeting of the American Ethnological Society. Seattle: University of Washington Press.

Suttles, Wayne, and Barbara Lane

1990 Southern Coast Salish. Pp. 485–502 in Suttles 1990.

Swan, James

1971 *Almost Out of This World: Scenes from Washington Territory, the Strait of Juan de Fuca, 1859–61.* Tacoma: Washington Historical Society.

Thompson, Laurence, and Claudine Poggi

ms. Klallam Dictionary. University of Hawaii, Department of Linguistics.

Thompson, Laurence, and Terry Thompson

1971 Clallam: A Review. Pp. 251–94 in *Studies in American Indian Languages*, ed. Jesse Sawyer. Berkeley: University of California Publication in Linguistics 65.

1972 Language Universals, Nasals, and the Northwest Coast. Pp. 441–56 in *Studies in Linguistics in Honor of George Trager*, ed. M. Estelle Smith. *Janua Linguarum*, Series Maior 52. The Hague: Mouton.

Thompson, Lucy

1991 *To The American Indian: Reminiscences of a Yurok Woman.* 1916. Reprint, Berkeley CA: Heyday Books.

Tollefson, Kenneth

1982 Northwest Coast Village Adaptations: A Case Study. *Canadian Journal of Anthropology* 3 (1): 19–30.

1987 The Snoqualmie: A Puget Sound Chiefdom. *Ethnology* 26: 121–36.

1989 Religious Transformation among the Snoqualmie Shakers. *Northwest Anthropological Research Notes* 23 (1): 97–102.

1989 Political Organization of the Duwamish. *Ethnology* 28: 135–49.

1992 The Political Survival of Landless Puget Sound Tribes. *American Indian Quarterly* (spring): 213–35.

1995a Potlatching and Political Organization among the Northwest Coast Indians. *Ethnology* 34 (1): 53–73.

1995b Duwamish Tribal Identity and Cultural Survival. *Northwest Anthropological Research Notes* 29 (1): 103–16.

1996 In Defense of a Snoqualmie Political Chiefdom Model. *Ethnohistory* 43 (1): 145–71.

ms. *Northwest Tribal Trilogy: Tlingit, Duwamish, Snoqualmie*. Ms in submission.

Tolmie, William Fraser

1963 *The Journals of William Fraser Tolmie: Physician and Fur Trader*. Vancouver: Mitchell Press.

Turner, Nancy J.

1975 *Food Plants of British Columbia Indians*. Part 1: *Coastal Peoples*. British Columbia Provincial Museum, Handbook 34.

Tweddell, Colin

1950 *The Snoqualmie-Duwamish Dialects of Puget Sound Salish*. University of Washington Publications in Anthropology 12.

1974 A Historical and Ethnological Study of the Snohomish Indian People. Pp. 475–694 in Horr 1974.

1984 A Componential Analysis of the Criteria Defining an Indian "Tribe" in Western Washington. Pp. 41–80 in *Western Washington Indian Socio-Economics: Papers in Honor of Angelo Anastasio*, ed. Herbert Taylor and Garland Grabert. Bellingham: Western Washington University.

Underhill, Ruth

1965 *Red Man's Religion*. Chicago: University of Chicago Press.

USA v. Washington State

1981 Civil # 9213. [Makah and Klallam re Hoko River] vols. 1 and 2; U.S. v. Lower Elwha Tribe, 642 F. 2nd 1141.

Walens, Stanley

1981 *Feasting with Cannibals: An Essay on Kwakiutl Cosmology*. Princeton: Princeton University Press.

Walker, Deward

1967 Mutual Cross-Utilization of Economic Resources in the Plateau: An Example from Aboriginal Nez Perce Fishing Practices. Report of Investigations 41. Laboratory of Anthropology, Washington State University, Pullman.

Walls, Robert

1987 *Bibliography of Washington State Folklore and Folklife*. Seattle: University of Washington Press.

Walter, George

ms. The Effects of the Boldt Decision on the Nisqually Indian Fishery.

Waterman, Thomas

1920 The Whaling Equipment of the Makah Indians. *University of Washington Publications in Anthropology* 1 (2): 1–67.

1922 The Geographical Names Used by the Indians of the Pacific Coast. *Geographical Review* 12 (2): 175–94.

1924 The Shake Religion of Puget Sound. Pp. 499–507 in Smithsonian Annual Report for 1922.

1930 The Paraphernalia of the Duwamish "Spirit-Canoe" Ceremony. *Indian Notes* 7 (2): 129–48, 295–312, 535–61.

1973 Notes on the Ethnology of the Indians of Puget Sound. Indian Notes and Monographs, Miscellaneous Series 59. New York: Museum of the American Indian, Heye Foundation.

Waterman, Thomas, and Collaborators
1921 Native Houses of Western North America. Indian Notes and Monographs, Miscellaneous Series 11. New York: Museum of the American Indian, Heye Foundation.

Waterman, Thomas, and Geraldine Coffin
1920 Types of Canoes on Puget Sound. Indian Notes and Monographs. New York: Museum of the American Indian, Heye Foundation.

Waterman, Thomas, and Ruth Greiner
1921 Indian Houses of Puget Sound. Indian Notes and Monographs, Miscellaneous Series 5. New York: Museum of the American Indian, Heye Foundation.

Watt, Roberta Frye
1931 *Four Wagons West: The Story of Seattle*. Portland: Binford and Mort Publishers.

Wells, Oliver
1987 *The Chilliwacks and Their Neighbors*. Ralph Maud, Brent Galloway, and Marie Weeden, eds. Vancouver BC: Talon Books.

White, Kris, and Janice St. Laurent
1996 Mysterious Journey: The Catholic Ladder of 1840. Special Issue: Catholic Missionizing in the West. *Oregon Historical Quarterly* 97 (1): 70–88.

White, Richard
1980 *Land Use, Environment, and Social Change: The Shaping of Island County, Washington*. Seattle: University of Washington Press.

Whitehead, Margaret
1981 *The Cariboo Mission: A History of the Oblates*. Victoria BC: Sono Nis Press.

Wickersham, James
1896 Pueblos on the Northwest Coast. *American Antiquarian* 18: 21–24.
1898 Nisqually Mythology: Studies of the Washington Indians. *Overland Monthly* 32: 345–51.
1899 Notes on the Indians of Washington. *American Antiquarian* 21: 269–375.

Wike, Joyce
1941 Modern Spirit Dancing of Northern Puget Sound. M.A. thesis, University of Washington.
1952 The Role of the Dead in Northwest Coast Culture. Pp. 97–103 in *Indian Tribes of Aboriginal America*, ed. Sol Tax. Proceedings of the 29th International Congress of Americanists.
1958 Social Stratification among the Nootka. *Ethnohistory* 5 (3): 219–41.

Williams, Johnson
1916 Black Tamanous: The Secret Society of the Clallam Indians. *Washington Historical Quarterly* 7: 296–300.

Wingert, Paul
1949 *American Indian Sculpture: A Study of the Northwest Coast*. New York: J. J. Augustin.

Wright, Robin, ed.
1991 *A Time of Gathering: Native Heritage of Washington State*. Seattle: University of Washington Press.

York, Annie, Richard Daly, and Chris Arnett
  1993 *They Write Their Dream on the Rock Forever: Rock Writings of the Stein River Valley of British Columbia*. Vancouver: Talon Books.
Zucker, Jeff, Kay Hummel, and Bob Hogfoss
  1983 *Oregon Indians: Culture History and Current Affairs—An Atlas and Introduction*. Portland: Oregon Historical Society Press.

INDEX

Page numbers in italics refer to illustrations.

forts, 84
Frog, 56
Ft. Nisqually, 39, 43

Galin, Anne, 7
gender, 33
Gibbs, George, 29, 46
gold rush, 42
Guemes Island, 79

Haeberlin, Herman, 3, 49, 147 n.1
Harmon, Alexandra, 37, 150 n.2
heart, 64, 107, 111, 150 n.17, 152 n.5, 153 n.20
Hilbert, Ron, 14
Hilbert, Vi, 2–6, 4, 75, 105, 150 n.13, 156 n.14
households, 20; at Nisqually 86–88
houses, 62, 79, 154 n.25. *See also* Oldman House
Howard, Mary Carolyn, 28
Hudson's Bay Company, 39

illness, 34

jobs, 44
Joe, Andrew Span, 52

Kanakas (Hawaiians), 43
Kane, Paul, 43, 84
Kanim, Jerry, *38*, 142
Khaals, 63, 67
Kinkade, Dale, 3, 153 n.10
kinship, 122
Kitsap, 94

Lahalbid, 84
Lahalet, 39
Le Clair, Frank, 83, 117
Levirate, 113, 127
Little Earths, 62, 133, 135, 136, 144, 153 n.19
Little Sam, 60
logjam, 18

mask, 116
matrilineals, 8, 19, 126, 152 n.1, 158 n.11
McIlwraith, Thomas, 69
mediums, 36, 74, 131

men, 96, 119
Methodists, 40
minmints, 71
mistake, in law, 48
Mourning Dove, 5
Mud Bay, 47
murder, 157 n.1

names, 6, 9, 21, 85, 90
nodal kindred, 90
Nooksak, 17, 40, 74, 99
Nusmatta, 70

Ober, Sarah, 46
odyssey, last, 1, 6, 36
Oldman House, 84, 115 n.9. *See also* houses
Old Pierre, 63
Orcas Island, 17
orphans, 123

paint, 24
Patius, 95
Patkanim, 146
pattern numbers, 14
Pentecostals, 46
persons, 10, 22, 57
Peter, Susie Sampson, 37, 51, 54, 152 n.8
pinky (insult), 92, 156 n.20
poles, 61
portages, 16, 18
posts, 83, 114, 153 n.9, 155 n.8
prophets, 40, 84, 95, 155 n.12
Protestants, 40, 152 n.13
pulse, 34

Qatuwas Festival, 106
Queen Susan, 158 n.3
Quintasket, Charles, 5, 154 n.29

racism, 42
rainfall, 6
Rat, 54
Rattlesnake, 119
renewals, 7, 19, 36, 147 n.4
river, 24
roof, 80–81, 154 n.1

Sahaptians, 128
Salishan, 13
salmon, 20, 149 n.9
Sampson, Martin, 31, 157 n.9
schwa, xiii
seasons, 97–98
Seattle, 101, 109, 146 157 n.5
Seattle, Jim, 94
selfishness, 25
Shakers, 131
shamans, 8, 33, 132; gestures of, 34, 132; killing of, 34; speech of, 158 n.16; sucking by, 35
Sicade, Henry, 83, 151 n.3
Sierras, 19
sigers, 20, 32
slaves, 23, 82, 92–93
Slocum, John, 32, 37, 48, 150 n.15, 153 n.15
Slocum, Mary Thompson, 32, 37
slox, 87, 155 n.14
Smith, Marian, 153 n.16
Sneatlum, 39, 83, 156 n.15
Snyder, Warren, 26
Solomon, Dora, 153 n.11
song, 75, 100
soul, 1; loss of, 8
Species Mother, 71
spirits, 21, 58–60, 72, 148 n.6; mean, 28, 94; traveling, 22, 31, 49; wealth of, 60
Spokan Gary, 39
stem kindred, 90
Stevens, Isaac, 46
Swanaset, 66

teeth, 117
throw (scramble), 101
tolt, 33
toys, 116, 121
towns, 10
training, 117
trance, 34
trembling, 145, 159 n.9
Tsalalkum, 39, 41
Tsalbit, 85
Tulalip, 41

Umiak, 109
Utsaladdy, 37

Wahalchu, Jacob, 3, 11, 76, 94, 148 n.8
wapato (root), 15
warmth, 2, 75
warriors, 94
Waskalatchy (the Frenchman), 39
Wawetkin, John, 155 n.10
Webster, Lawrence "Web," 3
weirs, 18
Whidbey Island, 44
Wike, Joyce, 49, 75
wisdom, 9, 91
women, 85, 96, 119, 154 n.3

Yelm, 39
Yelm Jim, 87, 155 n.13
Yokuts, 30
York boats, 105
Yurok, 107, 152 n.2